*For Dummies*
BESTSELLING BOOK SERIES

# Linux® Smart H
# For Dummi

MW00997573

## Linux Home Automated Projects That Get Your Feet Wet

| Project | What You Need | Chapter |
|---|---|---|
| Build personal video recorder | MythTV software, a spare computer, a sound card, a video card, an optical drive, and a video capture card | 6 |
| Stream music | Twonky Media software, a D-Link DSM-320 or Netgear MP101, and music | 7 |
| Have fun with a webcam | CamStream software, a webcam such as Logitech Orbit or QuickCam Pro 4000, a microphone, speakers, and a sound card | 8 |
| Automate lamps in your home | CM11A, a spare serial port, Heyu Software, and X10 module(s) | 13 |
| Set sprinklers on a timer with X10 wirelessly | CM17A, a spare serial port, X10 modules, an RR501 (in the CM18A kit), and Bottlerocket software | 14 |
| Use MisterHouse and X10 | MisterHouse software, a CM11A, and X10 modules | 15 & 16 |

## Linux Smart Home Projects for the Adventurous Spirit

| Project | What You Need | Chapter |
|---|---|---|
| Set up an IP PBX | A network, Asterisk software, the config files on this book's CD, and a SPA-3000 | 9 |
| Set up a weather station | Oww weather station software, a weather station unit, a weather vane, anemometer cups, a test cable, serial port adapter, and a straight-through cable | 10 |
| Automate thermostat controls | TXB16, TW523, CM11A, and either MisterHouse or Heyu software | 12 |
| Set up wireless networking | Wireless network card and a WAP (Wireless Access Point) | 3 & 4 |
| Set up routing | Network card and at least two computers (one may be the WAP) | 5 |

*For Dummies: Bestselling Book Series for Beginners*

# Linux® Smart Homes For Dummies®

Cheat Sheet

## Must-Have Hardware

**Note:** Before purchasing any hardware listed in this table, please read the related chapter for suggestions and warnings.

| Device | Use | Cost | Buy It Here | Chapter |
|---|---|---|---|---|
| Wireless network interface card | Wireless network access | $50–$100 | Local consumer electronics outlet, online store, or auction site | 3 |
| Video capture card or device | Personal video recorder | $150 and up | Local consumer electronics outlet, online store, or auction site | 6 |
| CD/DVD burner (optical drive) | Burning CDs and DVDs | $60 and up | Local consumer electronics outlet or online store | 6 & 7 |
| Sound card (Most motherboards have a sound card built-in, so an extra card is unnecessary.) | To play and record audio (music and movies) | $50 and up | Local consumer electronics outlet or online store | 6 & 7 |
| Speakers and a microphone | To play and record audio (music and movies) | $30 and up | Local consumer electronics outlet or online store | 6 & 7 |
| D-Link DSM-320 or Netgear MP101 | Play music | $50–$200 | Online stores or auctions | 7 |
| Logitech Orbit or Quickcam Pro 4000 | Webcam and video conferencing | $50–$160 | Online stores or auctions | 8 |
| SPA-3000 | Voice over IP | $90–$150 | Online stores or auctions | 9 |
| CM11A | X10 PC serial interface controller | $25 and up | Online stores or auctions | 12, 13 & 15 |
| X10 modules | Appliance and lamp control | $20 and up | Smarthome.com, local consumer electronics outlet, online store, or auction site | 13, 14 & 15 |
| CM18A kit | Wireless control of X10 modules | $15 and up | Online auctions | 14 |
| Wireless X10 modules (optional) | RF control of X10 | $15 and up | X10, Smarthome.com, and online auctions | 14 |

Copyright © 2006 Wiley Publishing, Inc. All rights reserved.

Item 9823-6.

For more information about Wiley Publishing, call 1-800-762-2974.

## For Dummies: Bestselling Book Series for Beginners

# Linux®
# Smart Homes
## FOR
# DUMMIES®

# Linux® Smart Homes

## FOR

# DUMMIES®

by Neil Cherry

Wiley Publishing, Inc.

Linux® Smart Homes For Dummies®

Published by
**Wiley Publishing, Inc.**
111 River Street
Hoboken, NJ 07030-5774
www.wiley.com

WILEY

# About the Author

**Neil Cherry** has been working with computers, computer electronics, and software since 1978. He has been playing with X10 since 1982. He began automating his home in 1992 when a friend gave him an X10 computer interface, and he started the Linux Home Automation Web site (www.linuxha.com) in 1996. When he's not riding his bicycle or playing with home automation, he works for AT&T Research Lab South, Middletown, NJ, as a Test Engineer. You can reach him by e-mail at linuxha@linuxha.com.

# About the Contributors

**Terry Collings** is the owner of TAC Technology, located in eastern Pennsylvania. He provides Linux consulting and training services to a variety of clients. Terry has been an adjunct faculty member at several colleges in his area where he taught A + and Network + certification courses. He also taught courses on UNIX, Linux, TCP/IP, and Novell Netware. Terry is the author of *Red Hat Enterprise Linux 4 For Dummies,* has co-authored three editions of Red Hat Networking and System Administration and contributed to several other Linux books. He was the technical editor for the following books: *KDE Bible, The Samba Book, UNIX Weekend Crash Course, Red Hat Linux 9 For Dummies, Solaris 9 For Dummies, Fedora Linux 2 For Dummies,* and *Linux Timesaving Techniques For Dummies.*

**Gurdy Leete** is a co-author of *OpenOffice.org For Dummies,* a technical editor for *Free Software For Dummies,* and the co-author of five other popular computer books. He's also an award-winning software engineer and a co-author of the Multitile plug-in for the GNU Image Manipulation Program (GIMP). Gurdy teaches digital imaging, graphic design, Web design, video, and animation at Maharishi University of Management in Fairfield, Iowa, where he has been a pioneer in using GNU/Linux applications in undergraduate art and design classes. His blog, titled *Free Software for Art, Music and Personal Creativity,* is at www.peaceloveandhappiness.org.

**Mary Leete** wrote *Free Software For Dummies* and co-wrote *OpenOffice.org For Dummies.* She has a B.S. in Computer Science and a Masters in Professional Writing, and she lives to write code as well as write about it. Mary has extensive experience as a systems analyst and programmer with a multitude of software on way too many platforms. She is also a freelance Web designer, a video producer, and an award-winning screenwriter, and she has written under contract for the producer of *The Buddy Holly Story,* among others.

# Author's Acknowledgments

I wish to thank my wife, Diane, for putting up with my years of experiments and for not allowing me to kludge together anything. She's kept me honest and helped make our home automation work better. Honey, I love you and I'll take you out to dinner but first just one more compile.

Thanks to Terry Collings and Gurdy and Mary Leete who helped by writing various chapters that I was unable to. They really helped to make this book possible.

Thanks to Nicole Sholly and Virginia Sanders, the editors who worked with me on this book. I doubt most people know the amount of work a book takes to get written and how much help the editors give to make a book successful. I really appreciate all the help — thank you very much and I hope I get *it* now. I'd also like to thank the rest of the folks at Wiley who are too numerous to mention. They do a lot of the work to help get a book put together and to the stores but seldom get mentioned.

Thanks to Deepak Dube for his kind words of encouragement, without which I wouldn't have thought I could write a book.

Thanks also to Donald Brookman and Vincent Miller, my friends who always ask the most pertinent questions. (Are we there yet?!)

## Publisher's Acknowledgments

We're proud of this book; please send us your comments through our online registration form located at www.dummies.com/register/.

Some of the people who helped bring this book to market include the following:

### Acquisitions, Editorial, and Media Development

**Project Editor:** Nicole Sholly

**Acquisitions Editors:** Kyle Looper, Tiffany Ma

**Copy Editor:** Virginia Sanders

**Technical Editor:** Dan DiNicolo

**Editorial Manager:** Kevin Kirschner

**Media Development Specialists:** Angela Denny, Kate Jenkins, Steven Kudirka, Kit Malone

**Media Development Coordinator:** Laura Atkinson

**Media Project Supervisor:** Laura Moss

**Media Development Manager:** Laura VanWinkle

**Editorial Assistant:** Amanda Foxworth

**Sr. Editorial Assistant:** Cherie Case

**Cartoons:** Rich Tennant (www.the5thwave.com)

### Composition Services

**Associate Project Coordinator:** Tera Knapp

**Layout and Graphics:** Carl Byers, Andrea Dahl, Denny Hager, Joyce Haughey, Stephanie D. Jumper, Barbara Moore, Heather Ryan, Alicia B. South

**Proofreaders:** Leeann Harney, Heidi Unger

**Indexer:** Techbooks

**Special Help:** Andy Hollandbeck, Pat O'Brien

---

### Publishing and Editorial for Technology Dummies

**Richard Swadley,** Vice President and Executive Group Publisher

**Andy Cummings,** Vice President and Publisher

**Mary Bednarek,** Executive Acquisitions Director

**Mary C. Corder,** Editorial Director

### Publishing for Consumer Dummies

**Diane Graves Steele,** Vice President and Publisher

**Joyce Pepple,** Acquisitions Director

### Composition Services

**Gerry Fahey,** Vice President of Production Services

**Debbie Stailey,** Director of Composition Services

# Contents at a Glance

# Table of Contents

# Introduction

**W**elcome to *Linux Smart Homes For Dummies.* To own and operate a Linux smart home means to control and monitor devices and information around your home by using a standard personal computer, Linux, and its vast array of open source tools. Having a Linux smart home is also about doing it yourself and getting your hands dirty — with the code, the hardware, and everything else in between. Don't worry if you aren't a hardware person; I don't make you break out a soldering iron to whip up a new interface. Also, don't worry if you aren't a software person; I don't hand out programming assignments. Your limits are your imagination, your pocketbook, and how much your spouse will let you get away with. You can start out small and build your way up to a larger system. This is not about spending big bucks, though I do try to keep it as professional looking as possible. Some home automation work looks like a cheap hack (wires hanging everywhere) or something that looks like it was slapped together at the last minute. My wife won't stand for that.

Home automation has high geek value and a lot of neat toys. In the past, basic home automation included turning on and off lights and some appliances. Later, things like security systems, fire alarms, sprinkler controls, and climate control (HVAC, or heating, ventilation and cooling) were added to be controlled by the system. With the advent of the Internet, it's now also about information and communications (data and voice networks). Although this book doesn't cover everything there is to know about home automation — after all, that's a huge topic and this is just one book — it gives you a sturdy base to start with.

## About This Book

Here are some of the things you can do with this book:

- ✔ Build a wireless network and connect it to the Internet. Part II covers installing a wireless network card in your computer, setting up a wireless access point, and routing and connecting to the Internet.
- ✔ Control your TV and music by adding servers to record and play back TV programs at your leisure and listen to music anywhere in your home.
- ✔ Build a better answering machine with a software Private Branch eXchange.

✔ Monitor the weather with your own weather station and software to collect and display local and Internet weather predictions.

✔ Control lights and appliances with X10 and X10 wireless modules from Linux.

✔ Use MisterHouse, the home automation server. It can control and monitor a number of interfaces, such as an *Infrared Remote* (IR) and X10, and newer interfaces are being added. In addition, you can monitor and manually control MisterHouse from the comfort of any Web browser.

✔ Use IR to control your entertainment and home automation system from the comfort of your remote control.

✔ Securely access your home automation from anywhere on the Internet.

# Foolish Assumptions

This book is not for everyone because it's for Linux users. It might be useful to other UNIX users, such as the BSD folks and Sun users, if they're clever enough to figure out the differences. However, I describe everything from the perspective of Linux. If you're a Windows user, you're really out of luck with this book (but you can check out *Smart Homes For Dummies,* 2nd Edition, by Danny Briere and Pat Hurley, from Wiley). To use this book, I expect that you

✔ **Know a little bit about the Linux OS, the distribution you have installed and the version of the Linux kernel that is installed and running.** There are many distributions, such as Fedora, Debian, Red Hat, SUSE, Unbuntu, and Slackware. You'll also see many versions of the Linux kernel, but if you have a recent distribution, then it's either version 2.4 or 2.6.

✔ **Have at least installed these development tools:**

- GNU C compiler
- Development libraries
- Perl programming language
- Perl modules and libraries
- bash shell

If you've installed everything or at least the entire development environment, you'll be fine.

✔ **Know how to log in as a normal user and as the user root and also how to bring up a shell or terminal (if you're using the GUI [X Window]).**

✔ **Are familiar with navigating the operating system by changing directories.**

 ✔ **Have a favorite editor and know how to use the basic editing commands, such as Add, Delete, Search, and Save.** (You *cannot* use a Windows editor on Linux files. Windows doesn't know how to deal with the Linux line endings. So don't do it!)

 ✔ **Are willing to purchase some hardware.** For instance, you must have extra serial and/or USB ports and hardware such as the X10 modules. It would have been nice if the hardware were free, but that isn't always possible. Most of it isn't too expensive.

 I can't tell you where to purchase most of these items, with the exception of the X10-compatible products, which you can purchase from `www.smarthome.com`, which offers excellent selection, service, and prices. (I don't work for them; I'm just a satisfied customer.) Most items are also available from online stores or online auctions. If you're good at bidding or searching, you can often save some money on used equipment. Either way, you can use a search engine with a few keywords to find various bits of information about where you can purchase or bid on various items.

 ✔ **Have a thirst for knowledge and a Do It Yourself (DIY) attitude.** Though Linux and the available packages are becoming easier to use and install, you do have to tinker with the hardware and software to get home automation properly running. The amazing thing is that after you have it running, you can ignore it until you want to add something else. Linux is a very stable OS and seldom crashes — even on my development machine where I tinker with lots of kernel settings.

# Conventions Used in This Book

I use a few conventions in this book. By *conventions,* I simply mean a set of rules I've employed in this book to present information to you consistently. When you see a term *italicized,* look for its definition, which I include so that you know what things mean in the context of Linux home automation. Sometimes, I give you information to enter on-screen; in this case, you need to type the **bold** text. Web site addresses and e-mail addresses are in `monofont` so that they stand out from regular text.

# What You Don't Have to Read

Because I've structured this book modularly — that is, it's designed so that you can easily find just the information you need — you don't have to read whatever doesn't pertain to your task at hand. You also don't have to read the Technical Stuff paragraphs, which parse out über-techie tidbits (which you might or might not be interested in).

# How This Book Is Organized

*Linux Smart Homes For Dummies* is split into seven parts. You don't have to read it sequentially, and you don't even have to read all the sections in any particular chapter. You can use the Table of Contents and the index to find the information you need and quickly get your answer. In this section, I briefly describe what you can find in each part.

## Part 1: Bringing the Future Home

Part I explores the possibilities of home automation, the fun and function of automated applications. Find out about controlling your environment, entertaining yourself, and watching the weather. You find out how to fill your toolkit with some great software that you can run on older hardware (and newer hardware, of course). This part helps you to find HA (home automation) software, get drivers, daemons, and dress up the rough stuff with a GUI front end.

## Part 11: Connecting Multiple Computers without the Wires

Wires, wires, everywhere, but not if my wife has her say! Part II is all about the network but without the wires. You delve into adding a wireless network card, the drivers, and the Linux wireless support tools. Next, you add a wireless access point that can even support that other operating system (cough, Windows, cough). Finally, routing with the big boys: You find out how to add dynamic routing to your network.

## Part 111: Entertaining Your Brain with a Little Help from Linux

The hills are alive with the . . . okay, okay, I'll stop singing. Part III delves into how to use a particular digital video recorder (MythTV); share music throughout your home with a media server (TwonkyMedia); install, view, and post pictures with a Web camera (USB Webcam); and take advantage of a smart phone system (Asterisk).

## Part 1V: Keeping a Linux Eye on the Sky

Weather-watching is made easy with your very own weather information resource. In Part IV, you keep an eye on the live local weather (with a One-wire weather station, or Oww) and get Internet weather reports. And you learn how to control your home's thermostat. No more excuses for not having an umbrella.

# Part V: X10-ding Your Environment with Home Automation

It's all part of my plan to control the world with the veteran X10 protocol, using lights, appliances, computer interfaces, and wireless modules as the building blocks of many home automation projects. Part V introduces you to some of the hardware to control lights and appliances and the software needed to allow Linux to control, monitor, and schedule device events. Prepare to control the world!

# Part VI: Controlling and Securing Your Automation Network

MisterHouse does it all! Part VI is all about MisterHouse, an open source home automation program written in Perl. It's extremely customizable because you can add your own Perl code. Additionally, you extend your control of X10, discover how to use the Web interface, and add a bit of Linux security so that you can access MisterHouse from anywhere you can access the Internet. I love it when a plan comes together.

# Part VII: The Part of Tens

Goodies! Every good *For Dummies* book has a Part of Tens, and this one is no exception. So here you find ten tasks you can automate (Chapter 19) and ten snappy home automation gadgets (Chapter 20). More toys for the tinkerin'.

# The CD appendix

The appendix is a quick-and-dirty guide to using this book's CD. It also lists and briefly explains the products and software included on the CD.

# About the CD-ROM

The CD contains all the open source software needed for the chapters in the book along with custom scripts provided, so you don't have to type in the scripts from the various chapters. If you're wondering about system requirements necessary to use the CD and run the software contained on it, check out the appendix.

# Icons Used in This Book

What's a *For Dummies* book without icons pointing you in the direction of really great information that's sure to help you along your way? In this section, I briefly describe each icon I use in this book.

The Tip icon points out helpful information that is likely to make your job easier.

This icon marks a general interesting and useful fact — something that you might want to remember for later use.

The Warning icon highlights lurking danger. With this icon, I'm telling you to pay attention and proceed with caution.

When you see this icon, you know that there's techie stuff nearby. If you aren't feeling very techie, you can skip this info.

This icon highlights the products and software you can find on the CD included with this book.

# Where to Go from Here

In a perfect world, you'd be able to follow the instructions in this book and have everything working on the first try, but this isn't a perfect world. If you run into any problems, find any errors, have suggestions, or just want to discuss Linux smart homes, please visit the Linux HA (that's HA as in *home automation* and not *ha ha*) Web site: www.linuxha.com/FD. There, you can find the latest software, links to various software sites, and the support forums for this book and Linux home automation. If you need to contact the author, send e-mail to linuxha@linuxha.com.

# Part I
# Bringing the Future Home

## The 5th Wave
### By Rich Tennant

SMART HOME OF THE FUTURE

©RICH TENNANT

"I'm setting preferences – do you want Turkish or Persian carpets in the living room?"

# In this part . . .

Making your home a smart home is the ultimate upgrade. But before you do anything with home automation, you need to find out what your options are and what tools you need.

Part I explores the possibilities of home automation. You discover ways to control your environment, entertain yourself, watch the weather, and more. You also find out how the software you already have can help you on your way, and I point you toward the software you might still need to acquire. The best part about some of this software is that you can even get that old clunker of a computer out of the storage closet, dust it off, and put it to work again!

# Chapter 1

# Exploring the Possibilities of Home Automation

*H*ome automation offers time-saving opportunities that can make your life more organized, more efficient, safer, and more fun. Dozens of free Linux software packages are available for home automation. These programs are often at the cutting edge of the field because Linux is often the platform of choice for programmers around the world in the field of home automation. Many of these programs are published under the GNU General Public License, which means they can be used by anyone freely, and because the source code is available, anyone can add new features to it. That is what programmers everywhere are doing at a fast rate, which makes this field exciting to be a part of. The practical uses for home automation are endless. This chapter covers an overview of how it works and its possibilities, and I get you started automating right away.

## Functional and Fun: Home Automation Applications

Every room of your home probably offers plenty of possibilities for home automation. Maybe the most well-known use is turning lights on and off — especially to dissuade any thieves from targeting your place when you aren't at home. But there are plenty of other uses. Here are some of the most popular and most exciting:

- ✔ **Automate chores** such as watering your lawn, opening and closing drapes, controlling your lights and appliances — even controlling your electric water heater.

- ✔ **Use motion sensors** to turn on floodlights and cameras outside your home. Or turn on lights indoors as you walk from room to room, create an automatic doorbell, and more.

- ✔ **Use water sensors** to inform you of leaking plumbing, both minor or major, while you're at home or away for the day or on vacation. (Why not have your computer call you to let you know?)

- ✔ **Control your lights and appliances remotely** via the Internet or a telephone.

- ✔ **Remotely adjust your thermostat** so you can warm up your home before you get there.

- ✔ **Zone your heat and automatically adjust it** to make your home comfortable in the areas that you're using, and energy efficient in those areas that you aren't.

- ✔ **Wirelessly beam your entertainment around your home**. For instance, be your own DJ and send your MP3 songs playing on your computer to any stereo or TV in your house. Or use the plasma TV in your den to view videos playing on your computer.

- ✔ **Use a smart phone** for your home communications with a digital receptionist, voice mail, call forwarding, call waiting, and more.

- ✔ **Videoconference** with your friends, family, and co-workers by using the Linux Ekiga application; see Chapter 8 for more about Ekiga.

- ✔ **Set up a home surveillance system** by using webcams.

- ✔ **Keep your eye on your home remotely** via webcams and the Internet.

- ✔ **Set up your computer to alert you to storms** in your area or any area you specify by e-mailing you or calling your cell phone or pager.

## Controlling your environment

Basically, any appliance or light that you can plug in or wire with a switch can be controlled to turn on (or dim, if applicable) remotely by using a system known as X10.

## An X10 overview

X10 signals are sent and received via the powerlines of your home and interpreted by specially made X10 modules. The two basic types of X10 modules are lamp modules for incandescent lights, which can enable your light to dim, and appliance modules, which don't dim. (You don't want to dim your coffee maker.) These modules come in various shapes and sizes. They might look like little white boxes, like the Lamp Module shown in Figure 1-1; they can look like a normal wall outlet; or they can look similar to a lamp socket, like the Socket Rocket.

**Figure 1-1:**
Use the X10
Lamp
Module to
control a
light by
using
various X10
controllers.

To use an X10 module, you plug in the lamp (or appliance) or screw a light bulb into it, and then you plug (or wire) the module into the wall or screw it into a lamp socket. These X10 modules interpret the X10 signal and determine whether the signal is meant for it, and if so, it can turn itself on or off or dim the light accordingly, based on the signal.

Using X10 technology, every appliance and every light in your home can be automated and controlled. X10 signals do not interfere with any electrical system because A/C current alternates its phases at 60 times per second, and X10 signals operate during the spare time between the phases!

To send the signals to control your X10 modules, you can use any one of the following or combinations of the following:

✔ **Remote control:** This works in conjunction with a transceiver that is plugged into the wall. Press the proper controls on your remote to tell the transceiver what appliances to turn on or off and what lights to dim or brighten.

 ✔ **Motion sensors:** Motion sensors can signal when motion is detected, and you can set a motion sensor's transceiver to send X10 signals to X10 modules (for instance, to turn on lights) or to an appliance (such as a camera).

 ✔ **Other sensors:** Water sensors can detect leaks and cause a chime to sound, for example, and rain sensors can delay the watering of your lawn. They operate similarly to motion sensors.

 ✔ **Touchtone controller:** This item controls X10 modules through touchtone signals, so you can control your system via your phone.

 ✔ **Desktop controller:** This inexpensive controller plugs into the wall and can control 8 to 16 X10 modules without a transceiver.

 ✔ **Computer:** You can control your X10 modules via your computer software in the following ways:

   • *Send and receive X10 signals over the powerlines from your computer.* For example, the CM11A computer interface, as shown in Figure 1-2, can control your modules by using Linux home automation software. A starter kit is available from www.x10.com for $49.99.

   • *Enable your computer to function as a remote control.* The Firecracker computer interface, also called CM17A, is compatible with Linux home automation software. This is one-way communication only. A starter kit is available from www.x10.com for $39.99.

**Figure 1-2:**
You can use the CM11A X10 computer interface with free Linux software to control your X10 modules.

### Controlling X10 modules with Linux software

By computerizing your X10 system, you gain the power to create sophisticated macros that can operate based on the input of more than one X10 device, such as opening the garage door if motion is sensed by the hall closet (where you keep your coat) between the time of 8:00 and 8:15 a.m. Or you can connect your system to the Internet so you can operate it from anywhere in the world without having to pay for a phone call.

With your computer controlling your system, you can also use features that might not be available with other controllers, such as using the Internet to control your X10 system from anywhere in the world or using your computer to operate a smart phone system that can call you if, for example, your basement floods.

The CM11A interface can be controlled by several programs, such as MisterHouse, as shown in Figure 1-3, or Heyu. For more information on how to set up your computer to control X10 modules, refer to Chapter 13.

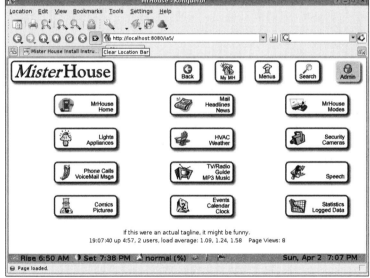

**Figure 1-3:**
Use
MisterHouse
to control
your X10
appliances
remotely,
even over
the Internet.

### Fun and functional ways to use X10

The uses of X10 are many and limited only by the imagination. For information on how to start building a simple X10 system, check out Chapter 13. After you get to know the basics, filling your home with all kinds of X10 systems is easy.

Some practical or just plain fun uses for X10 automation include these:

✔ Use a motion detector to switch on Robo-Dog, an X10 dog barking device to scare intruders, or hook up your motion detector to floodlights.

✔ Create an automatic doorbell with a motion detector and chime. Place the motion detector at your front door, front gate, or sidewalk to alert you of guests.

✔ Dim all the lights with the touch of a single button in your living room for a home-theater effect.

✔ Set up a motion detector to work in a bedroom during the night to turn on the bathroom lights as well as a lighted hallway path when your child needs to go to the potty.

✔ Automate your security by aiming X10 cameras outside your home so that they will turn on when tripped by motion detectors. If you want to get fancy, have your computer call you to alert you and watch your cameras from the Internet.

✔ Use sprinklers attached to motion detectors to scare off neighborhood dogs or deer. (However, this might be a magnet to every child in town!)

✔ Use X10 to start your coffee in the morning and open your window shades.

✔ Turn off all your lights with one click of a remote.

✔ Water your lawn automatically on schedule.

✔ Check the state of your car's muffler and exhaust system with an automated pan-and-tilt camera base.

✔ Decorate with X10-controlled Christmas lights that turn on and off to the beat of your music or other cues.

### Best places to find X10 products

X10 products are generally inexpensive. For example, you can buy a CM11A computer interface, a two-way transceiver module, a remote, a lamp module, and a credit card controller all bundled into one package for $49.99 at www.x10.com — plus free shipping!

X10.com is a great place to shop for home automation devices. Their prices are generally low and their sales are often incredible. (No, I don't get a commission.) However, don't get excited by their Sale Ending Soon banners or Buy Now — Only 4 Left! Don't feel like you need to rush. New sales start every day.

Smarthome (www.smarthome.com) and Radio Shack (www.radioshack.com) are two other suppliers of X10 products. And don't forget eBay for good deals.

Here's an interesting statistic: Roughly 95 percent of all X10 products are sold online. Maybe this will change as X10 rises in popularity — or maybe not.

## Taking your entertainment wherever you go

Here's the problem. Your favorite music is on your computer and you want to play it on your stereo in the den. Or you have MythTV (a Linux-based TiVo knock-off I describe in detail in Chapter 6) on your computer, but you want to watch it from your couch — not your swivel chair. Or, another problem: You set up your MP3 files on your computer to play in your den, but you want to control them with a remote — and your computer is 50 feet away on the other side of the house. This section covers a wide variety of incredibly easy (and cheap) entertainment solutions. And if you want information on streaming your music through the Internet, check out Chapter 7.

### Wirelessly sending TV and stereo signals from any TV, stereo, or CD player

For about $50, you can get an X10 wireless video sender from www.x10.com. The entire package consists of a video sender and video receiver, both of which look like small boxes with regular antennas and tiny dish-like antennas protruding from them, which can communicate with each other wirelessly throughout your home. The video sender also sends and receives stereo sound from your TV, CD player, or stereo — whatever takes standard RCA Audio In and Audio Out jacks — or coaxial cable.

The following steps show you how to hook up your wireless video sender to your DVD, VCR, stereo, TiVo, satellite receiver, or cable box to play on a TV or stereo:

1. **Connect the RCA jacks to the Audio and Video inputs and outputs of your video sender and video receiver, and connect them to the Video Out and/or Audio Out of your DVD player, VCR, TiVo, satellite receiver, CD player, stereo, or cable box and the Video In and/or Audio In of your stereo or TV.**

   If RCA connections are not available, coaxial cable inputs and outputs will do as well.

2. **Set the channel on the wireless video sender to either three or four, whatever channel the TV that is normally connected to the DVD player, VCR, or other device uses to receive the signal.**

3. **Set the channel on the wireless video receiver to the same channel on the wireless video sender.**

4. **Angle the flat antennas of the wireless video sender and receiver so they are facing each other.**

   It's okay if there are walls between them. Just pretend the walls are not there.

5. **Turn on whatever your wireless video sender and receiver are connected to and enjoy!**

   If the signal isn't as strong as you like, try adjusting the angles of the antennas or changing the channel numbers on both the sender and receiver. They need to be the same numbers.

### Wirelessly transmitting MP3 files

Using the wireless video sender, you can easily transmit your MP3 tunes wirelessly from your computer to any stereo or TV in your home — or by the poolside. The wireless video sender is also an audio sender. To hook up your computer to play your audio from your computer remotely on any TV or stereo, follow these steps:

1. **Plug the white and red RCA connectors of the video receiver into the RCA Audio In jacks of any stereo or TV equipped with them.**

   You can use coaxial cable if you need to.

2. **If your computer has RCA jacks for Audio Out, plug your red and white RCA cables into them; if it has a Video Out card with a place to screw on a coaxial cable, hook up a coaxial cable to it. Then skip to Step 5.**

3. **If your computer has no Audio Out jack that is compatible with RCA plugs or coaxial cable, find or buy a stereo tuner with Audio In and Audio Out RCA jacks on it and place it near your computer.**

4. **Buy a cable that has an earphone jack on one end and two RCA jacks on the other end and plug the headphone jack into your computer and the two RCA jacks into the Audio In jack on the back of the stereo.**

5. **Plug the white and red RCA cables into Audio Out jacks in the back of the stereo and plug the other end of the white and red RCA cables into the wireless video sender.**

6. **Set the channel number on your video sender and receiver to the same number — whatever number you want — or whatever works best.**

7. **Follow Steps 4 to 5 in the preceding section "Wirelessly sending TV and stereo signals from any TV, stereo, or CD player."**

Lots of good MP3 players with easy-to-use interfaces are available for use on the Linux desktop. XMMS, MPlayer, or Zinf Audio Player are a few. Any of these players will work with this system.

### Controlling your Linux MP3 player with an X10 remote control

It is possible to control your XMMS MP3 player running on your computer from a handheld remote up to 50–100 feet away (and through walls). This remote, called the Anywhere Remote, can control the following:

✔ Song selection

✔ Play/stop/fast forward/pause

✔ Volume/mute

✔ Balance

The Anywhere Remote is a universal remote that can do the following:

✔ Control your TV, CD player, DVD, cable box, and satellite receiver.

✔ Control your X10 modules up to 50–100 feet away and through walls (if you use it with a TM751 or RR501 transceiver, which is available at www.x10.com for about $13).

✔ Control your MP3 player on your computer remotely up to 50–100 feet away and through walls if you have the following:

   • A TM751 or RR501 transceiver, which costs about $13 from www.x10.com.

   • XMMS audio software comes with most Linux desktop distributions, as shown in Figure 1-4.

   • A computer capable of sending and receiving X10 signals. Refer to the "Controlling X10 modules with Linux software" section.

   • A program called x10mp3.

x10mp3 is free software that runs in Linux and is available for download at http://x10mp3.sourceforge.net. This software is the Linux version of the Windows program, Boom 2000, which controls the Anywhere Remote.

When you use the Anywhere Remote along with a video sender, you can send your MP3 music to any stereo or CD player in the house from your computer and control it remotely from up to 50–100 feet away. You can find the Anywhere Remote on www.ebay.com for about $10.

If you want to beam your music to a stereo directly from your iPod, special iPod transmitters are available for about $50. The sender attaches directly to the iPod and the receiver attaches to a stereo by using standard RCA connectors. This has nothing to do with Linux, however.

**Figure 1-4:**
Your
Anywhere
Remote
interfaces
with the
MP3 player
software
package,
XMMS.

### Wirelessly viewing Linux applications and videos on any TV

If you like to download videos to your computer (from Google Video, or MythTV, for example) and want to see them on a TV elsewhere in your house, you can easily do it. After all, your computer lives in your home office, and your plasma TV is in your living room (you wish). Your home office is crowded, and your living room can seat more people. Your desk chair is hard, and your couch is soft (or maybe not). So, if you have video on your computer that you want to enjoy in more comfort, you can hook up your computer to the wireless video sender. The only requirement to using the wireless video sender with your Linux computer is that you need to have a *Video Out card* — that means you need to have a coaxial cable connection or RCA Audio and Video outputs.

## Watching the weather

Whether or not you or someone in your family is a budding meteorologist, it is still handy to know what the weather conditions are — without having to get frozen or fried checking it out. A wide variety of home weather stations are available on the market, and they can give you accurate information concerning weather conditions. Some of these weather stations can interface with Linux software, so you can gather and store your information on your computer. Or you can create your own weather station by using information from the Internet. Having weather information right on your desktop or browser or being alerted by a text message on your cell phone can be handy.

## *Getting weather reports from your own weather station*

Weather stations come in all sizes and price ranges. For about $25, you can get a display that tells the temperature indoors and out and tells time. For about $50 to $100, you can get a display that tells temperature and gives you the local forecast via a wireless connection. These weather stations come with their own displays that are updated wirelessly every couple of minutes from the sensors outside your home. A good place to find a large variety of weather stations for sale is `www.weatherbarn.com`.

If you want to read the weather conditions outside your home on your PC by means of sensors for temperature, wind speed, wind direction, humidity, barometric pressure, rainfall, wind chill, and more, you can get this kind of weather station for around $200 to $500. Connecting your weather station with your computer can also enable you to share and manipulate your weather data. For more information on installing your own weather station, see Chapter 10.

## *Getting weather reports from the Internet*

Another way to get weather information is to have your computer automatically gather the information from the Internet. This allows you to have instant access to the following:

✔ The current weather conditions for your area

✔ The current weather conditions for any other area you designate, which might be useful if you want to keep track of your family around the country or around the world.

✔ The weather report for the next few days

✔ Severe storm warnings

Four popular means of having access to up-to-date and continuous weather information are as follows:

✔ **Installing and using a weather applet with your Linux desktop:** This is a tiny application that lives on your desktop and tells you the temperature, wind speed, and direction and uses an icon representing general weather conditions. If you double-click the applet, it brings up a window with more information, as shown in Figure 1-5.

✔ **Installing an extension for the Firefox Web browser that automatically gives you up-to-date and future weather information:** If you're a regular Web surfer, having weather reports on the browser can be useful. You can see icons representing current and future weather as well as a pop-up screen of the Doppler radar for your area and severe storm icons. Knowing when severe storms are expected can be an extremely handy feature — especially if you live in a mobile home.

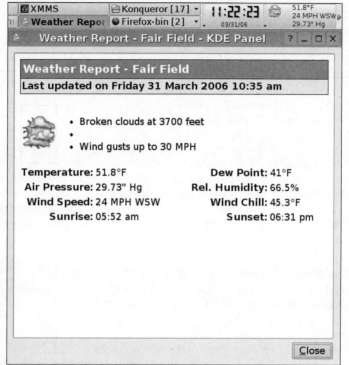

**Figure 1-5:**
Get up-to-date
weather
information
automat-
ically on
your Linux
desktop.

✔ **Getting weather updates from MythWeather:** A primary function of MythTV is to fulfill your need for a personal video recorder (PVR), but MythTV also has a program called MythWeather that you can use to get your current weather conditions and extended forecast. Access MythWeather by choosing the Weather option from the MythTV main menu; see Chapters 6 and 11 for more information.

✔ **Using StormSiren to alert you of storms by e-mail or text messages to your cell phone or pager:** This program automatically checks the National Weather Service for information on storms in the county or counties that you specify. If a severe weather alert exists, it e-mails you and sends instant messages to your cell phone or pager. For more information on StormSiren, see its homepage at `http://stormsiren.sourceforge.net`.

## *Creating a sophisticated phone system*

Sophisticated phone systems, like the kind large stores have that can direct calls automatically, can now be used in the home! These systems usually cost about $40,000 to install, but an enterprising businessman/programmer who needed one and did not have the cash to buy one just programmed one himself. He offered it to others as an open source program, named Asterisk, and since then over 300 programmers have contributed to it.

Asterisk is one of the best phone systems for businesses around, and it's free! Because Asterisk needs someone savvy with Linux to install it, another system based on Asterisk was created for home use: Asterisk@Home.

Asterisk@Home has the following features:

- ✔ Digital receptionist to direct calls automatically. For example, the call can be directed to your phone, your spouse's phone, or the kids' phones.
- ✔ Queue calls on hold and play music.
- ✔ Forward calls.
- ✔ E-mail voice mail messages.
- ✔ Send voice mail with Web access or phone access and more.

Running Asterisk at home requires the following items to work:

- ✔ Dedicated computer. (Old hardware is fine for this.)
- ✔ Broadband connection — the faster the better.
- ✔ VoIP (Voice over IP) phone lines, which are phones that work over the Internet, such as VoicePulse or BroadVoice. This costs about $10 a month per phone.
- ✔ Phones that are compatible with VoIP, which you can buy for as little as $60, but most cost from $100 to $150.

Asterisk can also be used in conjunction with MisterHouse, a free software application that controls X10 modules and more. For more information about running Asterisk, see Chapter 9.

# Using Linux to Your Advantage

Linux is on the cutting edge of home automation. Using Linux home automation enables you to

- ✔ **Save money:** Most Linux software is free to use, free to give away, free to modify, and even free to sell.
- ✔ **Access the cutting edge of home automation:** Asterisk, for example, is one of the top phone systems available for businesses today. And MisterHouse offers features that aren't available in any proprietary home automation software and is exploring the frontiers of voice activation for X10 devices. Plus MythTV lets you set up a free and feature-full TiVo-like system.

✔ **Explore lots of possibilities:** Lots of home automation software exists, but you can't usually try out the proprietary software without paying money — so that limits your exploration of it. With Linux, you can explore and try whatever you want without feeling a financial pinch. You are not locked into a single program.

✔ **Contribute to the growth of free software:** You can contribute to improving the home automation field by programming new features (if you are a programmer), by helping newbies on the forums, by suggesting new features, and more.

Linux home automation software published under popular licenses such as the GNU General Public License has the source code available for everyone to improve and add features to. This way, it can be advanced by professionals and amateurs alike. And the new features, which are added by programmers around the world, cause the software to grow, sometimes as effectively as if it were designed by a business plan and paid programmers spent every day working on it — maybe even more effectively. And its setup and maintenance costs are a fraction of what similar proprietary software costs.

To some people, Linux is a hobby, but it can be a career as well. Money-making opportunities are available for savvy entrepreneurs. Here are just a few possibilities:

✔ Setting up Asterisk phone systems for clients

✔ Creating Internet-accessible, home-surveillance systems

✔ Offering clients high-performance video streaming

Linux software offers a large range of home automation possibilities, which are fast becoming very powerful and have lots of mainstream applications.

Because the source code is freely available, bugs in the program are swiftly fixed by programmers all around the world. This factor often makes free software more robust than proprietary software. Also, it is much less vulnerable to viral attacks and other malicious software because Linux is inspired by the UNIX operating system, which had security built into it since ancient times — not added on after the system was already established.

Using Linux for home automation might require a bit more knowledge on your part, but in the long run, can be much more satisfying and rewarding.

# Chapter 2

# Filling Your Home Automation Toolkit with Linux Software

- - - - - - - - - - - - - - - - - - - - - - - - - - - - - - - - - - - - - - - - - - - - - - - - - - - - - -

*In This Chapter*

▶ Putting old hardware to work with new software

▶ Checking out the best Linux-based smart home software

▶ Controlling software from the command line

▶ Dressing up software with a graphical user interface

- - - - - - - - - - - - - - - - - - - - - - - - - - - - - - - - - - - - - - - - - - - - - - - - - - - - - -

*A*  tremendous amount of free Linux software is available for almost every aspect of home automation. In this chapter, I point out some of the best software you can use to turn your house into a really smart home, and I show you where to get the software.

# Using New Software on Old Hardware

One great feature of Linux is that you can pick and choose the parts of it that you want and mold it to work the way you want it. If you want to use it to control some simple task, you might find that you can use a stripped-down or lightweight version of Linux (such as Damn Small Linux), so that old clunker computer in your basement has plenty of power to do what you need. In this way, you can give new life to old computers that formerly seemed worthless. It's time to resurrect them from your computer graveyard and put them to work on highly useful tasks.

## Choosing a Linux distribution

The software I describe in this chapter works with many different distributions of Linux. If you haven't already chosen a version of Linux to use, here are some good choices:

✔ **Ubuntu Linux** (www.ubuntu.com): Ubuntu is currently one of the most popular Linux distributions. Like the other Linux distributions listed here, Ubuntu is available as a free download and offers thousands of free software applications and a big community of users you can consult for support. Ubuntu offers new versions of the distribution every six months, and it's easy to maintain and upgrade.

✔ **Gentoo Linux** (www.gentoo.org): Gentoo is a source-based distribution, which means that, rather than simply installing precompiled binary code, you typically compile every aspect of the system from source code. Your computer can take a long time to do that, but this process can give you much more control over your Linux software environment and makes it easy to always have the most current software packages.

✔ **Fedora Core** (http://fedora.redhat.com): Fedora Core is a widely used, well-tested, and stable distribution sponsored by Red Hat, one of the most prominent Linux software companies. Fedora Core offers an interesting mixture of stable and cutting-edge software.

✔ **SUSE Linux** (www.opensuse.org): SUSE Linux is a high-quality Linux distribution that originated in Germany and is now sponsored by Novell. SUSE Linux is distinguished by its polish, its attention to detail, and its easy-to-use YaST configuration tools.

✔ **Damn Small Linux** (www.damnsmalllinux.org): Damn Small Linux is a versatile, powerful, and very small Linux distribution that fits on a 50MB business card CD. It can be a great choice when you're looking for a lightweight version of Linux to install on older computer hardware.

## Choosing computer hardware

For the personal video recorder, MythTV, a faster computer is definitely better, and you need a TV tuner card. (The Hauppauge WinTV model 401 with dbx works well.) For recording one show at a time and playing it back later, you could probably live with a Duron 800 CPU and 256MB of RAM. To record a show while watching another show, you probably need a 1.4 GHz CPU and 384MB of RAM. To record two shows simultaneously, you probably need at least a 1.8 GHz CPU and 512MB of RAM. You probably want at least an 80GB hard drive.

The needs of other programs might be significantly less. For the Asterisk smart phone system, for example, you probably need only a 500 MHz processor, 64MB of RAM, and a 5GB hard drive.

# Finding Linux-Based Home Automation Software

Many free, Linux-based, home automation, software packages are out there, which is great, but so much is available in so many varying stages of completeness and usefulness that picking out what you need can be challenging. Furthermore, the world of home automation is a big world of diverse functionalities that includes software packages for

- Automated device control for lights, home appliances, and so on.
- Automated digital video recording and streaming.
- Motion detection.
- Remote control.
- Weather data measurement and thermostat control.
- Smart telephone systems.
- Webcams for home security and videoconferencing.

That's a lot of ground to cover, but putting it all together isn't hard if you know what to choose. So here I give you recommendations on some of the best software choices and tips to get you started quickly. In the rest of the book, I show you in more detail how to set up, configure, and customize everything to your liking.

## About X10

X10 is a standard that uses the electrical wiring in your home to communicate with and control lights, appliances, and other compatible devices. X10 signals are short, radio-frequency bursts that represent digital information and are carried over your power lines. Because X10 uses your existing electrical wiring, you don't need to rewire your home to automate your devices — you can simply plug X10 modules into your existing power outlets and then plug your lamp, appliance, or other device into the X10 module.

X10 devices come in a variety of flavors. The most widely supported by Linux currently are

- **CM11A:** The CM11A is manufactured by X10 Ltd. (www.x10.com). The company sells CM11A as part of its ActiveHome kits (but not the new ActiveHome Pro kits). The CM11A is also sold as the IBM Home Director. So software for the CM11A is compatible with ActiveHome and Home Director devices and with the UK version of the CM11A, called the

CM12U. The serial port in your computer connects via a serial cable to a CM11A device that plugs into your wall socket and controls other X10 devices via your home's power lines.

✔ **CM17A:** This small X10 computer interface is roughly the size of a Fig Newton. It's also known as the X10 Firecracker. It transmits radio frequency (RF) signals from your computer's serial port to a wireless transceiver that controls your X10 devices via your home's power lines. The Firecracker is available from www.x10.com.

You have lots of choices of free Linux software packages to automate the control of X10 devices in your home. In the following sections, I list some of the most popular and mature packages. With these packages, it's sometimes useful to customize the programming code, so I also list the computer languages in which they're written.

## Software for ActiveHome, HomeDirector, and Firecracker devices

If you're starting out automating your home, you might want to buy either the ActiveHome kit or HomeDirector kit, which includes the CM11A device that can enable your computer to send and receive X10 signals. Or you might want to use the Firecracker device, which can enable your computer to operate like an X10 remote. Both the Firecracker device and the ActiveHome kit are available at www.x10.com. (At the site, search for Firecracker or ActiveHome kit.) You can probably find the HomeDirector kit on eBay. Many programs are available to interface with the CM11A and CM17A. MisterHouse is probably the most amazing, as I demonstrate here. For more information about MisterHouse, see Chapters 15 and 16.

The New ActiveHome Starter kit that is sold at www.x10.com uses the CM15A, which currently has almost no Linux-compatible software written for it yet.

### MisterHouse

MisterHouse (http://misterhouse.sourceforge.net) is a very comprehensive home automation program. It features a nice Web interface, as shown in Figure 2-1, and you may control and monitor it from any Web browser. MisterHouse is a fun program that can do the following:

✔ Dispatch commands to X10 devices as a result of your voice input. (Yes, you can talk to your computer and have it open the drapes, water the lawn, turn lights on or off, turn the stereo or TV on or off, run your VCR, download your stock quotes, and lots more. You speak to it with words that it understands, and it performs whatever function you set up as a response.)

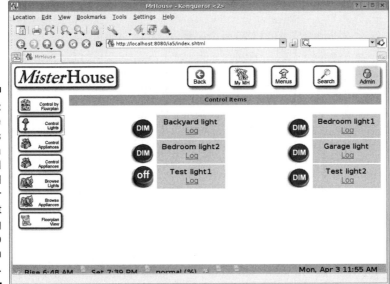

**Figure 2-1:**
MisterHouse
provides
you with a
Web-based
control
panel for
almost
anything
you want to
automate in
your home.

✔ Respond to input from X10 sensors, such as motion sensors or temperature sensors.

✔ Work as a timer (and calendar) to send X10 commands at the proper time to turn X10 devices on and off.

✔ Use free, text-to-speech software to make announcements.

✔ Respond to your verbal commands by using IBM's free ViaVoice voice-recognition engine.

✔ Read and write e-mail files and Web pages unattended.

✔ Send and receive instant messages via AIM, MSN, or Jabber.

✔ Read Web pages of TV schedules to program your VCR and show you reminders about upcoming shows.

✔ Control your RoboSapien, ESRA, and ER1 home robots, and lots more.

MisterHouse is written in Perl, which makes it fairly easy to customize if you want to do so.

### Project WiSH and x10Web

Project WiSH (http://wish.sourceforge.net) implements a universal device driver for the X10 protocol and currently supports CM11A, Firecracker, and some other X10 devices. The advantage of this approach is that you can use a single application with this device driver to talk to your X10 network without worrying about the type of X10 transceivers that are attached.

Project WiSH is available in two versions:

- ✔ x10dev (Version 1.X), a driver for Linux kernel 2.4.
- ✔ x10dev-2 (Version 2.X), a less mature driver for Linux kernel 2.6.7+ and kernel 2.4. This version works on the more recent Linux kernels, but it's more likely to contain bugs and doesn't support Firecracker.

The Project WiSH drivers are written in the C computer language. As shown in Figure 2-2, Project WiSH can be used with its x10Web package, which provides you with three graphical user interfaces (GUIs) that run in a Web browser: two depicting your X10 home network and one that displays temperature events reported by the SmartHome TempLinc, a sensor that transmits X10 signals based on temperature data that it collects. These GUIs are written in the Java programming language.

### Heyu

Heyu (`www.heyu.org`) is a command-line-based program that you can use to control your home's lights and appliances via X10 devices. It's written in the C computer language. You can, among other things, use Heyu to store a schedule of events and macros in the CM11A's memory, which it can execute even when not connected to the computer. In Chapter 13, you build a starter X10 kit by using Heyu.

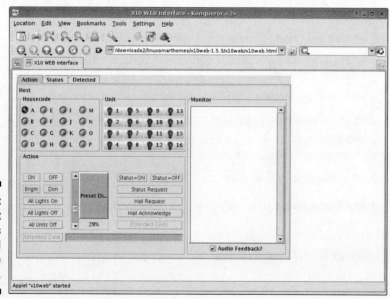

**Figure 2-2:**
Project
WiSH's
x10Web GUI
is simple
and direct.

### BlueLava

BlueLava (`www.sgtwilko.f9.co.uk/bluelava`) is a CGI script written in Perl that lets you control your X10 devices via a Web page, as shown in Figure 2-3. The script acts as a frontend for several command-line-based programs, including Heyu, BottleRocket, Flipit, and Project WiSH.

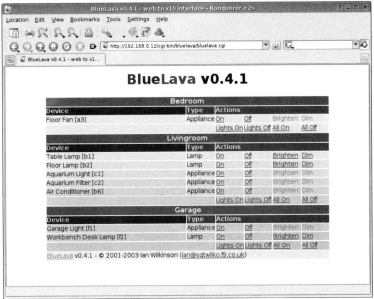

**Figure 2-3:**
BlueLava
gives you a
convenient
Web page
frontend to
command-
line-based
software
such as
Heyu and
Project
WiSH.

CGI stands for Common Gateway Interface. CGI scripts are usually small programs written in a computer language such as Python, Perl, Tcl, C, or C++. You upload a CGI script to a Web server where it is used by the HTML code in Web pages to run other programs on the server that are too complicated to be controlled directly by the HTML code. In other words, it acts as glue between HTML pages and other programs on the server.

## Software for X10 Firecracker devices (CM17A)

The tiny Firecracker is a cool, inexpensive device that can turn your computer into an X10 remote, and there are many good free software packages to control it via Linux. Here are some of the best.

### BottleRocket

BottleRocket (www.linuxha.com/bottlerocket) is a command line inter-face to Firecracker devices, and it's written in the C language. If you like, you may use BlueLava, WMX10, or CGI-x10 as a Web-based frontend to BottleRocket.

### CGI-x10

CGI-x10 (http://bubba.org/?option=cgi-x10) is a CGI interface to BottleRocket. It's written in Perl. Figure 2-4 shows the Web interface it creates.

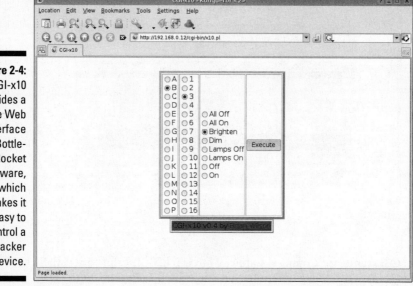

**Figure 2-4:** CGI-x10 provides a simple Web interface to Bottle-Rocket software, which makes it easy to control a Firecracker device.

### Flipit

Flipit (www.lickey.com/flipit) is a simple, command-line-based program for controlling Firecracker devices. It's written in the C programming lan-guage. If you don't want to run Flipit from the command line, you can use BlueLava as a Web page frontend to Flipit.

### TK10

TK10 (http://mywebpages.comcast.net/jfilerunner/tk10.html) is a graphical user interface frontend for BottleRocket, shown in Figure 2-5. It looks like the HR12A controller that's part of the Firecracker kit from www.x10.com. TK10 is written in Tcl/Tk.

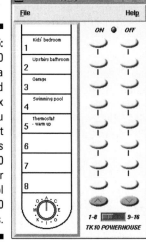

**Figure 2-5:**
Using TK10
as a
frontend
for Bottle-x
Rocket, you
can transmit
commands
to an X10
transceiver
to control
your X10
devices.

### wmx10

wmx10 (www.cs.uml.edu/~jhawkins/wmx10) is a WindowMaker/
AfterStep applet. It's a very small application that runs in a thumbnail-sized
window that runs on the desktop, and it allows you to control X10 modules
via BottleRocket. It's a nice graphical interface for BottleRocket, which is a
command line program. (WindowMaker and AfterStep are window managers
which are commonly available with many Linux distributions.) wmx10 is written in the C programming language.

## Home networking

Your home computer network is important for home automation because if
you set up your network with the right software, your whole network turns
into something like one big computer, with all the resources of every computer available at any computer in your home. Then you can quickly transfer
files to and from any computer, surf the Web from any computer, stream
media from any computer in your home to any other computer, remotely control devices hooked up to your computer, and more. GNU Zebra is a good
choice for turning your home network into an automated powerhouse.

### GNU Zebra

GNU Zebra (www.zebra.org) is free, high-performance software for routing
information on your computer network. It carries out routing of information
packets at higher speed than with traditional networking software. It's also
highly modular, using a separate computer process for each routing protocol.
This makes it easy to maintain and upgrade because each protocol can be

upgraded separately while the other protocols and the router remain online. GNU Zebra is written in the C programming language. For information on how you can use GNU Zebra to transform your computer network into a high-speed performer, see Chapter 5.

### Quagga

Quagga (www.quagga.net/about.php) is an offshoot of GNU Zebra. Some developers wanted to take GNU Zebra and improve it using their own development team instead of working with the GNU Zebra's development team. At present, Quagga is virtually the same as GNU Zebra, although that might change in the future.

## Digital video recorder and media center

With the right software, you can turn one or more of your home computers into a digital video recorder like TiVo. The free software package MythTV is a good choice for this. In Chapter 6, we show you how to build your own personal video recorder by using MythTV.

### MythTV

MythTV (www.mythtv.org) is a free Linux software package that allows you to record and play back TV shows on multiple computers on your home network. With MythTV, you can do the following:

✔ Pause, fast forward, and rewind "live" TV.

✔ Detect and skip commercials automatically.

✔ Play DVDs.

✔ Rip, categorize, and play audio files. (*To rip* an audio file is to copy data from one format to another, such as from a CD audio file to an MP3 file.)

✔ Read RSS news finds.

✔ View weather information whenever you want.

✔ And much more. . . .

MythTV also provides an electronic program guide for changing channels and selecting the programs you want to record.

MythTV is written in the C++ programming language.

### KnoppMyth

KnoppMyth (www.mysettopbox.tv/knoppmyth.html) aims to make the installation of MythTV easy. To quickly see what MythTV can do, you might try installing KnoppMyth on one of your computers.

Be aware that the default installation process repartitions your hard drive, erasing everything there. Be sure to back up anything you need to keep first.

## Motion detection

You can use one or more webcams along with motion-detection software to detect, for example, whenever someone enters your house. You can set things up to send this data to a program such as MisterHouse to automatically notify you whenever this happens.

Motion (`www.lavrsen.dk/twiki/bin/view/Motion/WebHome`) is a software package that monitors the video signal from one or more cameras and detects whether part of the pictures changes, thus detecting motion. With Motion, for example, you can use your webcam to detect when someone enters a room. Motion is a command-line-based tool written in the C computer language.

## Remote control

You can use Linux software to control your computer with an infrared remote control. Just by pressing a button on your remote control, you can send commands to computer applications, start programs, and more. This gives you a way, for example, to remotely control your computer's TV tuner card or CD-ROM (if your computer has them). You can also control other devices with the infrared port on your computer — if it has one. In this way, you can, for example, program your VCR or satellite tuner with your computer.

LIRC (`www.lirc.org` and `www.lirc.org/software.html`) stands for Linux Infrared Remote Control; it's a set of free Linux software packages that allow you to send and decode infrared signals to and from many popular infrared remote controls. The software is mostly written in the C programming language.

## Smart telephone system

With free Linux software such as Asterisk, you can transform your home phone into a smart telephone system that's capable of caller ID, voice mail, call forwarding, and many other fancy features. You can even put people on hold and make them listen to music while waiting!

### Asterisk

Asterisk (www.asterisk.org) is a PBX in software with many features, including voice mail, call conferencing, call queuing, support for three-way calling, caller ID services, and much more. (A *PBX* is a Private Branch eXchange, a private telephone switch that allows telephone extensions to connect to each other and the world outside.) Asterisk is written in the C programming language. For more information on using Asterisk as part of your home automation systems, see Chapter 9.

### Asterisk@Home

Asterisk@Home (http://asteriskathome.sourceforge.net) is a software project designed to enable home users to easily set up and operate an Asterisk PBX with a Web-based graphical user interface. It sets you up with FreePBX, a Web-based graphical user interface that lets you configure Asterisk without editing configuration files.

## Weather

You can use free Linux software to set up your own home weather station and become your own friendly neighborhood meteorologist.

One-wire weather (Oww; http://oww.sourceforge.net) is a Linux software interface to the Dallas Semiconductor 1-Wire weather station. (1-Wire is a low-cost computer bus system designed by Dallas Semiconductor.) With a home weather station and One-wire weather software you can monitor, record, and transmit wind speed, wind direction, temperature, precipitation, humidity, barometric pressure, and other weather data. It transports power and low-speed data over a single wire. The software is written in the C programming language.

## Webcams, home security, and videoconferencing

With this software, you can set up your webcam to monitor rooms in your home or to use for videoconferencing — to make your home safer, to have fun, to conduct business and more.

### CamStream

CamStream (www.smcc.demon.nl/camstream) gives you the ability to view your webcam in a Web page or ftp it in a local network. You can stream images from a single webcam or multiple webcams. CamStream is written in the C++ programming language.

### Ekiga

Ekiga (www.ekiga.org), formerly GnomeMeeting, is free Linux software that makes it possible for you to make free video calls and audio calls over the Internet. It can also call regular phones for a slight charge. Ekiga is a polished and proven program and easy to use. It has a Configuration Druid (that's like a wizard) that leads you through the setup step-by-step and gets you started without a hassle (hopefully). For more information on Ekiga, check out Chapter 8.

## Finding even more software

There's lots more Linux home automation software out there. For a big list of all kinds of Linux software for home automation, check out my Linux Home Automation pages at www.linuxha.com/athome/index.html#Software.

# Doing the Tough Work with Low-Level Software

Some of the software I discuss here, such as Heyu, is no-frills stuff that has no graphics and runs from a *command line* in a *terminal window*. If this is Greek to you, it isn't as bad as it sounds. You're probably used to running programs that have windows and menus that you control via the computer mouse. A *terminal window* is a program that emulates an old-fashioned, text-based computer from the days before computer windows, menus, and mice. You can typically bring up a terminal window by choosing it from a menu. If you're running Linux with the KDE desktop environment, for example, you might bring up a terminal window by choosing KDE⇨System⇨Terminal Program (Konsole). Then a window appears in which you can type commands. The current location in the window where you can type in a command is called the *command line*. For example, if you've already installed Heyu on your computer, at the command line in the terminal window you might type

```
heyu on a1
```

This would run the program Heyu with the parameters on and a1, so that Heyu would turn on the device at location a1.

To run some of the software I discuss here, you might need to compile it from source code by issuing some commands from a terminal window. A computer program's *source code* is the set of instructions that a computer programmer writes that direct the computer to do something. This set of instructions is transformed by a special program called a *compiler* into the numeric codes that can directly control the computer hardware. These numeric codes are called *object code.* So to compile the program's source code into object code and thus install the program onto your computer into a form in which it can run, you might need to type a series of commands in a terminal window, perhaps something like this:

```
./configure
make
make install
```

Note that you might have to type something different for a particular program, but generally, you will find the instructions for compiling your program in a file that comes with the source code and is labeled README or INSTALL or something like that. Then the computer will digest the lines of source code one by one and compile them into object code. When this is all done, you should be able to run your program.

# Dressing Up the Rough Stuff

Running a program from the command line might seem like driving a car with a stick shift. You can do it, but it's work. If this doesn't appeal to you, often the command-line-driven programs I discuss here can be dressed up with a graphical user interface (or GUI) that makes them much easier to use. For example, you can control Heyu via the Web page interface provided by MisterHouse. You can control Project WiSH with one of the two graphical interfaces provided by x10Web. You can use BlueLava as a GUI for Heyu, BottleRocket, Flipit, or Project WiSH. You can use Asterisk@Home to dress up Asterisk with the FreePBX Web page interface, and so on. In some cases, simply issuing commands from the command line might be easier, but usually, it's much easier to control everything from one of the GUIs.

# Part II
# Connecting Multiple Computers without the Wires

The 5th Wave                     By Rich Tennant

"That's it! We're getting a wireless network for the house."

# In this part . . .

You can have your fun and lose the wires, too! In Part II, you discover all about building the network setup without the hookup. You find out about wireless network cards, as well as the drivers and Linux wireless support tools you need to make your smart home wireless. I show you how to add a wireless access point, and I even discuss how to add dynamic routing to your network.

# Chapter 3

# Going Wireless

*W*ireless networking is all the rage, and for good reason: It makes working with a computer easy. With wireless networking, you can build a high-speed network that enables you to freely move around. At work, I have a wireless setup, which permits me to move around the building (inside and out) and carry my work with me. When working from home, I'm no longer stuck in my home office. I can move around the house or out in the back yard and continue to work. I still have various computers that must be hard-wired to the LAN. However, for computers that I want to move around or when I put a computer where no LAN cabling exists, wireless works great.

I start this chapter by introducing you to the basics of wireless networking. Then I show you how to select a card, upgrade your Linux kernel, install the wireless driver, and configure and secure your wireless network interface card (NIC).

## Wireless Networking 101

The starting point for your wireless decision-making is to gather a few items. (Don't rush and buy them just yet because it's not easy to mix and match wireless cards and Linux without knowing what and why you need it.) Here's a general list of what you need:

  ✔ **Wireless access point (WAP):** The WAP is the center of your network. (See Figure 3-1 for what a common, home network setup might look like.) It connects the wired network to the wireless network. Most WAPs have a lot of other useful extra features, such as network sharing and security. The network sharing feature allows you to have multiple computers accessing the Internet by using the single IP address provided by your ISP. A lot of good wireless network vendors are available, and you need to do some research before you buy.

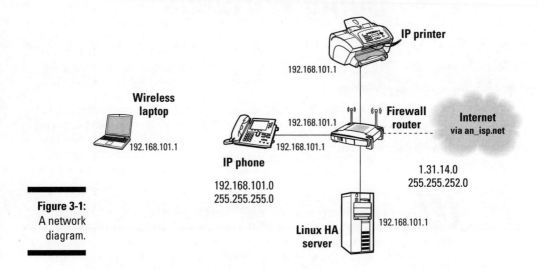

**Figure 3-1:**
A network
diagram.

I like the Linksys WRT54GL or WRT54GS (version V1 to V4, not V5 or GC). The Linux community has done a good job of extending the original open source Linksys code to provide tremendous power in a home router. Other vendors offer other models, but I don't cover them here (although I do have some). The WRT54GL is the router I use in Chapter 4. Before you purchase a WAP, look at that chapter, which contains some warnings about the various versions and a longer discussion about what a WAP is and what it can do for you.

✔ **A wireless network interface card (NIC) for each computer to be networked:** I recommend four types of cards: the PCMCIA card, the mini-PCI card, the USB card, and the PCI card. See the next section, "Wireless hardware components," for more details.

✔ **The appropriate driver for each card:** If you can find a *native Linux driver* (one written specifically for Linux) for your card, then I recommend that you use that. (I don't cover using native Linux drivers.) If you can't find a native driver, use the NdisWrapper solution I provide in this chapter. The native solution would give you better performance and provide better support for future driver upgrades. The NdisWrapper gives you hope when all else fails.

✔ **The computer(s) you're wirelessly networking:** This is a no-brainer. I describe the computers further in the next section.

## Wired versus wireless networking

Wireless networking is the easy way to set up a home network. If done correctly, it's relatively secure and easy to operate. My network at home is a mix of wired and wireless network devices. The network hardware that stays in one place (such as my TiVo, desktop computers, and servers) are networked with cables. My laptops (one for work, one for this book, and my Nokia N770 Internet tablet) all use the wireless network. Wireless makes it easier to move things around so that I'm not tied to my office. I can enjoy a nice day outside and still get my office work done.

Sometimes, too many wireless devices try to access the network, and the quality of your net-work connection decreases. This is why my server is on the wired network. For large networks, a mix of wired and wireless computers is acceptable. For a small, home network, wireless is fine unless all your neighbors also have wireless — then things get pretty interesting! There are eight wireless access points within 150 feet of my home. Security in this sort of situation is very important, not only so that others don't steal your bandwidth (and do things you might be blamed for), but also so that your devices don't accidentally join other networks. Diagnosing this kind of a problem can leave you stumped for hours.

Next, I describe the wireless hardware components you need. After that, I move on to a discussion of which wireless standard to use. Finally, I finish this section by telling you about wireless support you can expect from the Linux community.

## Wireless hardware components

I break down your choice of computers to three basic types (server, desktop, and laptop) and your choice of network interface cards to four (the PCMCIA card, the mini-PCI card, the USB card, and the PCI card).

You can argue that, with Linux, a server and a desktop are pretty much the same thing. I define a *server* as less of a desktop (little word processing and graphics use) and more of a computer used for file sharing, printer sharing, Web server, mail, and other services provided to users. Generally, I recommend that you add a wired PCI NIC to a server unless you don't expect a lot of traffic. For typical home use, wireless should be fine. My preference is for a PCI card verses a USB card for server use.

A *desktop computer* is your normal computer that sits on a desk. Generally, you use a desktop for word processing, browsing the Internet, and playing games. Again, I prefer the PCI to the USB for its speed, but the USB card tends to be cheaper; it's your choice.

A *laptop computer* is easy to move around, making a wireless network necessary. Here, you might have more of a choice with NICs. Most new laptops come with a wireless card built into the laptop. Internally, they have a mini-PCI slot to add a wireless card. Your next two choices of NICs for a laptop are PCMCIA or USB. My preferences, in order, are mini-PCI, PCMCIA, and USB. I particularly like the mini-PCI card because it's permanent and gives good performance. PCMCIA cards are plentiful, give good performance, and are inexpensive. USB cards are clumsy because they don't securely fit in the USB port of the laptop (and can easily fall out). If you move around, you have to be careful not to disconnect the USB card.

## Wireless network standards: 802.11

Okay, you've got your computer, you've figured out which bus to use, and now it's time to select the wireless standard (the one your NIC supports). In stores, you'll see a lot of pretty boxes with lovely jargon (geek-speak) on the side. Usually, the manufacturer states which wireless networking standard the device supports. You just want to make sure that all the network hardware you purchase supports at least one of the same standards. The wireless standards define the protocols that are used, the speeds at which information is sent, the frequency that's used, how many channels there are, and so on. You don't need to know all those details because I help you narrow it down to just one choice. There are currently four standards that are of interest. They are:

- ✔ **802.11a, 54 Mbps:** The standard used mostly by businesses. This one is expensive.

- ✔ **802.11b, 11 Mbps:** This is the older standard.

- ✔ **802.11g, 54 Mbps:** The current standard.

- ✔ **802.11n, 108 Mbps:** The newest standard that's being developed.

The speeds listed (Mbps stands for megabits per second) are the theoretical maximum speeds. The "n" standard is not complete. Most vendors are advertising pre-n equipment, and I haven't seen a whole lot of cards available yet. To make things more interesting, there are WAPs with single and multiple antennas. The multi-antenna setup is called MIMO (multi-in, multi-out). They promise to deliver better performance. I have a pre-n WAP with one antenna (a Netgear WGT634U running OpenWrt), but most new pre-n WAPs have MIMO.

The difficult part of this is that I'm writing the book in advance of when you'll be reading it. At this time, the 802.11g standard is the most popular standard. Most "g" equipment also supports the "b" standard. If wireless equipment — WAPs and NICs that support 802.11b and 802.11g (sometimes written as

802.11b/g) — encounters a mix of equipment that supports 802.11b only and 802.11b/g equipment, everyone drops down to the slower, 801.11b standard. This can be a pain if your neighbor has old equipment and is close enough to be noticed by your equipment. The 801.11n standard might be able to work around this, but I'm not sure of that yet. Most vendors will provide compatibility with their 802.11n equipment and the 802.11g and 802.11b equipment. For the rest of this chapter, I talk about 802.11g equipment because that is what I have, and it's the current defined standard.

## Linux wireless support

Wireless support for Linux is very confusing, but it is improving. When you want to build a wireless network with Windows, you purchase a NIC, and it comes with the drivers. However, you won't find any open source Linux drivers on the CD. That's because wireless NIC vendors have signed a non-disclosure agreement with the chipmakers, which means the source code must stay *closed source* (proprietary). For a while, many blamed the wireless chipmakers, claiming that they wouldn't share their chip information with the open source software (OSS) community.

The problem seems to be a side effect of one of the rules of the Federal Communications Commission (FCC, one of the communications regulatory agencies). The rule basically states that the user can't modify the power setting for software-defined radio devices. If all of the chip information were released, the setting would be user-modifiable.

So where does that leave you? Well, the OSS community is a pretty resourceful bunch, and the community reverse-engineered the operation of the drivers. It also seems that some of the manufacturers are pretty resourceful. They've figured out how to comply with the law but still help the OSS community. There are a number of OSS drivers for several chipsets; there is a software vendor that sells drivers; and there is the NdisWrapper package that covers some of the other wireless cards by using the Windows drivers to interface to the Linux kernel. Now that's creative!

So here you are, about to choose a chipset and NIC. Alternatively, the chipset and NIC might have already been selected for you. This happens when you have a Windows machine you'd like to use with Linux (you've already purchased an IC to work with Windows). Here are your choices:

- **Linuxant (`www.linuxant.com`):** Sells commercial drivers for many chipsets. They have a good reputation for their products.

- **Linux-wlan Project (`www.linux-wlan.org`):** Support for the Prism chipset.

# Of Linux, WiFi NICs, and chipsets

So why does the Linux community deal with chipsets? Well, as it turns out, the WiFi NIC manufacturers seem to change chipsets often. It's often easier to identify the chipset that the NIC uses rather than go by the NIC name and manufacturer (different versions use different chipsets). When I first put together my home's wireless network, I researched the most popular chipsets, gathered up a list of NICs that used the Prism2 chipset, and went about searching eBay for a decent price on those NICs. I won a bid for a Belkin F5D6001 (an 802.11b PCI NIC). I got it at a great price and proceeded to pull everything together I needed to replace my existing Floppy Firewall (www.zelow.no/floppyfw) with a Floppy Firewall/WAP by adding the wireless NIC and appropriate software. The WAP would allow the wireless and

wired client to talk to each other and the Internet. When the card arrived, I was surprised to find that the F5D6001 that I received didn't have the Prism2 chipset but instead had the ADMtek chipset (also known as ADM8211). At the time, the chipset wasn't supported under Linux. That means that Linux didn't have a device driver to talk to this NIC and chipset. Since that time, members of the OSS community have come up with a driver for the ADM8211. Instead, I decided to go with the Linksys WRT54GS WAP to replace my existing firewall. So, you should do research before you purchase a WiFi NIC to make sure that Linux can support the chipset on the NIC. If you're stuck with a NIC that is not supported, you can fall back to using NdisWrapper.

- **MadWifi (http://madwifi.org):** Support for the Atheros chipset.
- **Atheros (www.ath-driver.org):** Support for the Atheros chipset.
- **acx100, from TI (http://acx100.sf.net):** Support for the TI ACX100 chipset.
- **Broadcom (http://bcm43xx.berlios.de):** Support for the Broadcom bcm43xx chipsets.
- **rt2x00 (http://rt2x00.serialmonkey.com/wiki/index.php/Main_Page):** Support for the Ralink RT2400 and RT2500 chipsets.
- **Linux wireless LAN support (http://linux-wless.passys.nl):** Support for the Prism chipsets.
- **Intel (http://ipw2100.sf.net):** Intel-supported driver for the Intel Pro 2100BG chipset.
- **Intel (http://ipw2200.sf.net):** Intel-supported driver for the Intel Pro 2200BG chipset.
- **Prism (http://prism54.org):** Driver for the ISL38xx chipset.
- **NdisWrapper (http://ndiswrapper.sf.net):** Support for the NdisWrapper package.

As you can see, there are quite a few choices. Unfortunately for me, when it came time for me to decide, I was limited to just one (at the time, anyway). I had to use NdisWrapper because my laptop came with a built-in Broadcom chipset. Therefore, that's what I cover in this chapter. For some people, if none of the other chipset drivers work, they can fall back to NdisWrapper. The good news is if you find that one of the preceding links has a driver for your NIC, you can compile it without compiling the kernel. (Although you'll still need the kernel development package.) In addition, you can use WPA-Supplicant, but you need to make sure that the correct support is compiled into the package. (See the README file for details.)

So far, you've determined what type of NIC and what standard to use. Now it's time to look for an actual card. I recommend that you check out the site www.linux-wlan.org.

There you'll find the support details for the chipsets and NICs.

# Getting Started with NdisWrapper

NdisWrapper (on SourceForge) is a wireless networking software that you use to provide an interface between a Windows network device driver and the Linux kernel. It allows the Linux kernel to use Windows network device drivers as Linux's device driver. It has recently saved me: I have a nice new laptop that runs Windows (the one I'm writing this book on), and I've loaded Fedora 4 on the machine. I have the built-in Ethernet NIC working fine, but I desperately wanted to use the wireless NIC. Through research, I found that at the time there were no open source drivers for the built-in Broadcom chipset, and I couldn't replace the card with another because the BIOS (Basic Input/Output System, the built-in software that allows your computer to start and load the operating system) doesn't support anything but the Broadcom chipset.

This is where NdisWrapper came in: I followed the site's directions, recompiled the kernel, compiled NdisWrapper, and added WPA-Supplicant to handle the wireless security needed to connect to my WRT54GS WAP. I now have my laptop, running Linux, connected to my wireless network (yeah!). Oh, the drivers are the Windows driver provided by Broadcom. Yes, some rather resourceful folks on the NdisWrapper project figured out a way to interface the Windows NDIS driver to the Linux kernel. So now when you can't find a native Linux driver or an open source project to support your NIC, you can fall back to using the Windows driver (ick, but it works).

NDIS has been around since Windows 3.11. Its primary purpose is to define a standard Windows API for network interface cards. It allowed the higher-layer protocols (such as TCP/IP and Novell's IPX) to have a standard interface to the network cards. The NDIS standard is still being used for Windows NIC device drivers today. In the following sections, I show you how to get your wireless network up with NdisWrapper.

## Before you start

You need to get a few things together. Here's a list of what you need:

✔ Software (not found on the CD, distribution dependent)

- Windows 2000 or XP drivers (usually supplied with NIC)
- Linux kernel source code
- Linux kernel development package
- Development environment
- PCMCIA package (if you have a PCMCIA wireless NIC)
- Wireless tools

✔ Software (found on the CD)

- NdisWrapper
- WPA-Supplicant

✔ Hardware

- Wireless NIC
- Wireless access point
- Ethernet cables
- Home network and/or Internet access

The software not found on the CD is the software that comes with your Linux distributions (such as Fedora, Debian, or Slackware) or with the NIC. If you have installed everything when installing the distribution, you should have the development environment, the PCMCIA package, and the wireless tools. (Type **iwconfig** and press Enter at a command line prompt. If you get a `'command not found'` message, you need to install wireless-tools.) If they aren't installed, use your distribution's package manager to install them (for example, `yum`, `yumex`, `synaptic`, `dpgk`, or `apt-get`).

## Hardware setup

You need to install your NIC hardware into your computer. Follow the directions provided with the NIC. If your NIC is anything other than a PCMCIA or USB card, you need to turn off your computer. Make sure you go through the proper shutdown procedures before installing your card. I also recommend that you unplug the power cable. Some computers appear to be off but are actually still on. At this time, you might want to install the WAP hardware and any of your wired network connections. In Chapter 4, I explain how to set up a WAP (with a WRT54GL and OpenWRT software).

Prerequisite information:

- ✔ **IP network address and mask:** The IP network address is the easiest bit of information to get; most people use one of the reserved private network addresses (Google *RFC1918* for further details). I recommend using the 192.168.0.0 (255.255.255.0 mask). This allows you to have up to 254 devices on your network. The IP addresses 192.168.0.1 through 192.168.0.254 are for host use while 192.168.0.0 and 192.168.0.255 are reserved for special use. I chose this network because a lot of new equipment comes configured by default with this network address.

- ✔ **Service Set Identifier (SSID):** The SSID is an ID that is used by 802.11 networks to advertise the presence of a WAP. There is some debate as to whether it's a good idea or bad idea to permit the SSID to be advertised. Pretty much it boils down to this: If you don't advertise it, the *script kiddies* (amateurs) won't see it, but that won't stop a more professional attacker. I use the advertisement because it makes it easier to get my friends' machines working and it makes the diagnosis a little easier.

- ✔ **Wireless channel number:** You must select a wireless channel number. In the United States, by default, most wireless devices use channel 6. In my neighborhood, eight WAPs are within reach of my home. This usually means that within about 150 feet of my wireless device there is a WAP that is advertising its SSID. That also means that at least seven other users are using the same channel at the same time. It's like having a conversation with 14 people — not everyone can talk at the same time. By selecting another channel, you might be able to limit the conversation to just your equipment. You'll have to experiment if you begin to have performance problems and you notice many SSIDs when you search for a WAP.

- ✔ **Security mode (WPA Pre-Shared key/WPA Radius/Radius/WEP):** You need to select a security mode. You can set up none, which is wildly insecure because anyone walking down the street can use your wireless connection for whatever nefarious deeds he or she wishes to commit. You can set up WEP, which is a short step up from no security. (WEP can be broken easily by an attacker in a few minutes' time.) Alternatively, you can use WPA Pre-Shared key, Radius, or WPA Radius. (Both Radius and WPA Radius require a radius server.) I use the WPA Pre-Shared key, but only because I didn't want to set up the Radius server.

- ✔ **Passkey or shared key:** The last item is the passkey, shared key, or both (depending on the security mode). These keys are like passwords. This is information that you want to keep private. Share it only with those who must connect to your wireless network.

## NdisWrapper drivers

Compared to compiling the kernel, compiling NdisWrapper is much easier! Just type in the following at the command line prompt:

1. **Become `root` by typing** su -. **When prompted for a password, enter root's password.**

2. **Type** cd **and press Enter to change directory to `root`'s home directory.**

3. **Untar the `ndiswrapper` package by typing** tar xvf /media/disk/ chapter/ndiswrapper-1.11.tar.gz **and pressing Enter.**

4. **Change directory to `ndiswrapper-1.11` by typing** cd ndiswrapper-1.11 **and pressing Enter.**

5. **To ensure you're working with a clean setup, type** make clean **and press Enter.**

6. **Begin the install (don't worry — it will compile the code also) by typing** make install **and pressing Enter.**

This compile is pretty simple. Just type in each of the commands, and you'll have NdisWrapper compiled and installed in no time. The harder part is getting the Windows drivers. Here are some pointers:

✔ You want to use the Windows 2000 or Windows XP drivers. (The XP drivers are preferred.)

✔ If you have a CD that came with your NIC, getting the drivers is as easy as copying the correct directory to your machine and then changing to the directory that contains the .sys and .inf file endings.

✔ If you have a laptop that came with Windows installed and you have no install CD, you have to visit the laptop manufacturer's Web site and download the drivers. I had to use Wine (a Windows compatibility layer for Linux) to install the drivers under Linux. If you use Wine, don't worry that it fails to install; it leaves behind the files under ~/.wine/ drive_c/SwSetup/SP30290A/. The location might vary, but the initial ~/.wine/drive_c/ should stay the same.

If while compiling NdisWrapper you get a warning message (in Step 6 of the previous steps) that your kernel is compiled with the 4K stack option, proceed to the section "Compiling a Custom Kernel" and compile a new kernel. After you've rebooted (you need to reboot to use the new kernel) and you're running the new kernel, return to Step 5 of the previous steps and proceed forward. If you receive no such warning, you can just continue with the steps. And then you can skip the section on compiling your kernel. Remember that it makes a good reference for the future if you ever need to recompile the kernel.

# Configuring NdisWrapper

After you've copied the Windows drivers from your CD (or other method), you're ready to configure NdisWrapper. Just follow these steps:

1. **Insert the CD (that came with your NIC) into your CD drive. If it doesn't automount, type** mount /dev/cdrom /mnt/disk -r **at the command line prompt and press Enter.**

2. **Type** cd /media/disk/ **and press Enter to change directory to the mounted disk.**

3. **Find the Windows driver for your card.**

   You have to search the CD that came with your NIC. Search for file names that end in .inf. You can use the command find . -name *.inf to help you find likely candidates.

4. **When you find a likely candidate, change to the directory that contains the XP (preferred) or 2000 drivers and type** file *.inf.

   This directory will have files with the extension .inf and .sys. You should see at least one file that is described (from the file command's output) as Windows INF file. Make note of that file name; it's the one you need in a minute. I use bcmw15a.inf in my example.

5. **To install the Windows drivers with NdisWrapper, type** ndiswrapper -i bcmwl5a.inf **and press Enter.**

   This will read the bcmw15a.inf file, find the device drivers, and then install them into the correct directories under Linux. (You don't need the Windows CD when you boot Linux.)

6. **To verify the installed drivers, type:**

   ```
   ndiswrapper -l
   Installed drivers:
   bcmwl5a    driver installed, hardware present
   ```

   This tells you that NdisWrapper has installed the bcmwl5a drivers and that the hardware is present. (NdisWrapper found the NIC on the machine.)

   If you encounter errors, you probably booted into the wrong kernel. Double-check your work and make sure you're on the new kernel. (Type **uname -a** — the output should have today's date if you compiled it today.)

7. **Use** modprobe **to install the ndiswrapper driver into the kernel by typing** modprobe ndiswrapper **and pressing Enter.**

This part may seem a little confusing. The earlier command installed the Windows drivers on your hard disk. Now you've installed the NdisWrapper driver in the kernel. This driver wraps an interface around the Windows driver so Linux can talk to NIC.

8. **Make sure the NdisWrapper driver installed properly by typing** dmesg | grep ndiswrapper **and pressing Enter.**

   This returns some information about the installation of the module, allowing you to double-check that everything is okay.

9. **Create a module alias for ndiswrapper by typing** ndiswrapper -m **and pressing Enter.**

In my example, I used the Broadcom Airforce One 54g drivers (bcmwl5). In the XP directory, I found a number of .inf files. The bcmwl5a.inf file was the only file that was identified as a Windows .inf file (type **file \***), so that was the one for me to choose.

# Compiling a Custom Kernel

Well, if you're reading this, it probably means you need to build a *custom kernel* (a kernel where you add drivers or other features not compiled into the default kernel). If you received no warning during your compile of NdisWrapper (Step 6 of the "NdisWrapper drivers" section), compiling a custom kernel is unnecessary, and you can move on to the "Getting Started with WPA-Supplicant" section. If you're here for some other reason, such as you need a kernel with new features, by all means, read on.

Building your first kernel is a bit scary, but eventually you might need to create a custom kernel to support a new piece of hardware or some other feature. The process isn't scary because it's difficult but rather because it's slow and frustrating. The one thing you should never do is to go into the config file (using make xconfig) and start turning off many things all at once. You should make changes gradually, one at a time. The proper way to build the kernel is tightly tied to three things: the distribution (Red Hat, Fedora, Debian, SUSE, and so on) you're using; the version of the kernel (2.4 or 2.6) you're using; and the boot loader you're using (LILO or GRUB). So despite the instructions I have here, I still recommend using your favorite search engine with the following parameters: the kernel compile or build, your kernel version (2.4 or 2.6), and the distribution you're using. Then double-check my instructions before building a new kernel. This can save you endless hours of frustration. Although I'm confident with the information presented, a new change might occur between the time I'm writing this and the time you're reading this. In addition, you need to make sure you handle the boot loader correctly. The two that I'm aware of are LILO and GRUB. There are others, but they aren't as common. I've documented LILO and GRUB later in the chapter. In addition, as a last precaution, download and burn a recovery CD before you start building a new kernel. Use you favorite search engine with the parameters *Linux recovery CD.*

Most modern Linux distributions put the freshly built kernel into /boot. In my examples, that's where I put them. I describe only the kernel builds for Fedora with a 2.4 or 2.6 kernel, for Debian with a 2.4 or 2.6 kernel, or the use of a vanilla 2.4 or 2.6 kernel. (A *vanilla kernel* is not associated with a distribution.) This should cover just about everyone. The Fedora instructions should cover Fedora -based distributions such as Red Hat and Centos. The Debian instructions should cover Debian-based distributions such as Ubuntu and Knoppix.

## Backing up your current kernel

Before you start compiling your custom kernel, take the time to make a backup copy of your current running kernel. If something goes wrong in the process of creating your custom kernel, you'll be happy you did. To back up your current kernel, follow these steps:

1. **At a command line, type** uname -r.

   This returns your kernel version. Mine returned 2.6.15-1.1833_FC5, which I use throughout this example. You need the kernel version so you know what kernel version to back up.

2. **Change directories to /boot by typing:**

   ```
   cd /boot ; ls
   ```

3. **Make a copy of your old kernel. (I'm using vmlinuz-2.6.15-1.1833_FC5 in my example.)**

   ```
   cp vmlinuz-2.6.15-1.1833_FC5 vmlinuz-2.6.15-1.1833_FC5.bak
   ```

   If you're missing this file (your kernel), you've got problems that I can't fix (sorry). This could mean you've got a special distribution and you'll need to investigate that further. (Google is your friend.)

4. **Make a copy of your old initrd file. (I'm using initrd-2.6.15-1.1833_FC5 in my example.)**

   ```
   cp initrd-2.6.15-1.1833_FC5 initrd-2.6.15-1.1833_FC5.bak
   ```

   This step is important to those kernels that support initrd. This started in kernel 2.6, so it's important for machines with kernel 2.6.

5. **Make a copy of your old `System.map` file. (I'm using `System.map-2.6.15-1.1833_FC5` in my example.)**

```
cp System.map-1.6.15-2.1833_FC5 System.map-1.6.15-2.1833_FC5.bak
```

Don't worry if you don't have the files in Steps 5 and 6; if they're missing, you can skip these steps.

6. **Make a copy of your old configuration file. (I'm using `config-2.6.15-1.1833_FC5` in my example.)**

```
cp config-2.6.15-1.1833_FC5 config-2.6.15-1.1833_FC5.bak
```

Later in the chapter, in the "Configuring LILO" and "Configuring GRUB" sections, I explain how to add the correct statements for LILO and GRUB.

## *The compiling*

Compiling the kernel can be a bit scary. It takes quite some time (about an hour and a half on a 1.6 GHz machine) and a lot of disk space (up to 1GB of disk space for Fedora FC5). Unfortunately, it's necessary; to use NdisWrapper, you need to have the 4K stacks turned off. (In Fedora, it defaults to on.) In this section, I outline directions for doing this in five versions of Linux. (See the "Linux kernel version information" sidebar for a note about versions, and be sure to back up your current running kernel before you begin; see the preceding section for that.) Here is a summary of what you'll be doing:

1. Download the latest kernel source package for your distribution.

   At the time I was writing this, the 2.6.15 kernel just became available. I started with 2.6.12 only a few months earlier. Therefore, you most likely will be downloading a different version of the kernel source package. This is not a problem. I've also replaced the site names with `mirror.edu`. You really need to visit the distribution mirrors page and look for the closest mirror to you. Adjust the instructions that follow to fit the kernel version you're running. For example, if you download `kernel-2.6.15-1.1831_FC5.src.rpm`, replace the `2.6.12-1.1390` with `2.6.15-1.1831` and/or `2.6.12` with `2.6.15` in the instructions.

   This version might not match the version of the kernel you're currently running, but that's okay. As long as you aren't trying to upgrade from a 2.2 to a 2.4 or a 2.4 to a 2.6 kernel, you should be okay. Check for a mirror close to you:

   - Fedora: `http://fedora.redhat.com/Download/mirrors.html`
   - Debian: `www.debian.org/distrib`
   - Vanilla kernels: `www.kernel.org`

If you type **uname -r**, it will tell you whether you are currently running a version 2.4 or 2.6 kernel. Earlier versions such as 2.2 are not supported with NdisWrapper.

2. Install the kernel source, configure it, build the kernel and modules, and install it.

Of course, the installing, configuring, and building differs a bit from version to version. In the following sections, I outline the instructions for Fedora 2.6, Debian 2.6 and 2.4, and vanilla 2.6 and 2.4. They're all quite similar and are based on the more detailed steps included in the "Fedora 2.6" section; I note differences where applicable.

3. Configure LILO or GRUB (boot loaders) and reboot.

*Do not reboot,* though, until you have made the appropriate changes to your boot loader. You'll be adding entries so that if there is something wrong with your kernel you'll be able to safely reboot and choose the backup option in the boot menu.

### Fedora 2.6

To install the kernel source, configure it, build the kernel and modules, and install it in Fedora 2.6, follow these steps:

1. **Download the latest and greatest kernel source or the exact one that matches what you are currently running; for example:**

```
wget ftp://ftp.mirror.edu/pub/fedora/linux/core/updates/4/SRPMS/
      kernel-2.6.12-1.1390_FC5.src.rpm
```

The kernel `2.6.12-1.1390_FC5` isn't even close to being the latest and greatest; it's just an example.

The FTP site is at `http://fedora.redhat.com/Download/ mirrors.html`. Visit that page to find a mirror nearest you. To find out what version you are currently running, type in **uname -a**.

2. **Install the kernel with the rpm command, like this:**

```
rpm -ihv kernel-2.6.12-1.1390_FC5.src.rpm
```

3. **Change directories by typing this at the command line:**

```
cd /usr/src/redhat/SPECS/
```

4. **Prep a new rpm with rpmbuild -bp, like this:**

```
rpmbuild -bp --target=i686 kernel-2.6.spec
```

This unpacks everything and applies all the patches contained in the kernel source `rpm` that you just downloaded and installed (in Steps 1 and 2).

5. **Time to change directories again; type this at the command line:**

```
cd ../BUILD/kernel-2.6.12/linux-2.6.12/
```

6. **Copy the appropriate `config` file from the `configs` directory:**

```
cp configs/kernel-2.6.12-i586.config config.bak
```

If you're unsure, just copy the i586 version as I've done here.

7. **Run the `sed` these commands to replace the 4K stacks with 8K stacks:**

```
cat config.bak | \
sed -e 's/CONFIG_LOCALVERSION=""/ CONFIG_LOCALVERSION="_FC5"/' | \
sed -e 's/\(CONFIG_4KSTACKS\).*/# \1 is not set/' > .config
cp Makefile Makefile.bak
sed -e 's/^EXTRAVERSION = - prep.*/EXTRAVERSION = -1.1390/' \
< Makefile.bak >Makefile
```

The gobbledygook that follows `sed` is a regular expressions string to find the commented line and uncomment it. If you need to make other changes to the kernel, such as including other drivers, now is a good time to do so. (Type **make xconfig** before Step 8.) If you are unsure, just continue with my current instructions.

8. **Type make oldconfig to accept your current changes:**

```
make oldconfig
```

9. **Type make rpm, which can take a long time depending on the speed of your machine:**

```
make rpm
```

On my no-name brand 1.6 GHz machine, it took about one and a half hours.

10. **When the `make` command has finally completed (and had no errors), change directories:**

```
cd /usr/src/redhat/RPMS/i386/
```

11. **Install the new kernel with the `rpm` command:**

```
rpm -ivh kernel-2.6.121.1390-1.i386.rpm
```

12. **Now change directory to `/boot`:**

```
cd /boot
```

This is where your shiny new kernel sits, waiting for you to reboot to put it in service. Don't reboot yet! You still have a few more steps.

13. **Run the `mkinitrd` command:**

```
mkinitrd initrd-2.6.12-1.1390_FC5 2.6.12-1.1390_FC5
```

This command creates the initial `ramdisk` images for preloading the kernel modules.

14. **Change the directory to grub and jump to the "Configuring GRUB" section of this chapter to continue with the final steps *before* rebooting:**

```
cd grub/
```

## Debian 2.6

These commands follow along the same route as the Fedora commands. (Refer to the preceding set of steps for details.) I know the commands differ a little bit, but they still perform the same basic steps to configure (the make menuconfig), compile, and install the kernel. Again, don't reboot until you've completed the LILO instructions. Open a terminal window (a command line prompt) and enter these commands as shown here:

1. `apt-get install kernel-package ncurses-dev fakeroot wget bzip2`

2. `cd /usr/src`

3. `wget http://www.kernel.org/pub/linux/kernel/v2.6/ linux-2.6.16.tar.bz2`

4. `tar xjf linux-2.6.16.tar.bz2`

5. `cd linux-2.6.16/`

6. `cp .config config.bak`

7. `cat config.bak |`

   `sed -e 's/\(CONFIG_4KSTACKS\).*/# \1 is not set/' > .config`

8. `make menuconfig`

9. `make-kpkg clean`

10. `fakeroot make-kpkg --revision=custom.1.0 kernel_image`

11. `cd ../`

12. `deb http://www.backports.org/debian/ woody module-init-tools initrd-tools procps`

13. `apt-get update`

14. `apt-get install module-init-tools initrd-tools procps`

15. `dpkg -i kernel-image-2.6.16_custom.1.0_i386.deb`

16. `cd /boot/`

17. `mkinitrd -o /boot/initrd.img-2.6.16 2.6.16`

You're almost finished now, but don't reboot yet! See the "Configuring LILO" section for further instructions.

# Linux kernel version information

If you're using a distribution such as Fedora, you might have noticed many numbers associated with the Linux kernel version. (Type **uname -r** to see what I'm talking about specifically.) The first kernel used with Fedora Core 5, for example, is 2.6.15-1.2054_FC5. Here's how to translate this into something a little more useful:

✔ Version 2

✔ Patch level 6

✔ Sublevel 15

✔ Extra version -1.2054

✔ Local version _FC5

So if someone asks the person with this system what version of Linux she's using, she would say 2.6. The 2 is the major and the 6 is the minor version number. The version and patch level are the official names from the kernel's Makefile. The sublevel 15 is the 15th official release of kernel 2.6. The extra and local version are used internally by the distribution, in this case Fedora. Fedora uses them to indicate that this is their

official numbered release (1.2054). And for the distributions version number FC5, the underscore is just used as a separator. In this chapter, I refer to these numbers as V (Version), P (patchlevel), S (sublevel), E (extra version), and L (local version).

Further confusion can be avoided if you understand one more piece of information. When someone asks what version of Linux you're running, don't say Fedora FC5 or Debian Sarge. Fedora and Debian are *distributions.* The *version* of Linux is the information I explain here. To add further fuel to the fire (of confusion), some distributions add special methods to compile the kernel. Hence, the sections explaining the steps for Fedora and Debian. The section on the vanilla kernel is for those who don't need the special instructions (such as Fedora before FC4). These are generally distributions not derived from Fedora or Debian (two of the largest distributions). I can't know all the methods for compiling the kernel for a distribution, but the ones I outline probably cover most users' needs.

## Debian 2.4

These commands follow along the same route as the commands in the "Debian 2.6" section. I know — the commands do differ a little bit, but they still perform similar steps as the "Debian 2.6" instructions.

1. `apt-get install kernel-package ncurses-dev fakeroot wget bzip2`

2. `cd /usr/src`

3. `wget http://www.kernel.org/pub/linux/kernel/v2.4/linux-2.4.23.tar.bz2`

4. `tar xjf linux-2.4.23.tar.bz2`

5. `cd linux-2.4.23/`

6. `make menuconfig`

7. `make dep`

8. `make-kpkg clean`

9. `fakeroot make-kpkg --revision=custom.1.0 kernel_image`

10. `cd ../`

11. `dpkg -i kernel-image-2.4.23_custom.1.0_i386.deb`

You've done most of the work now, but don't reboot yet! See the "Configuring LILO" section for further instructions.

## Vanilla 2.6

These commands are very similar to the commands in the "Fedora 2.6" section but are meant for users not covered by the "Debian 2.6" or "Fedora 2.6" instructions. The commands differ a little, but they perform similar steps to configure, compile, and install.

1. `cd /usr/src`

2. Download your tarball from `ftp.XX.kernel.org`, where XX is your country code.

3. `bzip2 -dc linux-2.6.0.tar.bz2 | tar xvf -`

4. `cp old.config .config`

5. `make oldconfig`

6. `make`

7. `make modules_install`

8. `cp arch/i386/boot/bzImage /boot/vmlinuz-2.6.0`

9. `cp System.map /boot/System.map-2.6.0`

Don't reboot yet! See either the "Configuring LILO" or "Configuring GRUB" section for further instructions. To find out whether you have LILO or GRUB, use the following commands:

   a. Type **type lilo** and press Enter.

   b. Type **type grub** and press Enter.

## Vanilla 2.4

Because the Linux kernel is constantly being updated, I use `kernel-2.4.y` to represent the current version of the kernel in these steps. Still, these commands work along the same lines as the commands in the previous sections. The commands differ a bit, but they do perform the basic configure, compile, and install. Don't reboot until you've completed the LILO or GRUB instructions.

1. `wget http://www.kernel.org/pub/linux/kernel/v2.4/ linux-2.4.y.tar.gz`

2. `mv linux-2.4.x.tar.gz /usr/src/`

3. `cd /usr/src/`

4. `tar -xzvf linux-2.4.y.tar.gz`

5. `cd linux-2.4.x`

6. `make xconfig`

7. `make dep`

8. `make`

9. `make modules`

10. `make module_install`

11. `make install`

12. `make clean`

    You're near the end now, but do not reboot! See the "Configuring LILO" or "Configuring GRUB" section for further instructions. To find out whether you have LILO or GRUB, use the following commands:

    a. Type **type lilo** and press Enter.

    b. Type **type grub** and press Enter.

## Configuring LILO

Some distributions use LILO (Linux Loader) as their boot loader program. If your system uses LILO, you need to add the new kernel information to the `/etc/lilo` file. Just follow these steps:

1. **Back up your `lilo.conf` file:**

```
cp /etc/lilo.conf /etc/lilo.bak
```

2. **Break out your favorite editor and add the following lines to your `config` file:**

```
image = /boot/vmlinuz-2.6.15-1.1833_FC5.bak
    label  = Backup Kernel
    initrd = /boot/initrd-2.6.15-1.1833_FC5.bak
    root   = /dev/hda1
#
image = /boot/vmlinuz-V.P.S-E_L
    label  = Linux Smart Homes For Dummies
    initrd = /boot/initrd-V.P.S-E.L
    root   = /dev/hda1
```

Here's an explanation of these lines of code:

- The first entry is your backup entry. I had you make copies of the files (in the "Backing up your current kernel" section, earlier in the chapter).

- The `image` line contains the name of your new custom kernel (`vmlinuz-V.P.S-E_L`; some kernels might not have the `-E.L` ending), which can be found in your `/boot` directory. It's a good idea to double-check (type **ls -l /boot**) that you have the correct spelling and make sure that the files really exist in that directory.

- The `label` line is what will be printed on boot to give you a choice of which kernel to use.

- The `initrd` line is only used by 2.6 kernels, so if you're using a 2.4 kernel, you won't need to include that line. Therefore, you can delete the line or put a # in front of the line to comment it out.

- The last line, the `root` entry, tells LILO what disk to boot off. If you're in doubt, use the already installed (original) entry as an example. That one had to work because otherwise you wouldn't have been able to boot into Linux.

3. **Make sure that the LILO file has the prompt and timeout commands in the LILO file and that they aren't commented out.**

   Lines that start with a hash (#) are commented out.

4. **Make sure the timeout is a reasonable amount of time to select the kernel.**

   I usually use something like 30 seconds.

5. **When you're satisfied with all the settings, save the file.**

6. **Execute this command:**

   ```
   /sbin/lilo
   ```

   If you get no errors, you're ready to reboot. If you get errors, check to see that you typed in the path/file name correctly in the previous steps or that the files are really where you think they are. (For example, use the command **ls /boot/initrd-V.P.S-E.L** to check for the `initrd-v.p.s-e.l file`.)

7. **Log in as `root` and type the following:**

   ```
   reboot
   ```

8. **When you are comfortable that the new kernel works, you can go back to edit the `/etc/lilo.conf` file and change the default line to something like this:**

   ```
   default = "Linux Smart Homes For Dummies"
   ```

The test between the quotes can be anything you want. Just make sure that it makes sense and that it matches the `label` of the kernel you want to be the default kernel. (See the `label` entry in Step 2). Again, make sure you save the file.

9. **After you make the changes in Step 8, type:**

```
/sbin/lilo
```

This makes your changes permanent so that the next time you boot, you automatically boot to this kernel.

To find out more about the LILO, type `man lilo` or `info lilo` (at the command line).

## Configuring GRUB

GRUB is my preference for my Linux machine's boot loader. It has many really useful options to recover from mistakes (such as spelling the kernel name wrong). You can do this from the boot prompt when you discover you spelled it wrong; it would be a very bad thing if you couldn't fix the error — because you need to load Linux to fix the problem, but you can't load Linux because it's spelled wrong. . . . GRUB does away with that problem.

1. **Back up a copy of the `/boot/grub/grub.conf` file:**

```
cp /boot/grub/grub.conf /boot/grub/grub.bak
```

2. **Break out your favorite editor and edit `/boot/grub/grub.conf`. Add the following lines to the end of the file:**

```
#
title Backup Kernel
    root (hd0,0)
    kernel /vmlinuz-2.6.15-1.1833_FC5.bak ro root=LABEL=/ rhgb quiet
    initrd /initrd-2.6.15-1.1833_FC5.bak
#
title Linux Smart Home For Dummies
    root (hd0,0)
    kernel /vmlinuz-2.6.15-1.1833_FC5 ro root=LABEL=/ rhgb quiet
    initrd /initrd-2.6.15-1.1833_FC5
```

Here's what's happening in this code:

- The `title` line contains the string to be displayed at the boot prompt (the graphic or text version of the prompt).

- The next line, `root`, tells GRUB what disk to boot off. If you're in doubt, use the original entry as an example. That one had to work because otherwise you wouldn't have been able to boot into Linux.

- The next entry tells GRUB where to find the new kernel (`vmlinuz-V.P.S-E_L`) which can be found in your `/boot` directory. I always recommend double-checking (type **ls -l /boot**) that you have the correct spelling and that the files really exist in that directory.

- The next line, `initrd`, is used by the 2.6 kernels. If you're using a 2.4 kernel, you can skip adding this line. You can either delete the line or put a **#** in front of the line to comment it out.

3. **Make sure that the GRUB file has the correct timeout command and that it isn't commented out.**

    Lines that start with # are commented out.

4. **Make sure the timeout is a reasonable amount of time to select the kernel.**

    I usually use something like 30 seconds.

5. **In your editor, save the file and exit the editor.**

6. **When you're comfortable that this kernel works reasonably well, you can change the default line (mine is 0, which is the first title entry) to the entry number of your new kernel so that grub will boot that kernel if grub times out.**

    This allows you to have unattended reboots and the computer will come up on the default kernel of your choice.

7. **As root, type:**

```
reboot
```

    After you reboot, if you had a warning message during the compile of NdisWrapper, make sure you go back and recompile NdisWrapper. (See Step 5 of the "NdisWrapper drivers" section in this chapter.)

# Getting Started with WPA-Supplicant

WPA-Supplicant is a program that provides your wireless connection with its authentication. When you connect to a wireless access point (WAP), you might need to authenticate who you are before you are permitted to connect to the WAP. (A secure setup requires authentication.) To secure your network, it's best to use the best authentication available. Unfortunately, some of the devices you might need to connect to your WAP might not support the best method, and you might have to settle for weaker authentication. I advise you to use something better than plain old Wireless Equivalent Privacy (WEP), such as WiFi Protected Access (WPA), because WEP has already been cracked, and certain automated tools that are available allow people to break in and connect to WEP networks in minutes.

# Compiling WPA-Supplicant

Compiling WPA-Supplicant is straightforward and requires only that you
make one change to the config file. Just follow these directions:

1. **Untar the wpa_supplicant package:**

   ```
   tar zvf wpa_supplicant-0.5.1.tar.gz
   ```

2. **Change directories to wpa_supplicant-0.5.1:**

   ```
   cd wpa_supplicant-0.5.1
   ```

3. **Use sed (a stream editor) to uncomment (remove the #) the line that
   includes support for the NdisWrapper driver:**

   ```
   sed -e 's/^#CONFIG_DRIVER_NDISWRAPPER=y/
           CONFIG_DRIVER_NDISWRAPPER=y/' <defconfig
           >.config
   ```

   This is one line — sorry it doesn't fit nicely onto the page. There is no
   space between the / and the first C on the next line.

4. **Compile wpa_supplicant by typing:**

   ```
   make
   ```

5. **Change to root by typing:**

   ```
   su -
   ```

6. **Install the wpa_supplicant package by typing:**

   ```
   make install
   ```

Yep, that's it for compiling and installing. If you aren't using the NdisWrapper,
break out your favorite editor and make the appropriate change for your
device driver instead of the NdisWrapper (in Step 3 of the previous steps).

# Configuring WPA-Supplicant

After you have compiled and installed WPA-Supplicant, you can configure it
for your particular needs. Here is where you need your shared key or passkey
if it's required. (Earlier in this chapter, in the "Hardware setup" section, I ask
you to gather the SSID and the shared key or passkey; here's why.) Open the
file /etc/wpa_supplicant.conf with your favorite editor and add one
of the following network statements. The statements appear between the
network={ and } in each example and are arranged from strongest to
weakest:

✔ **Most secure:** In this example — WPA PSK encryption — you replace the string "*SSID*" with your SSID (you need the double quotes). WPA PSK provides good security, and I recommend it as the minimum security level to use to set up your wireless network.

```
# WPA PSK example
network={
   ssid="SSID"
   psk="Pass_key"
   key_mgmt=WPA-PSK
   proto=WPA
   priority=5
}
```

✔ **Not that secure:** This example is WEP security. Although it is better than plain text, it's still weak. Here you add your SSID (in place of "*SSID*"; include the double quotes) and your shared key (in place of "*Shared_key*").

```
# Shared WEP key connection (no WPA, no IEEE 802.1X)
network={
   ssid="SSID"
   key_mgmt=NONE
   wep_key0="Shared_key"
   wep_key1=0102030405
   wep_key2="1234567890123"
   wep_tx_keyidx=0
   priority=5
}
```

✔ **Very insecure:** This last one is a plain text example, which provides basically no security. Just add your SSID (in place of "*SSID*"; include the double quotes), and you're ready to go. I repeat, this is very insecure!

```
# Plaintext connection (no WPA, no IEEE 802.1X)
network={
   ssid="SSID"
   key_mgmt=NONE
}
```

There are more network setups, and they are progressively more secure. However, they require further infrastructure, such as a Radius server. The rest of the examples can be found in the README file in the `wpa_supplicant-0.5.1` directory. Therefore, if you need more security, there are examples that cover it in that file.

# Installing the startup script

Now you're on to the final part, the startup script. The startup script brings up the network at boot so that you can begin to use it right away. I included the startup script on the CD, and you will need to edit a portion of it for your home setup. Just follow these directions:

1. **If you're not already root, switch user (that's what *su* stands for) to root by typing:**

   ```
   su -
   ```

   When prompted for a password, enter root's password.

2. **Copy the rc file from the CD to /etc/rc.d by typing:**

   ```
   cp /media/disk/chapter03/rc.wifi /etc/rc.d/rc.wifi
   ```

3. **Change the file permissions to owner - read/write/execute by typing:**

   ```
   chmod 700 /etc/rc.d/rc.wifi
   ```

   The 700 tells Linux that only the owner can read, write, or execute the file. Everyone else (group and other) won't be able to do anything with the file. To find out more about the chmod command, type **man chmod** at the command line.

4. **Open /etc/rc.d/rc.wifi with your favorite editor and make changes to the following section at the top of the script:**

   ```
   WLAN='wlan0'
   ADDRESS='static'
   # The IP address of this machine's wireless interface
   IP='192.168.2.17'
   # Default Gateway address
   GATEWAY='192.168.2.254'

   # This must match your WAP
   SSID='YOUR_SSID_HERE'

   # This must match your WAP
   CHANNEL='6'
   ```

   This customizes the script for your needs:

   - I recommend leaving the WLAN variable alone. (Anything with an = is a shell variable.)

   - Change the ADDRESS variable to the IP address you want your wireless device to use. Just make changes to the strings between the single quotes. (For example, change '192.168.2.17' to '192.168.0.4'.) I'm using 192.168.2.17 in my example; my network is 192.168.2.0 with a network mask of 255.255.255.0.

- The GATEWAY variable contains the IP address of the gateway (router) to the Internet. In my example, it's 192.168.2.254. I set up this IP address for the LAN side of my WAP, which is my Internet gateway.

- The SSID is the SSID used in my WAP, and channel 6 is the default channel for most 802.11 equipment sold in the United States. If you have trouble with your equipment because of many other WAPs near your home, I recommend using another channel, but otherwise leave it be.

5. **Add the `/etc/rc.wifi` script to the `/etc/init.d/network` script by opening `/etc/init.d/network` with your favorite editor and finding the section of code that looks like this:**

```
# Initialize the networking hardware.  If your network driver is a module
# and you haven't loaded it manually, this will be deferred until after
# the hotplug system loads the module below.
if  [ -x /etc/rc.d/rc.inet1 ]; then
  . /etc/rc.d/rc.inet1
fi
```

6. **After this section (and before the `;;`), add this code:**

```
#My wireless card stuff
if  [ -x /etc/rc.d/rc.wifi ]; then
  . /etc/rc.d/rc.wifi
Fi
```

7. **When complete, save your changes and exit the editor.**

8. **When you're comfortable with all the changes, you can reboot into the newest kernel.**

Your wireless network should start up.

# Chapter 4

# Creating a Wireless Access Point

● ● ● ● ● ● ● ● ● ● ● ● ● ● ● ● ● ● ● ● ● ● ● ● ● ● ● ● ● ● ● ● ● ● ● ● ● ● ●

*In This Chapter*

▶ Getting to know the wireless access point

▶ Opening the OpenWrt software

▶ Upgrading your Linksys WRT54GL

▶ Configuring your wireless access point

▶ Touring OpenWrt

● ● ● ● ● ● ● ● ● ● ● ● ● ● ● ● ● ● ● ● ● ● ● ● ● ● ● ● ● ● ● ● ● ● ● ● ● ● ●

*I*n Chapter 3, I introduce you to wireless networking (802.11 a, b, g, and n). If you need a refresher or you haven't read it, you can check it out. Don't worry, I'll wait. Although the information in Chapter 3 isn't totally necessary to install the OpenWrt software, it's still good to know. The one thing you must know for this chapter is that the wireless access point (WAP) is the center of the wireless network. Although computers can connect together in an ad-hoc mode (sort of an "anyone can connect directly to anyone" network), most wireless networks are set up in infrastructure mode. *Infrastructure mode* has the WAP as the central point to which all the clients (your PC, for example) connect. This is the network design that I describe in this chapter. Here I show you how to use the Linksys WRT54GL as a WAP with OpenWrt firmware (runs Linux).

I'd really love to describe setting up other things such as SNMP (a way to get statistics about the WAP), FreeRADIUS (A RADIUS server for added security) and tcpdump (a network sniffer program), but there isn't enough room in this chapter for all that. I cover the Quagga dynamic routing suite in the next chapter, and I need the whole chapter to do it.

## *Discovering the Linksys WRT54GL*

The WRT54GL is a WAP, broadband router/firewall, and four-port switch. It provides firewall capabilities, wireless access support for 802.11b (11 Mbps) and 802.11g (54 Mbps) products, and bridging or routing on the wireless LAN, and the four-port switch can be used for your home LAN. (You might some-times see the WRT54GL referred to as a *WAP* and other times as a *router*. They mean the same thing. In this chapter, however, I always call it a WAP.) The stock Linksys firmware, also Linux, is fine and provides many features that most users need.

For folks who need only the WRT54GL's standard functionality, switching to a third-party firmware doesn't make much sense. However, by using the third-party firmware OpenWrt (which I describe further in the next section), you can add extra functionality, and support for the firmware will come from the open source community long after Linksys stops supporting the WRT54GL. I chose the WRT54GL specifically because it's available for purchase from Linksys. (Actually, OpenWrt supports a number of other WAPs, too. There is a long line of Linksys WRT WAPs that are supported, but many are no longer being sold. Still, good deals can be had on auction sites.)

The Linksys WRT54GL is a small, powerful computer built as a WAP and has the following features:

 ✔ 200 MHz 32 bit MIPS processor

 ✔ 16MB of RAM

 ✔ 4MB of flash memory (the WAP's file system)

 ✔ 802.11b/g wireless access point

 ✔ Built-in four-port switch

 ✔ WAN/Internet port

 ✔ Uses only 23 watts

It runs Linux and OpenWrt — the White Russian RC5 release — using the Linux 2.4.30 kernel and a variety of open source tools to make it a very com-plete system.

The WAP's main purpose is to take the packets off the ether and then send and receive them to the wireless or wired LAN. The WRT54GL has the extra feature, as most WAPs do, of being able to send packets to the Internet. The addition of routing and firewall software helps to keep local traffic local to the wired or wireless LAN and properly handle sending traffic out onto the Internet. In addition, the firewall can have *holes poked* in it to allow certain types of traffic to originate out on the Internet and connect to a specific com-puter behind the firewall. I talk about this further in Chapter 18, but I also show you how to do that in the "Touring OpenWrt" section, later in this chap-ter. My example permits ssh (secure shell) to connect to your Linux Home Automation server.

In the past, you had to purchase a separate wireless device called a *wireless Ethernet bridge* (no acronym this time) that enabled you to connect wired devices, such as a wired game machine, to the wireless network and back to a wired network. (Ditching the wires is always a real plus with my wife!) This device bridges the two networks together. You can easily do this with the OpenWrt software; essentially, that means that you can use your WRT54GL as a WAP or a bridge. Note, though, that bridging requires two WAPs, so I don't cover that. The OpenWrt Wiki (`http://wiki.openwrt.org`) can provide help on setting up a WAP for bridging.

# Discovering OpenWrt

A few years ago, Linksys came out with the WRT54G line of WAP firewall/ routers and used Linux as the OS for the device. In accordance with the GPL, Linksys made available the source code it used for the firmware. Several projects were born from that source code, and one of them is the OpenWrt distribution (`http://openwrt.org`).

The OpenWrt distribution is for wireless WAPs. It has various software packages that can be added after you install the firmware. It's meant to be small and customizable, a minimalist approach to building a WAP. OpenWrt actually supports quite a few router models from various vendors: Linksys, Netgear, Motorola, ALLNET, ASUS, Buffalo, Dell, Microsoft (yeah, go figure), and ViewSonic. Both Linksys and Netgear actually have quite a few products that are based on the Linux operating system. I also have a Netgear WGT634U running OpenWrt.

The Linksys Wrt family is the most popular of the WAPs, and OpenWrt has support for a number of versions of the Wrt family. Recently, Linksys released a new model, the WRT54GC, the WRT54G v5, and the WRT54GS v5. None of these has enough memory to run Linux. They aren't trying to rip people off; they're just trying to compete with other vendors. At the same time, they also changed the WRT54G v4 to the WRT54GL, which they still sell. So, as you can see, they haven't ignored the Linux community. (Thank you, Linksys.) Table 4-1 shows some products in the WRT family, indicating which OpenWrt does or doesn't support.

So what does OpenWrt provide that the Linksys firmware doesn't provide? In addition to the support from the OpenWrt community for patches, fixes, and upgrades to your WRT54GL, you can add extra tools, such as ttcp, the test TCP/IP utility that can be used for performance testing, among other things. On the other hand, maybe you'd like to gather information about your router via SNMP (Simple Network Management Protocol). This can be useful to see what your daily, weekly, and monthly traffic looks like. It's the flexibility that makes OpenWrt so useful.

| Table 4-1 | Availability of OpenWrt Product Support |
|---|---|
| *Product Name* | *Supported?* |
| WRT54GC | No |
| WRT54GL | Yes |
| WRT54G (v1.0 - v4.0) | Yes |
| WRT54G (v5.0) | No |
| WRT54GS (v5.0) | No |
| WRT54GS (v1.0 - v4.0) | Yes |
| WRT54GP | No |

The best choice of router is between these two models:

✔ **WRT54GL, supported by OpenWrt:** The WRT54GL is quite similar to the WRT54G v4.0. If you find code for the WRT54G v4.0 but not the WRT54GL, you can use the WRT54G v4.0 code because it is the same.

The WRT54GL is the easiest to get because it's in stores. Be careful, though, not to confuse the WRT54GL with the v5.0 or the GC model, which can be found on the shelf, side by side with the GL product. If you find two nearly identical WRTs that are priced dramatically differently, expect the cheaper one to be a GC or v5.0. The WRT54GL has its name written clearly on the box: "Model No.: WRT54GL." It also has a green and black graphic on the front that starts with "Open Source."

✔ **WRT54GS (v1.0 - v4.0), supported by OpenWrt:** The GS part of the family has more memory. Don't install software for it on the WRT54GL; there probably won't be enough memory.

Starting in the v4.0 of the G and GS family, Linksys improved the performance, so the best choice of hardware to get from this list is the WRT54GS v4.0. It has the best performance and the most RAM and flash storage.

Other models are supported, in progress, or not supported. Visit the OpenWrt site for further hardware details (http://wiki.openwrt.org/TableOfHardware).

# Preparing to Install and Configure Your WAP

Before you start, you need to have the following material:

- ✔ **Linksys WRT54GL WAP:** I discuss the WAP in the preceding section.

- ✔ **OpenWrt firmware:** White Russian RC5 (on the CD).

- ✔ **A wireless network interface card (NIC):** If you're installing the wireless NIC, use the manufacturer's instructions to properly install the NIC.

- ✔ **The appropriate driver for your OS, configured and working:** Use either a native Linux driver or the NdisWrapper (see Chapter 3 for further details).

- ✔ **The Chapter 4 worksheet shown here:** The worksheet (on the next page) is the place to write down all the information that you need to properly configure the WAP. The diagram (below) shows a typical wireless setup. Some of the information you will create on your own, and some of it you will get from your ISP. I explain further as you review the information.

I also included the worksheet on the CD, so you can print it (if you want) and fill in the data. It's named `Chapter4_worksheet.pdf`.

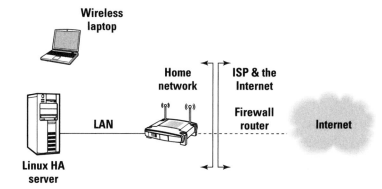

**LAN Worksheet**

Hostname:

Root password:

IP address:

Netmask:

Default Gateway:

DNS server(s):

**WAN/Internet connectivity Worksheet**

Connection Type:

IP Address:

Netmask:

Gateway:

Redial Policy:

Redial Timeout:

Username:

Password:

MTU:

DNS Server(s):

**Wireless Worksheet**

Enable:

SSID:

Channel:

Key:

Encryption type:

I've broken up the information on the worksheet into three parts:

- ✔ **The LAN:** This is your network in your home.

- ✔ **The WAN or the Internet:** This is the information that your ISP provides you.

- ✔ **The wireless network:** Again, this is in your home.

In the following sections, I explain what information to put into the worksheet and where to put it. I explain what everything means and where you can get the information. Now is a good time to plug in the power to your WAP. I recommend that you connect the PC that you will use to configure the WAP to the number 1 port of its switch. (See Figure 4-1.) There should be a network cable provided with the WRT54GL. It isn't a good idea to use the wireless connection because the WAP isn't configured, and when upgrading the firmware, a simple glitch in the wireless could cause you to *brick* your WAP (that is, to render it useless). Now, on to the worksheet; you get part of the information you need from your broadband provider, and the rest you make up. (Don't worry; I provide you with defaults.)

**Figure 4-1:**
Initially
connecting
your PC
to the
WRT54GL.

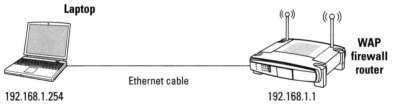

Laptop

WAP
firewall
router

Ethernet cable

192.168.1.254          192.168.1.1

*Note:* Although I can't teach you the science of networking in this book, I can give you defaults that will allow you to use the network without too much understanding. If you're interested in networking, you can check out *Networking For Dummies,* 7th Edition, by Doug Lowe, or *Home Networking For Dummies,* 3rd Edition, by Kathy Ivens (both from Wiley Publishing).

## LAN information

Because you're creating a LAN, you need to select an IP address, an IP mask, and a gateway. The default IP address for your WAP is 192.168.1.1, the mask is 255.255.255.0, and the gateway is 192.168.1.1 (the address of the WAP). This IP network (192.168.1.0 and mask 255.255.255.0) is part of the RFC1918 (Address Allocation for Private Internets). The address space is set aside to be used on private networks (as you have in your home) and is sometimes referred to as *private address space.* This means that you can't share this network information (a route) to this network out to the Internet because other people might also use this address space. The WAP's firewall software provides a way to translate the private addressing to the IP address that your ISP provides you. This is how you avoid sharing the private address space information. The outside world sees only the IP address that your ISP has provided. The WAP handles the technical details of juggling the information, so everything gets to where it needs to go.

Here's a list of the information on the worksheet, with a brief explanation of each:

- ✔ **Hostname:** The name you want to give your WAP. Some people use Greek gods, others the name of candy bars. It's your choice.

- ✔ **Root password:** The password needed to log in as `root` on the WAP. You need this for administering the WAP. Again, it's your choice.

- ✔ **IP address:** The default is 192.168.1.1. The first device on your network (the WAP) is getting the first address (.1), so its IP address is 192.168.1.1. The next device gets .2, and so on.

- ✔ **Netmask:** The default is 255.255.255.0. The maximum address you can use on this network is .254. The .255 is reserved for broadcast messages. A *broadcast* means everyone on your network sees the message. A *network mask* helps an IP network figure out the network portion of the address (192.168.1.0 in my example) and the host address (the .1 in my example). See the sidebar on IP addresses and masks in Chapter 5.

- ✔ **Default gateway:** The default is 192.168.1.1. The gateway is referred to as the *default route*. If you don't know how to get to an IP address, send your request to the gateway, and the gateway will do its best to deal with it. For PCs on the LAN, it will be the LAN IP address of the WAP.

- ✔ **DNS server(s):** DNS stands for Domain Name System. It is a system that stores information associated with domain names (like `wiley.com` or `linuxha.com`). It is used to convert names, which humans understand, to IP addresses, which computers understand. If you don't have a local DNS (one you set up), leave this blank.

If you understand IP networking, you don't have to use the defaults, but I recommend that you avoid the address spaces 172.16.0.0 through 172.31.255.255 and 10.0.0.0 through 10.255.255.255 because many ISPs use these address spaces in their networks. Seeing the same IP network in two places can be very confusing.

Your WAP does the Network Address Translation (NAT) for you, so the ISP doesn't see your private network. This keeps the network working properly. If that doesn't make sense to you, don't worry. You can just use the defaults, and it'll work fine.

TIP

## But my Linux PC isn't on 192.168.1.0

If you already have a home network and it isn't using the 192.168.1.0 IP network, you need to add a virtual interface to your Linux PC with that network. The good news is that you won't need to add any additional hardware or perform a whole lot of magic commands to be able to add this network. Simply open a terminal window and type **su -** and press Enter. Enter root's password when asked and then type **ifconfig**

**eth0:1 192.168.1.9** and press Enter. You've just added a second network to your Linux server. You can now use your browser on your Linux PC to connect to your WAP. This is necessary because when you set your WAP parameters to its factory defaults, it will reset itself back to 192.168.1.1. You won't need the eth0:1 interface all the time — only when you set the WAP back to its defaults.

# *WAN information*

In the WAN/Internet section, OpenWrt has support for these Internet connections types: None, DHCP, Static, and PPPoE. Here, I explain these connection types (see "Connection Type" on the worksheet) and describe the other settings according to connection type.

### *None*

The connection type None is for the user who won't be connecting the WAP to anything other than his or her local network. You use it for wired and wireless connectivity to your local network. You can take advantage of the extra port (the Internet port) by reconfiguring the WAP from the command line. You can do this after you've configured your WAP later in this chapter. Then, visit this URL: http://wiki.openwrt.org/OpenWrtDocs/ Configuration. Proceed to the "Ethernet switch configuration" section of the Web page and configure your WAP for "all ports lan (VLAN0)," as found on the Web page.

     Connection Type: None

That's pretty much it for the WAN/Internet. Simple is good. There is nothing to fill in for the rest of the WAN/Internet section of the worksheet (so just leave it blank).

### DHCP

The connection type DHCP is for the user whose ISP provides DHCP. I'm using this setup. My cable provider provides me with all the information (IP network, IP address, mask, DNS servers, and gateway) via DHCP.

> Connection Type: DHCP

The screen also provides a place for IP address and netmask. These are optional, but I must warn you that even if you know your IP address and mask that they can change. So I don't recommend filling them in.

### Static

The connection type Static is for the user whose ISP provides a static IP address (the IP address never changes).

> Connection Type: Static

Everything you need will come from your ISP. Anything your ISP doesn't supply should be left blank. Here is a list of what you should get:

- ✔ IP address: Supplied by your ISP
- ✔ Netmask: Supplied by your ISP
- ✔ Default gateway: Supplied by your ISP
- ✔ DNS server(s): Supplied by your ISP (you can have more than 1)

### PPPoE

The connection type PPPoE (Point-to-Point Protocol over Ethernet) is for the user whose broadband provider provides connectivity via PPPoE.

> Connection Type: PPPoE

PPPoE is similar to DHCP in that much of the information is dynamic. PPPoE has mechanisms that give you an IP address, a mask, a gateway, and your DNS server list. But the ISP will provide you with some information. Anything not supplied can be left blank, or just use the default I mention. Here is the list:

- ✔ Redial policy: (default is Keep Alive)
- ✔ Redial timeout: (default is 30)
- ✔ Username: Supplied by your ISP
- ✔ Password: Supplied by your ISP
- ✔ MTU: (default is 1500)

If your ISP supports Linux, it'll provide you with all this information. If not, you might have to do a little surfing of the search engines to find out some of the parameters (such as the MTU). The default parameters should work otherwise.

## Wireless information

You need a lot of information, and at first, you might want to start out simple — simple being

- ✔ Wireless interface: Enabled
- ✔ ESSID broadcast: Show
- ✔ ESSID: Set to something other than Linksys
- ✔ Wireless channel: 6
- ✔ Mode: Access Point (also known as Infrastructure)
- ✔ Encryption type: Disabled

This will get you up and running. It will allow you to test the hardware in the WAP and the PC that you're using to connect to the wireless network. But I don't recommend leaving it that way. This setup is very insecure, and it's used by at least four of my neighbors (argh!). So after you've checked everything out, fill in the proper data:

- ✔ **Wireless interface (default is Enabled):** If you don't need the wireless interface, disable it, but otherwise, enable it. It is the main point of this chapter.

- ✔ **ESSID broadcast (default is Show):** Now, there is some argument as to whether or not you should broadcast your ESSID. My opinion is that broadcasting makes it easier for my guests to find my WAP, so I leave it on.

- ✔ **ESSID (default is Linksys; *change this!*):** Now the subject of what gets broadcasted (the ESSID) is a lot easier. Most people who purchase a WAP leave it set to its defaults. There are several WAPs with Linksys in my neighborhood (and I bet I can guess their password, too). My advice to you is to change it to something unique because that way it's easier to use and you aren't left wondering why you can't connect to Linksys. (*Hint:* There are too many other folks using Linksys as their ESSID.)

- ✔ **Wireless channel number (default is 6):** As far as the channel is concerned, leave it to its default of 6. If you have too many neighbors using 6, try some other number until you find one that works better.

- ✔ **Mode (default is Access Point):** Leave the mode set to Access Point because that's the way you need to set it up. This is not on the worksheet because I want you to set up the WAP as an access point.

✔ **Encryption type (default is Disabled; you should really enable this):** This is currently a secure type of encryption, but it does require more work on your PC to properly set it up. And for my favorite subject, encryption type, I recommend using at least the minimum of WPA-PSK. Earlier, I recommend Disabled, but that was just for the initial setup. After you have your setup working, I recommend you change this to Enabled. The extra work is worth the extra peace of mind it gives you.

✔ **Passkey or shared key:** Your choices are WPA Pre-Shared key, WPA RADIUS, RADIUS, and WEP. RADIUS is a server that you'll need to install. (It's one of the available packages.) I don't cover that in this book, so don't use the RADIUS settings. When you select your key, make sure it's a decent key that can't be easily guessed. Mine is . . . I'm not telling! If you've disabled the encryption type, you can leave this blank.

If you're using a JavaScript-blocking application (such as NoScript in Firefox), make sure that you enable it for this site (`http://192.168.1.1/`). Without it, you won't be able to do much with OpenWrt's Web interface because it relies on Javascript.

# Upgrading Your WAP to OpenWrt

These instructions assume you're using the original Linksys firmware for your WAP. If you're using another third-party firmware, the instructions will be different, and I recommend you visit the third party's Web site for upgrade instructions. If you already have your WAP configured, make sure you copy the important information such as IP addresses, masks, DNS, hostname, ESSID, channel number, encryption type, and key. You can use the worksheet to write down your existing information. You need to reset the WAP to its factory defaults; otherwise, very odd problems can occur.

Now that you've written down the important information and reset the WAP to factory defaults, it's time to start the upgrade — but first, read the following points that can save you trouble while you perform the upgrade.

It's very important that the upgrade process not be interrupted while it's going on. So here are a few rules to follow:

✔ **Don't use the wireless connection to perform your upgrade.** If you're knocked off the wireless connection while in the middle of the upgrade, you can *brick* (render useless) your WRT54GL. There are recovery methods, but they're difficult to perform.

✔ **Don't let your cables (the power or Ethernet) hang out.** Dangling cables can trip someone. Make sure that the cables can't entangle even your own feet. One kick, and it's a brick!

✔ **Don't upgrade during inclement weather.** If a thunderstorm or other weather event might knock out the power, I advise you not to do the upgrade until the weather is better.

✔ **Don't wander off.** During the upgrade of my WRT54GL, Firefox popped up a message saying that the script was taking too long and asked whether I would like to continue or cancel. I clicked continue several times until my router finally rebooted. When your router finally finishes the upgrade, it will reboot on its own. (The power link light will start blinking, and other lights will follow.) I don't know whether the script continues on its own or whether the script simply stops and waits for your reply. (I wasn't going to take a chance; I'm not as thick . . . as a brick.)

After you make sure you aren't committing any of the preceding list of *don'ts,* here is what you *do* to perform the upgrade:

1. **Open a terminal session on your computer.**

2. **Type** su - **and press Enter (enter the password for** root**).**

3. **If you aren't using the 192.168.1.0 network, type** ifconfig eth0:1 192.168.1.19 **and press Enter.**

   If you are using the 192.168.1.0 network, you can skip this step.

   This step is really important if you aren't using the 192.168.1.0 network. This step enables you to get to the WRT54GL when it's reset to its factory setting. This is because the WRT54GL is on the 192.168.1.0 network. Its address will be 192.168.1.1 when it's done.

4. **Connect your WRT54GL to your local LAN and use port 1. (Refer to Figure 4-1.)**

   *Do not* connect your Internet connection at this time. You do that later.

5. **Open your browser to your WRT54GL's IP address.**

   If it's a WRT54GL that you've had for a while, use your existing address. If it's a brand new WRT54GL, use the URL http://192.168.1.1/. You'll be greeted by the Linksys Setup page. (See Figure 4-2.)

6. **Reset the** config **to its factory defaults by starting at the main Web page. Click the Administration link.**

7. **Click the Factory Defaults link.**

8. **Click OK.**

9. **It might be necessary to re-enter the URL** http://192.168.1.1/ **into your browser if a timeout error appears in your browser.**

10. **Click the Administration link.**

11. **Click the Firmware Upgrade link. (See Figure 4-3.)**

**Figure 4-2:**
The Linksys
Setup page.

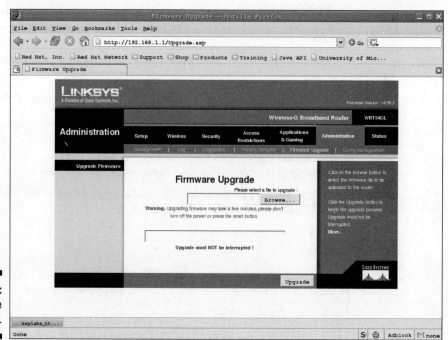

**Figure 4-3:**
Firmware
upgrade.

12. **Click Browse and look on the CD for the binary file: `openwrt-open-wrt-wrt54g-squashfs.bin`.**

    It's under the `chapter04/OpenWRT/bin` directory.

13. **Select upgrade and wait. (See Figure 4-4.)**

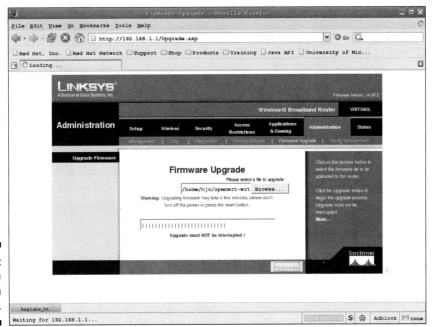

**Figure 4-4:** Firmware upgrade in progress.

14. **Wait patiently by your computer!**

    This will take several minutes. (It took me less than five minutes, but it did seem like forever.)

# Configuring Your WAP

After you have OpenWrt on the WRT54GL (see the preceding section), you can configure it. Just follow these steps:

1. **In your browser, open the URL `http://192.168.1.1/`.**

   You're greeted by the OpenWrt welcome screen. (See Figure 4-5.)

2. **Click the >>Router Info<< link near the top of the page.**

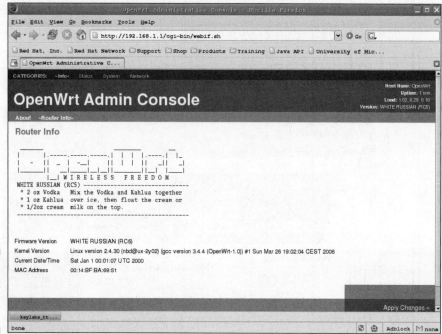

The router will ask you to enter a new password for root. root is your login name. (It's lowercase.)

3. **Carefully enter your password (once in each entry box). Click the Save Changes button when you're done.**

4. **Click the white Systems link.**

5. **Enter your hostname from your worksheet.**

   You can name it just about anything you want.

6. **Change the boot_wait to Enable.**

7. **Change the Language entry to the language of your choice.**

8. **Click the Apply Changes link and then click the Save Changes button.**

9. **Click the Network link.**

   You're greeted by the LAN configuration screen. (See Figure 4-6.)

10. **Enter your IP address, netmask, and default gateway from your LAN worksheet.**

    You can also add local DNS servers (if any). Most homes don't have a DNS server. Yeah, I have one; I have many devices.

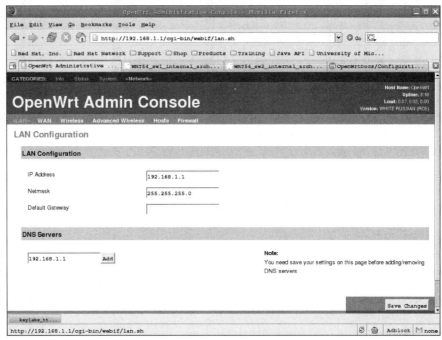

**Figure 4-6:**
OpenWrt
LAN config
page.

11. **Click the Save Changes button.**

    Don't click the Apply Changes link at this time because it might drop your connection.

12. **Reconnect with your browser and enter the login ID (root) and password (the new password you just entered).**

13. **Click the WAN link.**

    You're greeted by the WAN configuration screen. (See Figure 4-7.)

14. **Select your connection type and enter your WAN/Internet information from the worksheet.**

    The page will change appearance to match the connection type.

15. **Click the Save Changes button.**

16. **Click the Wireless link.**

    You're greeted by the LAN configuration screen. (See Figure 4-8.)

17. **Enter the information from the Wireless worksheet, click Apply Changes, and then click Save Changes.**

    Now you can connect your Internet cable to the Internet port on your WAP.

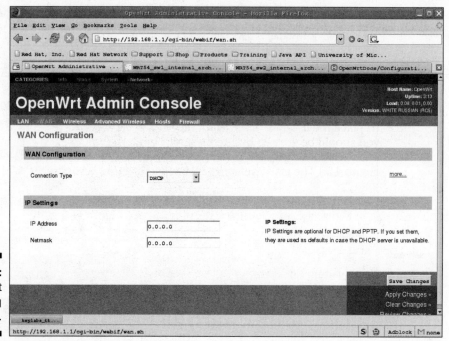

**Figure 4-7:**
OpenWrt
WAN config
page.

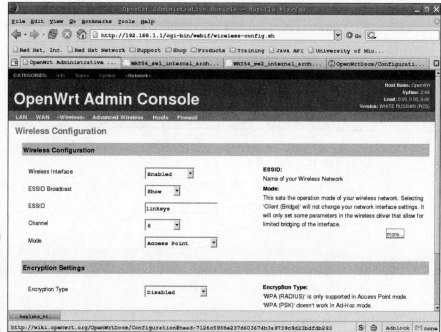

**Figure 4-8:**
OpenWrt
wireless
configur-
ation page.

# Touring OpenWrt

After configuring your WAP, you probably want to take a tour of it. If you want to have a look at the command line interface, open a terminal window and type **ssh root@*192.168.1.1*** (replace the IP address with new your LAN IP address). I don't describe that here because the Web interface will cover most of your needs, but it's nice to know it's there. Enter the URL `http://192.168.1.1/` (replace the IP address with your new LAN IP address) in your browser and you should be greeted by a request for your login ID and password. Enter **root** and the password. After that, you'll be greeted by the main Web page. (Refer to Figure 4-5.) The main Web page features these links across the top:

- ✔ **Info:** This is the general information shown on the main page in Figure 4-5, which appears earlier in this chapter.

- ✔ **Status:** Clicking this link shows you the router's status for Connections, LAN DHCP, and Wireless. (See Figure 4-9.)

- ✔ **System:** Click this link to see system settings, passwords, and installed and available software and firmware upgrades. (See Figure 4-10.)

- ✔ **Network:** Click this link for the LAN, WAN, Wireless, DHCP, and Firewall settings (Refer to Figure 4-6.)

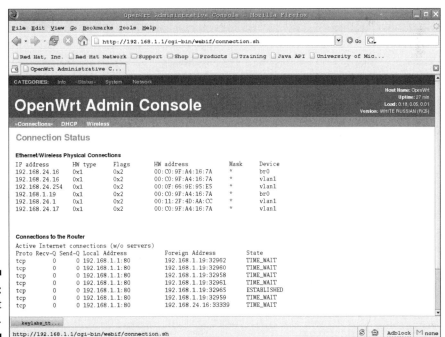

**Figure 4-9:** OpenWrt status page.

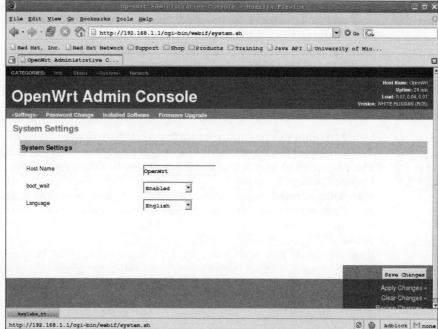

**Figure 4-10:**
OpenWrt
system
page.

One of the nice things about OpenWrt is that the pages aren't spread out. Everything is kept simple.

There are two screens I'd like to direct your attention to. The first is the Configured Hosts screen, which you access by clicking the Network link and then the Hosts link. On this page is a Static IP Addresses section (for DHCP), as shown in Figure 4-11. Here, you can enter the MAC address (usually found on the device, such as an IP camera) and assign it an IP address. Entering this information here ensures that the same IP address is given to the device every time. Otherwise, DHCP can give it any address that's available. You enter the MAC address (which looks like this: AA:00:04:00:04:01) and the IP address and click the Add button. On my network, I have a long list of cameras, printers, and other devices. It's important to know the IP address of anything that has a Web server because you can't easily guess it.

The second screen is the Firewall Configuration screen. To see it, click the Firewall link (which is next to the Hosts link). In Chapter 18, I show you how to set up ssh on your Linux server so that you can securely access it from anywhere on the Internet. To do that, you must *punch a hole* in your firewall.

Normally, ssh uses port 22, but that port quickly comes under attack, so I advise you to use another port number, such as 13218 (which is the example from Chapter 18). On the Firewall page (see Figure 4-12), select Forward from the New Rule drop-down list and then click the Add button. Now, select Destination Ports and click the Add button. This adds a new field. In this field, enter the port number **13218**; in the Forward field, enter the IP address of your Linux server; and in the Port field, enter **13218**. When you're satisfied with the information, click the Save button.

I want to point out one more important link: the Installed Software link. From the main page, click the System link and then click the Installed Software link. You'll be greeted by a long list of installed and available software. Click the Update Package Lists link so that you can get an updated list of what's available. Then scroll down past what's installed to what's available. That's a pretty impressive list. Remember that you can't install it all because you have only about 2MB of flash memory free for packages. Also be wary of removing packages; think before you remove anything. If you remove something important, you could turn your WAP into a *brick* (a useless piece of equipment).

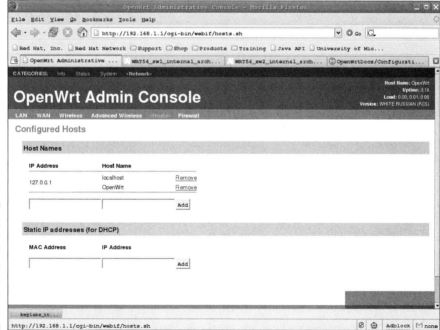

**Figure 4-11:** Enter your IP addresses here to ensure consistency.

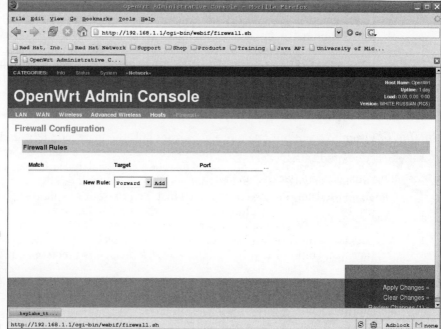

**Figure 4-12:**
The
OpenWrt
firewall
page.

# Chapter 5

# Routing Network Traffic for Free

. . . . . . . . . . . . . . . . . . . . . . . . . . . . . . . . . . . . . . . . . . . . . . .

. . . . . . . . . . . . . . . . . . . . . . . . . . . . . . . . . . . . . . . . . . . . . . .

*A*llow me to set expectations very quickly for this chapter. If you're expecting this to help with you Cisco Certified Internetwork Expert (CCIE) studies, it won't. In this limited space, I can introduce you only to the Quagga routing suite and a little bit of IP networking. I limit my discussion to IPv4 (the current standard) and not IPv6 (the new standard) to limit the amount of confusion. For the average home user, this chapter is probably overkill. For the intellectually curious, this is fun. (Yeah, I know, it's a strange idea of fun.)

In some places, I skip over some details for the sake of brevity. I'd like to explain it more thoroughly, but to do so would take several chapters on IP networking. For more information, check out *Networking For Dummies,* 7th Edition, by Doug Lowe, and *Home Networking For Dummies,* 3rd Edition, by Kathy Ivens (both by Wiley Publishing, Inc.).

# A Brief Introduction to IP Routing

Most home users have very simple needs for IP routing. You normally type in a URL, and the packets get there and back without too much worry. Sometimes you can't get there because a site has been *slashdotted* (when too many users converge on a site at the same time). Then maybe you'll break out to a *shell* (a command line prompt) and try the command `traceroute somehost` to see whether you can get to the site. You might notice that the name you enter is converted to numbers, and you see several lines of numbers with various information. The conversion from name to number is done by the Domain Name System (DNS). TCP/IP and IP routing handle the part where it goes from your PC to the end point and back. When your PC has the IP number, it checks its routing table and sends it to the appropriate device to route to the next place. That router does the same thing, and so on.

In the code listings of this chapter, you see long listings of text — some of it is bold text. The text in bold is the command that you can type at the command line (terminal window). If you type the command, you need to press Enter after the command. Before the command, you will see a prompt; after you press Enter, you will see the output of the command. It should look similar to what you see in the listing. It's exactly the same as working at the command line.

If you're running a Linux box and it's connected to a broadband router (which is another term for the WRT54GL wireless access point; I refer to it as a *router* in this chapter), you might see something like Listing 5-1 in your local routing table.

### Listing 5-1: Typical Routing Information on a Linux PC

```
$ route -n
Kernel IP routing table
Destination     Gateway         Genmask         Flags Metric Ref    Use Iface
192.168.1.0     0.0.0.0         255.255.255.0   U     0      0        0 eth0
169.254.0.0     0.0.0.0         255.255.0.0     U     0      0        0 eth0
0.0.0.0         192.168.1.254   0.0.0.0         UG    0      0        0 eth0
```

This setup is a *default route* (the 0.0.0.0 Destination and 0.0.0.0 Genmask). If your Linux PC doesn't have a specific route to the network you're trying to reach, the PC sends its traffic to the gateway that the default route points to (192.168.1.254). The gateway then looks in its routing table, does the same lookup, and tries to resolve the route. This is repeated until the traffic reaches its destination or no route exists for the traffic. This works well because the intelligent routing device (a router) exists in your ISP and has lots of information on how to get from here to there.

In small networks (bigger than your typical home network), a default routing won't work because no one router has all the information about all the others. One solution is to create static routes. In Linux, you can do that as shown in Listing 5-2.

### Listing 5-2:    Creating Static Routes under Linux

```
$ route add -net 192.168.100.0/24 gw 192.168.1.32
$ route
Kernel IP routing table
Destination     Gateway         Genmask         Flags Metric Ref    Use Iface
192.168.100.0   192.168.1.32    255.255.255.0   UG    0      0        0 eth0
192.168.1.0     0.0.0.0         255.255.255.0   U     0      0        0 eth0
169.254.0.0     0.0.0.0         255.255.0.0     U     0      0        0 eth0
0.0.0.0         192.168.1.254   0.0.0.0         UG    0      0        0 eth0
```

With the first route command, I've added a static route to network 192.168.100.0 to the routing table. The /24 means it's a 24-bit mask or 255.255.255.0. (That's 24 bits of ones in binary.) If Linux wants to send packets to a device on the 192.168.100.0 network, it sends those packets to the 192.168.1.32 router. No longer will these packets be sent to the 192.168.1.254 router; the 192.168.1.32 router has the more specific route to the destination.

Okay, so you have default routing and static routing, and all is well with the world, right? Well, not really. At some point, managing all those static routes becomes too difficult for the network administrator. Look at Figure 5-1.

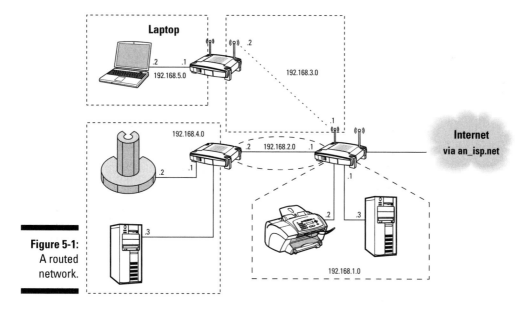

**Figure 5-1:**
A routed
network.

In the figure, you have five networks (I'm not sharing my routes with the Internet) that all need to know how to get to each other. Say you're at your laptop (192.168.5.2) and you need to connect to your Super computer (192.168.4.2; what, doesn't everyone have a Super computer?). You still use the default routing on your laptop and on your Super computer. However, for the routers in between, the solution is to use dynamic routing. *Dynamic routing* exchanges information about the networks to build the local routing table. When a connection is lost, the information is shared with all the routers participating in the dynamic routing. This allows the routers to know whether there is more than one way to a network or whether the route is lost. I didn't put a direct connection between the two routers on the left of Figure 5-1, but if I did so, all the routers would know about it, and each would know the best path to get to the other networks. That's the job of the routing protocols.

# Getting Acquainted with Quagga

A *quagga* is an extinct half horse/half zebra animal that lived in South Africa. Quagga is also a routing software suite. The reason for the name is that the original routing suite was called Zebra. Kunihiro Ishiguro started the Zebra project with the intent of bringing support for dynamic routing to Linux. In 2003, the Quagga project (www.quagga.net) *forked* (broke off from the original project) from Kunihiro's work when work on the Zebra project seemed to slow down. Quagga has continued, and Zebra seems to have stopped any updates. The current maintainers of Quagga are Paul Jakma, Vincent Jardin, Andrew Schorr, Hasso Tepper, Greg Troxel, and David Young.

The Quagga suite is a routing package, which contains the software for the routing protocols:

- **Routing Information Protocol (RIP):** This is referred to as an *Interior Gateway Protocol* (IGP). An IGP is used to route in an autonomous system such as a corporate network (a network under one company's control).

  RIP v1 and v2 support IPv4 (the current IP and addressing used on the Internet); RIPng (RIP next generation) supports IPv6 (IPv4's replacement, which is bigger, better, and more secure).

- **Open Shortest Path First (OSPF):** This is also an IGP.

  OSPFv2 supports IPv4; OSPFv3 supports IPv6.

- **Intermediate System to Intermediate System (IS-IS):** This protocol is an IGP, too.

  isisd (the Linux IS-IS routing daemon) supports IPv4 and IPv6.

- **Border Gateway Protocol (BGP):** BGP is an *Exterior Gateway Protocol* (EGP), which routes between autonomous systems (each under a different company's control). BGP is the routing protocol of the Internet, and it scales well to handle the size of the routing table, which has more than 175,000 routes at the time of this writing.

  bgpd (the Linux BGP routing daemon) supports IPv4 and IPv6.

If you're connecting your Linux box to a corporate network, you'll probably be using OSPF or RIP (probably v2). If you're connecting your Linux network to an ISP that will share routes with you, use BGP. For home use, OSPF or RIP is fine.

# Installing Quagga via a Package Manager

I've just begun to notice that many of the packages (Quagga included) are now turning up in formats that are easier to install via your distribution's package manager (no compiling). Although the package made available might not be the latest and greatest beta version (and that can be a good thing), it is a version that is generally compatible with your distribution. The package manager makes it easier to install the software packages. It also takes care of installing or upgrading any of the other packages that the new software you're installing relies on. If you can use your distribution's package manager, do so. Because I'm using Fedora, I use that as an example.

The first thing you need to do is to find out whether the package is available for your distribution. For Fedora FC5, you can use the yum command, as shown in Listing 5-3. Here, I'm searching for the package quagga. yum will search an online database for names and descriptions containing quagga.

**Listing 5-3:    Using yum to Search for Quagga and the Results**

```
$ yum search quagga
Loading "installonlyn" plugin
Searching Packages:
Setting up repositories
core                                          [1/3]
extras                                        [2/3]
updates                                       [3/3]
Reading repository metadata in from local files


quagga-contrib.i386              0.98.5-4              core
Matched from:
quagga-contrib
contrib tools for quagga
Contributed/3rd party tools which may be of use with quagga.
http://www.quagga.net
```

*(continued)*

### Listing 5-3 *(continued)*

```
quagga.i386                    0.98.5-4              core
Matched from:
quagga
Quagga is a free software that manages TCP/IP based routing
protocol. It takes multi-server and multi-thread approach to
resolve the current complexity of the Internet.

Quagga supports BGP4, BGP4+, OSPFv2, OSPFv3, RIPv1, RIPv2,
and RIPng.

Quagga is intended to be used as a Route Server and a Route
Reflector. It is not a toolkit, it provides full routing
power under a new architecture. Quagga by design has a
process for each protocol.

Quagga is a fork of GNU Zebra.
http://www.quagga.net


quagga-devel.i386              0.98.5-4              core
Matched from:
quagga-devel
Header and object files for quagga development
The quagga-devel package contains the header and object files
neccessary for developing OSPF-API and quagga applications.
```

If you make your *query* (the thing you're searching for; quagga in this case) too broad, you might end up with a list of unrelated packages. In that case, you need to change your query to be more explicit (such as using the file quagga.i386). Listing 5-3 includes three files, quagga-contrib.i386, quagga.i386, and quagga-devel.i386, and they all happen to be directly related to Quagga. Because the description matches, you can install these packages. The last package contains all the source code, which you might not want, so it's optional. There are additional options to query the packages further. Use the manual pages (also called *man pages*) for your package manager to get further information on the available options.

To install a package on Fedora FC5, type the yum command, as shown in Listing 5-4. Here I'm installing the quagga-devel.i386 package, one of the three packages I want to install to get Quagga running on my PC.

### Listing 5-4:    Using yum to Install quagga-devel.i386

```
# yum install quagga-devel.i386
Loading "installonlyn" plugin
Setting up Install Process
```

```
Setting up repositories
core                                                                     [1/3]
core                   100% |========================| 1.1 kB       00:00
extras                                                                   [2/3]
extras                 100% |========================| 1.1 kB       00:00
updates                                                                  [3/3]
updates                100% |========================|  951 B       00:00
Reading repository metadata in from local files
primary.xml.gz         100% |========================|  223 kB       00:00
updates      : #################################################### 714/714
Added 314 new packages, deleted 0 old in 3.29 seconds
Parsing package install arguments
Resolving Dependencies
--> Populating transaction set with selected packages. Please wait.
---> Downloading header for quagga-devel to pack into transaction set.
quagga-devel-0.98.5-4.i38 100% |========================| 13 kB       00:00
---> Package quagga-devel.i386 0:0.98.5-4 set to be updated
--> Running transaction check

Dependencies Resolved

=============================================================================
 Package              Arch      Version         Repository         Size
=============================================================================
Installing:
 quagga-devel         i386      0.98.5-4        core               455 k

Transaction Summary
=============================================================================
Install      1 Package(s)
Update       0 Package(s)
Remove       0 Package(s)
Total download size: 455 k
Is this ok [y/N]: y
Downloading Packages:
(1/1): quagga-devel-0.98. 100% |========================| 455 kB       00:00
Running Transaction Test
Finished Transaction Test
Transaction Test Succeeded
Running Transaction
  Installing: quagga-devel                  ######################### [1/1]

Installed: quagga-devel.i386 0:0.98.5-4
Complete!
```

If you want to, you can include more than one package name and each will be
installed. On Debian, the package manager is dpkg or apt-get. On other distributions, you can type **apropos "package manager"** and press Enter, and
you should get a list of information about your package manager(s).

# Compiling and Installing Quagga

Quagga works fine on the default kernel, so you don't need to recompile the kernel, but Quagga supports a few extra features that might not be turned on by default in your kernel. In my 2.6.15 kernel, the CONFIG_NETLINK and CONFIG_IP_MULTICAST are enabled. You can check the `.config` file in your kernel source directory or the `.config` file in your `/boot` directory. If you need to recompile your kernel, follow the directions in Chapter 3. Remember to edit your boot loader and to reboot to use the new kernel.

When you're satisfied with the running kernel, you can compile the Quagga suite with these steps (it looks scary, but this is a simple install):

1. **Open a terminal window.**

2. **Type** su - **and press Enter. Type the `root` password when prompted.**

3. **Type** tar zxvf quagga-0.99.3.tar.gz **and press Enter.**

   This unpackages Quagga.

4. **Type** cd quagga-0.99.3 **and press Enter.**

   This changes the directory to quagga-0.99-3.

5. **Type** ./configure –enable-vtysh **and press Enter.**

   In this step, you configure the software. You'll notice that there is an extra option for Step 5. This option enables the compiling of the `vtysh` command (see the list of options after these steps). This command makes it easy to edit all the Quagga configuration files at one time. It looks similar to DEC and Cisco routers' command line interfaces. Without it, you would need to use telnet to connect to each port (one of the ports listed in `/etc/services`). Then issue the commands related to each protocol in that routing daemon separately.

   - `--enable-snmp`: This turns on SNMP (Simple Network Management Protocol) support.

   - `--disable-ipv6`: This option turns off support for all IPv6 routing.

   - `--disable-zebra`: This turns off support for the Zebra routing manager.

   - `--disable-ripd`: Choose this option to turn off support for the RIP (v1 and v2) protocol.

   - `--disable-ripngd`: With this, you turn off support for the RIPng (IPv6) protocol.

- `--disable-ospfd`: This turns off support for the OSPF (v2 and v3) protocol.

- `--disable-ospf6d`: This turns off support for the OSPF IPv6 protocol.

- `--disable-bgpd`: This turns off support for the BGP (v4 and v4+) protocol.

- `--enable-isisd`: Finally, this one turns on support for the IS-IS protocol.

By default, the configure script sets up the necessary files so Quagga can compile all the routing protocols except IS-IS. There are more options; just type **./configure –help** to view them. The default options are fine in most cases. If you know which protocol support you want, you don't need to disable them. I don't recommend disabling the zebra route manager (`--disable-zebra`), because it manages your routing table. It also allows you to redistribute routing information among routing protocols. (Yes, you can run more than one routing protocol.) Also, enable `vtysh` because it makes configuring Quagga and your routing protocol(s) much easier to do.

6. **Type** make **and press Enter.**

   This compiles all the necessary files.

7. **Type** make install **and press Enter.**

   Here you install the manual (man) pages, routing daemons, necessary support files, and programs for Quagga.

8. **Break out your favorite editor, open the file /etc/services, and add these lines to the end of the file:**

   ```
   zebrasrv      2600/tcp   # zebra service
   zebra         2601/tcp   # zebra vty
   ripd          2602/tcp   # RIPd vty
   ripngd        2603/tcp   # RIPngd vty
   ospfd         2604/tcp   # OSPFd vty
   bgpd          2605/tcp   # BGPd vty
   ospf6d        2606/tcp   # OSPF6d vty
   ospfapi       2607/tcp   # ospfapi
   isisd         2608/tcp   # ISISd vty
   ```

   The /etc/services file associates a name with various TCP and UDP port numbers (such as e-mail on port 25). Quagga needs it to support the configuration of the daemons.

# Installing Quagga on Your WRT54GL

If you have OpenWrt installed on your WRT54GL, you can install Quagga. It's one of those extra features that OpenWrt adds (I mention it in Chapter 4). Just follow these steps:

1. **Open your browser to the URL for your WRT54GL.**

   Mine is still `http://192.168.1.1/`.

2. **Log in with the username `root` and the password you chose.**

3. **Click the System link and then the Installed Software link.**

4. **Scroll down to the section where you see `quagga-bgpd` (it's almost at the end of the page); if you can't find it, scroll back up to the top of the page and click the Update Package Lists link.**

   This updates the available packages. You need to be connected to the Internet for this to work properly. When you find the links, you should see something like the screen in Figure 5-2. Notice in Figure 5-2 that the packages `quagga`, `quagga-ospfd`, and `quagga-vtysh` are missing. That's because I installed them and have them working between my WRT54GL and Linux PC.

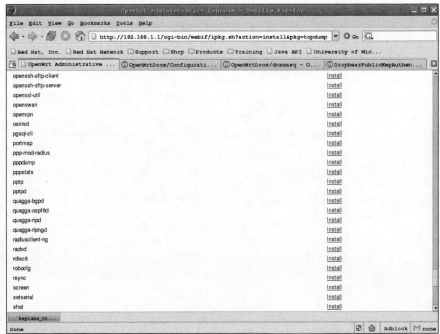

**Figure 5-2:**
Package
Install
on the
WRT54GL.

5. **Install the** quagga **package first (you must install it), and then install the** quagga-vtysh **package (which I highly recommend).**

6. **Decide which protocols to install, and then, to install each package, click the install link next to the package name, wait for it to complete, and select the next package.**

In the "Configuring Quagga" section of this chapter, I refer to the OSPF protocol daemon (the program that runs under Linux, see the section "Getting Acquainted with Quagga" for a list of protocols). You can have more than one daemon running; just remember that each daemon takes up precious RAM and flash space, so choose wisely.

7. **When you're done, you need to use ssh to connect to your WRT54GL by typing** ssh root@192.168.1.1 **in a terminal and pressing Enter.**

Adjust the IP address to suit your needs.

# Routing with Quagga

The Quagga site has several daemons, two of which monitor and maintain route daemons and tables (watchquagga and zebra). The rest are the daemons that exchange routing information:

- **watchquagga** is the watchdog program that monitors the status of the Quagga routing daemons. If a daemon is *dead* (has crashed) or is unresponsive, watchquagga restarts the daemon.

- **zebra** is the daemon that handless the kernel routing table management and redistribution among different routing protocols.

- **ripd** is the daemon that manages RIP version 1 (RFC1058) and version 2 (RFC2453). It supports IPv4.

- **ripngd** manages RIPng (RFC2080). It supports IPv6.

- **ospfd** manages OSPFv2 (RFC2328). It supports IPv4.

- **ospf6d** manages OSPFv3 (RFC2740). It supports IPv6.

- **isisd** is the daemon that manages IS-IS (RFC1195). It supports IPv4 and IPv6.

- **bgpd** manages BGPv4 (RFC1771). It supports IPv4 and IPv6.

- **vtysh** is the user command line for debugging, monitoring, and configuring all the route daemons and Zebra. It's a lot like the command line for DEC and Cisco routers.

Here, I've taken the liberty of including only one of the relevant RFC references because there are many (especially for BGP). As you can see, several routing protocols are supported. With the zebra daemon, you can run multiple routing daemons and redistribute the routing protocols into each other, including kernel and static routes.

# Configuring Quagga

Each daemon has its own port and its own configuration file, each with similar commands. You can use telnet to connect to each port and configure each daemon separately. The port assignments can be found in /etc/services (you add them during the installation process, which I describe in "Compiling and Installing Quagga," earlier in the chapter). This method is annoying because you need to configure each daemon individually, and then debug and monitoring commands can be typed only on the Zebra daemon. Quagga provides you with a solution: the command vtysh. vtysh connects you to all the daemons at the same time. From a command line prompt, you type the vtysh command shown in Listing 5-5.

## Listing 5-5:    The vtysh Command Example

```
$ vtysh

Hello, this is Quagga (version 0.99.3).
Copyright 1996-2005 Kunihiro Ishiguro, et al.

Quagga# ?
  clear        Reset functions
  configure    Configuration from vty interface
  copy         Copy from one file to another
  debug        Debugging functions (see also 'undebug')
  disable      Turn off privileged mode command
  end          End current mode and change to enable mode
  exit         Exit current mode and down to previous mode
  list         Print command list
  no           Negate a command or set its defaults
  ping         Send echo messages
  quit         Exit current mode and down to previous mode
  show         Show running system information
  ssh          Open an ssh connection
  start-shell  Start UNIX shell
  telnet       Open a telnet connection
  terminal     Set terminal line parameters
  traceroute   Trace route to destination
  undebug      Disable debugging functions (see also 'debug')
  write        Write running configuration to memory, network, or terminal
Quagga#
```

When you're connected, you can type a number of different commands. I demonstrate the help command (?) in Listing 5-5. Commands use tab completion, so you can type as few characters as are needed to make the command unique. *Tab completion* is where you type out part of the command and press the Tab key; either the rest of the command will appear or, if you press Tab a second time, possible completions will be recommended. An example command is show running-config, which I've abbreviated to sh run (see Listing 5-6). This command displays the current running configuration (as opposed to the startup-config).

**Listing 5-6:  The show run Command and the Results**

```
Quagga# sh run
Building configuration...

Current configuration:
!
hostname Quagga
hostname ospfd
log syslog
!
password cisco
enable password cisco
!
interface eth0
 ip ospf cost 10
 ipv6 nd suppress-ra
!
interface lo
!
interface sit0
 ipv6 nd suppress-ra
!
router ospf
 ospf router-id 0.0.0.1
 network 192.168.1.0/24 area 0.0.0.0
 network 192.168.24.0/24 area 0.0.0.3
!
line vty
!
Quagga#
```

The two hostnames (Quagga and ospfd) are a little freaky (I get to that in a minute), but otherwise the commands will look familiar to those who have configured DEC or Cisco routers. The OSPF commands are specific to OSPF. BGP, RIP, and IS-IS each have a set of unique commands. The hostname, log, service, password, enable, and line commands are global commands. To begin configuring the router, type the command conf t, as shown in Listing 5-7.

**Listing 5-7: The conf t Command and Results**

```
Quagga# conf t
Quagga(config)# ?
  access-list  Add an access list entry
  bgp          BGP information
  debug        Debugging functions (see also 'undebug')
  dump         Dump packet
  enable       Modify enable password parameters
  end          End current mode and change to enable mode
  exit         Exit current mode and down to previous mode
  hostname     Set system's network name
  interface    Select an interface to configure
  ip           IP information
  ipv6         IPv6 information
  key          Authentication key management
  line         Configure a terminal line
  list         Print command list
  log          Logging control
  no           Negate a command or set its defaults
  password     Assign the terminal connection password
  route-map    Create route-map or enter route-map command mode
  router       Enable a routing process
  router-id    Manually set the router-id
  service      Set up miscellaneous service
  table        Configure target kernel routing table
  username
Quagga(config)# int eth0
Quagga(config-if)# exit
Quagga(config)# end
Quagga#
```

After typing **conf t** (short for "configure terminal") and pressing Enter, you'll be dropped into the router's configuration line editor. Notice that the prompt has changed. This prompt tells you that what you're editing, sort of like a mode description. I typed **?** (help) to display the available commands. I next typed **int eth0**; notice that the prompt changed from Quagga(config) to Quagga(config-if). That's because I changed from the global mode (config) to the interface mode (config-if). I can then type the necessary commands to configure the interface. To get back to the global mode, I can type **exit**, I can end the configuration session with the command **end**, or I can type another command (**router ospf**, for example) to enter another mode. After you've ended your configuration session, you should inspect your work. To do this, type **show running-config**. If you're happy with your changes, type **copy running-config startup-config**. This saves your changes to the appropriate files. These files can be found either in the directory /etc/quagga or /usr/local/etc (installation dependent). Sample configuration files will also be located in this directory.

# Routing About

Now that you have a general feel for how to get around in Quagga, it's time for a concrete example of real routing. Figure 5-3 shows you what I built:

✔ I've chosen the routing protocol OSPF for no particular reason other than that's what I was using. This setup contains three OSPF areas: area 1, area 3, and area 0.

✔ The broadband router isn't participating in the OSPF routing; it's just doing its normal default routing. It contains two static routes to the 192.168.1.0 and 192.168.2.0 networks. These were required; a router that doesn't know how to get to a route will drop the packet.

✔ My Linux HA server, named Quagga, is participating in two OSPF areas (0 and 3) and is redistributing the default route.

✔ The WRT54GL, called OpenWrt, is also participating in two areas (0 and 1).

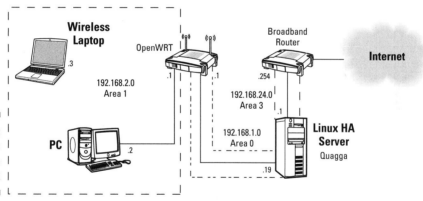

**Figure 5-3:** Routing in your home network

Listing 5-8 contains the information I gathered from the server Quagga. At this point, I have OSPF up, running, and exchanging OSPF information. I started with the information about interface configuration. Then I looked at the Linux kernel routing tables. I then connected to the routing process on the Quagga server via the vtysh command. I displayed the running configuration and its view of the routing tables and some OSPF information.

Listing 5-8:    Various Networking Commands on the Linux PC

```
[root@Quagga ~]# ifconfig
eth0     Link encap:Ethernet  HWaddr 00:11:22:33:44:55
         inet addr:192.168.24.1  Bcast:192.168.24.255  Mask:255.255.255.0
         inet6 addr: fe80::211:22ff:fe33:4455/64 Scope:Link
         UP BROADCAST RUNNING MULTICAST  MTU:1500  Metric:1
         RX packets:490215 errors:0 dropped:0 overruns:0 frame:0
         TX packets:406717 errors:0 dropped:0 overruns:0 carrier:0
         collisions:0 txqueuelen:1000
         RX bytes:490751549 (468.0 MiB)  TX bytes:48340714 (46.1 MiB)
         Interrupt:18 Base address:0xa000

eth0:1   Link encap:Ethernet  HWaddr 00:11:22:33:44:55
         inet addr:192.168.1.19  Bcast:192.168.1.255  Mask:255.255.255.0
         UP BROADCAST RUNNING MULTICAST  MTU:1500  Metric:1
         Interrupt:18 Base address:0xa000

lo       Link encap:Local Loopback
         inet addr:127.0.0.1  Mask:255.0.0.0
         inet6 addr: ::1/128 Scope:Host
         UP LOOPBACK RUNNING  MTU:16436  Metric:1
         RX packets:90605 errors:0 dropped:0 overruns:0 frame:0
         TX packets:90605 errors:0 dropped:0 overruns:0 carrier:0
         collisions:0 txqueuelen:0
         RX bytes:11751977 (11.2 MiB)  TX bytes:11751977 (11.2 MiB)

[root@Quagga ~]# route -n
Kernel IP routing table
Destination     Gateway         Genmask         Flags Metric Ref    Use Iface
192.168.100.0   192.168.24.254  255.255.255.0   UG    0      0        0 eth0
192.168.2.0     192.168.1.1     255.255.255.0   UG    20     0        0 eth0
192.168.1.0     0.0.0.0         255.255.255.0   U     0      0        0 eth0
192.168.24.0    0.0.0.0         255.255.255.0   U     0      0        0 eth0
169.254.0.0     0.0.0.0         255.255.0.0     U     0      0        0 eth0
0.0.0.0         192.168.24.254  0.0.0.0         UG    0      0        0 eth0

[root@Quagga ~]# vtysh

Hello, this is Quagga (version 0.99.3).
Copyright 1996-2005 Kunihiro Ishiguro, et al.

Quagga# sh run
Building configuration...

Current configuration:
!
hostname Quagga
log syslog
!
service advanced-vty
!
```

```
password Zebra
enable password Zebra
!
interface eth0
 ip ospf cost 10
 ipv6 nd suppress-ra
!
interface lo
!
interface sit0
 ipv6 nd suppress-ra
!
router ospf
 ospf router-id 0.0.0.1
 network 192.168.1.0/24 area 0.0.0.0
 network 192.168.24.0/24 area 0.0.0.3
 default-information originate always metric 110
!
ip forwarding
!
line vty
!
Quagga# sh ip route
Codes: K - kernel route, C - connected, S - static, R - RIP, O - OSPF,
       I - ISIS, B - BGP, > - selected route, * - FIB route

K>* 0.0.0.0/0 via 192.168.24.254, eth0
C>* 127.0.0.0/8 is directly connected, lo
K>* 169.254.0.0/16 is directly connected, eth0
O   192.168.1.0/24 [110/10] is directly connected, eth0, 02:18:07
C>* 192.168.1.0/24 is directly connected, eth0
O>* 192.168.2.0/24 [110/20] via 192.168.1.1, eth0, 02:01:46
O   192.168.24.0/24 [110/10] is directly connected, eth0, 02:15:09
C>* 192.168.24.0/24 is directly connected, eth0
K>* 192.168.100.0/24 via 192.168.24.254, eth0
Quagga# sh ip ospf route
============ OSPF network routing table ============
N    192.168.1.0/24       [10] area: 0.0.0.0
                          directly attached to eth0
N IA 192.168.2.0/24       [20] area: 0.0.0.1
                          via 192.168.1.1, eth0
N    192.168.24.0/24      [10] area: 0.0.0.0
                          directly attached to eth0


============ OSPF router routing table ============
R    0.0.0.3              [10] area: 0.0.0.0, ABR, ASBR
                          via 192.168.1.1, eth0


============ OSPF external routing table ============
```

*(continued)*

**Listing 5-8** *(continued)*

```
Quagga# sh ip ospf neighbor

    Neighbor ID Pri State        Dead Time Address      Interface
                RXmtL RqstL DBsmL
0.0.0.3         1 Full/Backup    30.985s 192.168.1.1    eth0:192.168.1.19
                0    0     0
Quagga# quit
```

Now it's time to look at the other router, OpenWrt, shown in Listing 5-9. I performed the same commands and recorded similar information as I did for my Quagga server. The one difference with this information is that I first had to use ssh to get to the OpenWrt machine. After I had logged in, I performed all the same commands as I did previously.

**Listing 5-9:   Various Networking Commands on the WRT54GL**

```
[root@Quagga ~]# ssh root@192.168.1.1
root@192.168.1.1's password:


BusyBox v1.00 (2006.03.27-00:00+0000) Built-in shell (ash)
Enter 'help' for a list of built-in commands.


 _____         _____       _
|      |.-----.-----.------.|  |  |  |.-----.|  |_
|  -   ||  _  |  -__||  _  ||  |  |  ||  _  ||   _|
|_____||   __|_____|__|__||__|__|__||__|__||____|
        |__| W I R E L E S S    F R E E D O M
WHITE RUSSIAN (RC5) ------------------------------
 * 2 oz Vodka   Mix the Vodka and Kahlua together
 * 1 oz Kahlua  over ice, then float the cream or
 * 1/2oz cream  milk on the top.
--------------------------------------------------
root@OpenWrt:~# ifconfig
br0       Link encap:Ethernet  HWaddr 00:AA:BB:CC:DD:EE
          inet addr:192.168.1.1  Bcast:192.168.1.255  Mask:255.255.255.0
          UP BROADCAST RUNNING MULTICAST  MTU:1500  Metric:1
          RX packets:15062 errors:0 dropped:0 overruns:0 frame:0
          TX packets:6486 errors:0 dropped:0 overruns:0 carrier:0
          collisions:0 txqueuelen:0
          RX bytes:1942161 (1.8 MiB)  TX bytes:646914 (631.7 KiB)

eth0      Link encap:Ethernet  HWaddr 00:AA:BB:CC:DD:EE
          UP BROADCAST RUNNING PROMISC MULTICAST  MTU:1500  Metric:1
          RX packets:27415 errors:0 dropped:0 overruns:0 frame:0
          TX packets:7339 errors:0 dropped:0 overruns:0 carrier:0
          collisions:0 txqueuelen:1000
          RX bytes:4307536 (4.1 MiB)  TX bytes:775963 (757.7 KiB)
          Interrupt:4

eth1      Link encap:Ethernet  HWaddr 00:AA:BB:CC:DD:ED
```

```
               UP BROADCAST RUNNING ALLMULTI MULTICAST  MTU:1500  Metric:1
               RX packets:0 errors:0 dropped:0 overruns:0 frame:175852
               TX packets:13182 errors:11 dropped:0 overruns:0 carrier:0
               collisions:0 txqueuelen:1000
               RX bytes:0 (0.0 B)  TX bytes:2104674 (2.0 MiB)
               Interrupt:2 Base address:0x5000

lo             Link encap:Local Loopback
               inet addr:127.0.0.1  Mask:255.0.0.0
               UP LOOPBACK RUNNING  MTU:16436  Metric:1
               RX packets:0 errors:0 dropped:0 overruns:0 frame:0
               TX packets:0 errors:0 dropped:0 overruns:0 carrier:0
               collisions:0 txqueuelen:0
               RX bytes:0 (0.0 B)  TX bytes:0 (0.0 B)

vlan0          Link encap:Ethernet  HWaddr 00:AA:BB:CC:DD:EE
               UP BROADCAST RUNNING ALLMULTI MULTICAST  MTU:1500  Metric:1
               RX packets:15062 errors:0 dropped:0 overruns:0 frame:0
               TX packets:6486 errors:0 dropped:0 overruns:0 carrier:0
               collisions:0 txqueuelen:0
               RX bytes:2002409 (1.9 MiB)  TX bytes:672858 (657.0 KiB)

vlan1          Link encap:Ethernet  HWaddr 00:AA:BB:CC:DD:EC
               inet addr:192.168.2.1  Bcast:192.168.2.255  Mask:255.255.255.0
               UP BROADCAST RUNNING MULTICAST  MTU:1500  Metric:1
               RX packets:12344 errors:0 dropped:0 overruns:0 frame:0
               TX packets:852 errors:0 dropped:0 overruns:0 carrier:0
               collisions:0 txqueuelen:0
               RX bytes:1811185 (1.7 MiB)  TX bytes:70674 (69.0 KiB)

root@OpenWrt:~# route -n
Kernel IP routing table
Destination     Gateway         Genmask         Flags Metric Ref    Use Iface
192.168.2.0     0.0.0.0         255.255.255.0   U     0      0        0 vlan1
192.168.1.0     0.0.0.0         255.255.255.0   U     0      0        0 br0
192.168.24.0    192.168.1.19    255.255.255.0   UG    20     0        0 br0
0.0.0.0         192.168.1.19    0.0.0.0         UG    110    0        0 br0
root@OpenWrt:~# vtysh

Hello, this is Quagga (version 0.98.4).
Copyright 1996-2005 Kunihiro Ishiguro, et al.

OpenWrt# sh run
Building configuration...

Current configuration:
!
log syslog
!
service advanced-vty
```

*(continued)*

**Listing 5-9** *(continued)*

```
!
password Zebra
enable password Zebra
!
interface br0
!
interface eth0
!
interface eth1
!
interface lo
!
interface vlan0
!
interface vlan1
 ip address 192.168.2.1/24
!
router ospf
 ospf router-id 0.0.0.2
 network 192.168.1.0/24 area 0.0.0.0
 network 192.168.2.0/24 area 0.0.0.1
!
ip forwarding
!
line vty
!
OpenWrt# sh ip route
Codes: K - kernel route, C - connected, S - static, R - RIP, O - OSPF,
       I - ISIS, B - BGP, > - selected route, * - FIB route

O>* 0.0.0.0/0 [110/110] via 192.168.1.19, br0, 01:03:21
C>* 127.0.0.0/8 is directly connected, lo
O   192.168.1.0/24 [110/10] is directly connected, br0, 02:05:48
C>* 192.168.1.0/24 is directly connected, br0
O   192.168.2.0/24 [110/10] is directly connected, vlan1, 02:05:57
C>* 192.168.2.0/24 is directly connected, vlan1
O>* 192.168.24.0/24 [110/20] via 192.168.1.19, br0, 02:05:48
OpenWrt# sh ip ospf route
============ OSPF network routing table ============
N    192.168.1.0/24        [10] area: 0.0.0.0
                           directly attached to br0
N    192.168.2.0/24        [10] area: 0.0.0.1
                           directly attached to vlan1
N IA 192.168.24.0/24       [20] area: 0.0.0.0
                           via 192.168.1.19, br0


============ OSPF router routing table ============
R    0.0.0.1               [10] area: 0.0.0.0, ABR, ASBR
                           via 192.168.1.19, br0
```

```
============ OSPF external routing table ============
N E2 0.0.0.0/0                [20/110] tag: 0
                              via 192.168.1.19, br0

OpenWrt# sh ip ospf neigh

Neighbor ID    Pri   State         Dead Time   Address        Interface
               RXmtL RqstL DBsmL
0.0.0.1          1   Full/DR       00:00:33    192.168.1.19
               br0:192.168.1.1    0     0     0
OpenWrt# quit
root@OpenWrt:~# exit
Connection to 192.168.1.1 closed.
[root@Quagga ~]#
```

Listings 5-8 and 5-9 show actual data from working setups. Here's one thing to remember: On my Linux server, Quagga, I found it necessary to turn on IP Forwarding. To turn it on at the command line, type

```
echo "1" >/proc/sys/net/ipv4/ip_forward
```

This enables forwarding until your next reboot. To make it permanent, edit `/etc/sysconfig/network` and add to the end of the file this line:

```
FORWARD_IPV4 = YES
```

Under Fedora, you need to edit `/etc/sysctl.conf` instead. Just change the 0 to a 1, as I did on this line:

```
net.ipv4.ip_forward = 1
```

Then, the next time you reboot, the kernel will have IP forwarding enabled.

# Part III
# Entertaining Your Brain with a Little Help from Linux

The 5th Wave          By Rich Tennant

"The best thing about MythTV is I'm able to answer 50 percent more 'Jeopardy' questions than before."

# In this part . . .

There's a party in this part, and you're invited. Here you set up a digital video recorder known as MythTV, control music throughout your home with help from TwonkyMedia, and get rolling with a USB Webcam. The only thing left to do is call your friends over, and make sure somebody's bringing the pizza and nachos — which you can do after you set up Asterisk, the smart phone system.

What are you waiting for? It's time to get this part started!

# Chapter 6

# Building a Personal Video Recorder with MythTV

*O*ne of the things I like about running Linux as my operating system is the availability of a large number of open source, free programs. One such program I use is MythTV; with it, I have converted an old, rarely used PC to a personal video recorder (PVR), and now it's one of the most used PCs in my house.

Most people know what a PVR is, and many people have commercial versions such as TiVo or proprietary PVRs supplied by the cable or satellite companies. With a PVR, you can pause live TV and record whatever you desire whenever you desire. Typically, you have to pay a subscription fee to TiVo or your cable or satellite provider for the privilege of using its PVR. But, if you have an old PC, you can build your own PVR for little or no cost — and you won't have to pay a subscription fee either — by downloading and installing MythTV. MythTV lets you build your own PVR, download TV programming information, watch, pause, and record live TV, as well as schedule recordings. But MythTV can do so much more: With MythTV, you can gain complete control of all your online media content and access the Internet for news and weather information. This chapter shows you how to build your MythTV system.

*Note:* The MythTV program is very complex and could fill an entire *For Dummies* book alone. The information in this chapter tells you how to set up and configure a basic MythTV system. I highly recommend that you do some research on your own and explore the MythTV information that is available on the Web. A good place to start is the MythTV official site at www.mythtv.org.

# Building Your MythTV PVR

In the following sections, you find out how to set up your PC hardware to use with MythTV. You must meet some specific hardware requirements before you can install and configure MythTV. After you configure your hardware, you download, install, and configure MythTV.

## Selecting the hardware

The first consideration for using MythTV is choosing and configuring the hardware that the system will use. Your hardware must meet some basic requirements, and I include a list of required hardware items and their purposes.

You can set up MythTV in several different configurations by using one PC as the master *backend* unit (not connected to the TV) and another as the *frontend* unit (connected to the TV). Or, you can use one PC for both the backend and frontend units. In this chapter, you find out about using one PC for both the backend and frontend units. Just about any recent PC that is capable of running Linux should have enough processing power to run MythTV. The following list shows the basics. Following the list of generic hardware types, I list the specific hardware I used when I set up my system.

### Generic hardware types

This list shows generic types of hardware that you need to set up your system with MythTV:

- ✔ **CPU:** Pentium II class or higher CPU. (This includes AMD CPUs, as well.)
- ✔ **RAM:** A 256MB minimum.
- ✔ **Hard drive:** Any ATA 66/100/133, 30GB or larger for storing video.
- ✔ **Sound card:** An onboard or a PCI card. (Nearly any card will work.)
- ✔ **Video card:** An onboard or a PCI/AGP card. (The card must have a TV out port to connect to TV.)
- ✔ **Optical drive:** Required only if you want to play or record CD/DVDs.
- ✔ **Video capture card:** Used to get the video into your PC. MythTV supports many kinds.

Because it isn't possible for me to discuss every type of hardware that might work with MythTV in this section, I recommend that you check out `http://mythtv.org/docs/mythtv-HOWTO-3.html#ss3.1` (to find more detailed information about hardware requirements) and `http://pvrhw.goldfish.org/tiki-pvrhwdb.php` (to find a list of many hardware configurations known to work with MythTV). You can save yourself a lot of time and aggravation if you configure your system with hardware that is known to work with MythTV.

I followed my own advice and made sure that my hardware would work before I downloaded, installed, and configured MythTV.

### *My system-specific hardware*

Here's the specific hardware I am using on my system:

- **Motherboard:** Shuttle AK32A
- **CPU:** AMD Athlon 1800
- **RAM:** 1GB pc133
- **Hard drive:** Seagate 7200rpm ATA100 80GB
- **Sound card:** onboard AC97
- **Video card:** XFX GeForce FX 256mb TV/DVI AGP
- **Video capture:** Plextor PX-M402U
- **Optical drive:** Generic DVD+/-RW, CD-RW, DVD-ROM, CD-ROM
- **NIC:** onboard Realtek

Regardless of which hardware you decide to use, be sure to properly install and configure it before you begin to install and configure MythTV. I can't know what hardware you're using, so I leave it to you to be sure it's working properly. I can only repeat; be sure you select hardware that is known to work with MythTV!

# *Installing MythTV*

When you have hardware that is compatible with MythTV and you know it is properly configured, you're ready to install MythTV. My instructions are based on using Fedora Core 4 (FC4) as the Linux distribution, but you can also run MythTV with SUSE or Debian and Debian-based distributions such as Knoppix or Linspire.

*Note:* If you're running FC4 or SUSE, you can follow the instructions here using yum for the installation. If you're running Debian or a Debian-based distribution, you can use the apt-get command instead of yum to do your installation.

Before you begin the installation, you have some prep work to do:

- **Install the drivers required by your specific hardware and be sure your hardware is working properly.** You are using hardware supported by MythTV, aren't you?

✔ **Install the LIRC packages if you plan to use a remote control with your system (perhaps one came with your capture device).** Go to `www.myth tv.org/docs/mythtv-HOWTO-8.html` for details. (You don't need to use a remote; you can use keyboard commands to control MythTV.)

✔ **Make sure that you have free space on your system hard drive.** You need this space to hold your TV recordings. You should probably have at least 20GB free for this purpose. (The MythTV program will use about 100MB.)

✔ **Create a user on your system called mythtv.** You will log in as this user to configure and run MythTV.

✔ **Create a directory /mnt/store.** This is where MythTV will save your recordings.

✔ **Be sure that `mysql` is installed on your system.** If it isn't, you need to install it.

✔ **Enable NTP on your system.** This ensures that your system time will always be accurate.

✔ **Be sure your system is updated with the most recent packages.** You can run `yum upgrade` to do this.

✔ **Set up the atrpms and freshrpms repositories for use with `yum`.** You can edit the `/etc/yum/conf` file, or you can place a configuration file for each repository in `/etc/yum.repos.d`.

In the code examples, the first character indicates the command prompt. A dollar sign ($)indicates a non-root user. A pound sign (#) indicates the root user. You don't type these characters — only the text following these characters.

Now you're ready to begin the installation; just follow these few steps:

1. **Open a terminal window and log in as root.**

2. **At the command prompt, type**

```
# yum install mythtv-suite
```

The installer searches the rpm repositories and will finds the necessary packages and any required dependencies.

3. **When you are asked whether you want to install the selected packages, answer Yes to continue.**

When the installer says `Complete!` and the command prompt returns, the installation is complete. The next step is to configure MySQL.

## Configuring MySQL

For MythTV to work properly, you must have MySQL installed, properly configured, and running. If you haven't already installed MySQL, do it now. If you have it installed, go ahead and configure it. First, you want MySQL to start whenever you start your PC. You can issue the following command as the root user to ensure MySQL always starts:

```
# chkconfig mysqld on
```

Then you can start MySQL immediately by entering

```
# service mysqld start
```

Now you need to set the root password for MySQL by entering the following command. Be sure to use your own password where it shows `'Enter your desired password here'`. (The single quotes are required.)

```
# mysql -u root mysql
        mysql> UPDATE user SET Password=PASSWORD('Enter
        your desired password here') WHERE user='root';
        mysql> FLUSH PRIVILEGES;
        mysql> quit
```

Then you must create the database that MythTV will use by entering the following command:

```
$ mysql -u root -p < /usr/share/doc/mythtv-
        0.18.1/database/mc.sql
```

(When prompted, enter the password you just set previously.)

You are now ready to configure MythTV.

## Configuring the MythTV backend server

To configure the MythTV backend server, you run a program called `mythtv-setup`. Just follow these steps:

1. **Log in as the mythtv user you create earlier. (Refer to the preparatory tasks I list in the "Installing MythTV" section.)**

2. **From a terminal prompt, enter the following command:**

```
$ mythtv-setup
```

The program starts and opens to a window asking whether you want to clear your capture card settings.

**3. Highlight Yes and press Enter.**

Next you are asked whether you want to clear channel settings.

**4. Select Yes and press Enter.**

The program opens to the main settings menu, which lists five options:

- General
- Capture Cards
- Video Sources
- Input
- Channel Editor

You've got the `mythtv-setup` program up and running.

### Adjusting the main settings

In many cases, you don't need to change the default settings. In the following subsections, I briefly explain the five menu choices and explain in more detail those settings that you need to change, providing illustration where necessary. Use your up- and down-arrow keys to move through the menus and additional pages; press Enter or the spacebar to select.

#### General

You use these settings to set the IP address and port numbers of your backend server as well as other settings. Because you're setting up a PC that is both the backend and frontend of your MythTV system, you don't need to change any settings here. Selecting General opens eight additional pages. Feel free to open them and have a look at their purposes. Remember that you don't need to change any settings for your configuration here. Press Esc to go back to the main settings menu.

#### Capture Cards

Choosing the Capture Cards option opens a page that shows your video capture cards. Because this is the first time running `mythtv-setup`, no cards are configured and the highlight is on the (New capture card) option. Press the spacebar to select this choice. When the Capture Card Setup window (shown in Figure 6-1) opens, follow these steps to configure your card:

**1. Use the up- or down-arrow keys to highlight the Card Type field and the right- or left-arrow keys to move through the list of supported cards; when you find your card, press Enter or the spacebar to select it.**

The window returns to the Capture Card display window, and your capture card is listed.

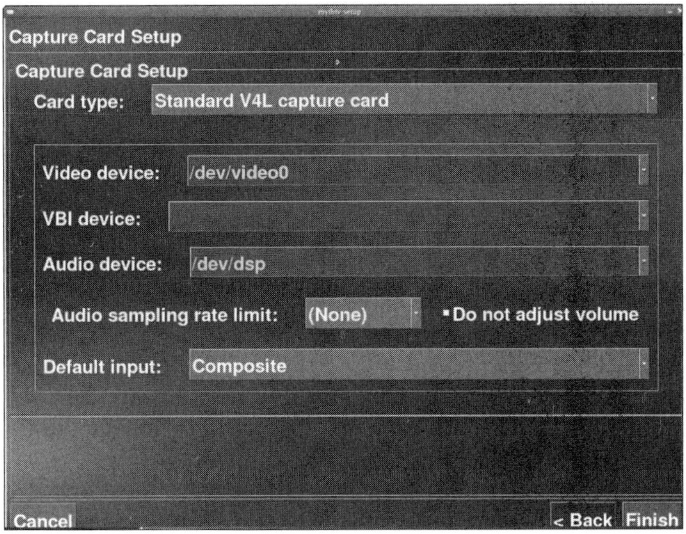

**Figure 6-1:**
The Capture
Card Setup
window for
selecting
your
capture
card.

2. **Press Enter when the card is highlighted to go back to the Capture Card Setup window for your capture card and make any changes needed.**

   Your video device should be listed in the Video Device field, typically as /dev/video0, and your audio device should be listed as /dev/dsp. You might need to set the default input type according to the signal coming into the card. The signal might be either Composite or S-Video.

3. **Press Enter or the spacebar to accept your changes and then press Esc to return to the main settings menu.**

### Video Sources

Selecting the Video Sources option opens a window that displays the video sources. Because this is your first time here, no video sources are set up yet, and New video source is highlighted. Press the spacebar or the Enter key. The Video Source Setup window appears. See Figure 6-2.

To configure the video source, follow these steps:

1. **Use the up- or down-arrow keys to move the highlight to the Video Source Name field and enter the name you want to give this video source.**

   I called mine Dish Network because this is where I get my programming.

2. **Enter your Zap2it username and password in the User ID and Password fields, respectively.**

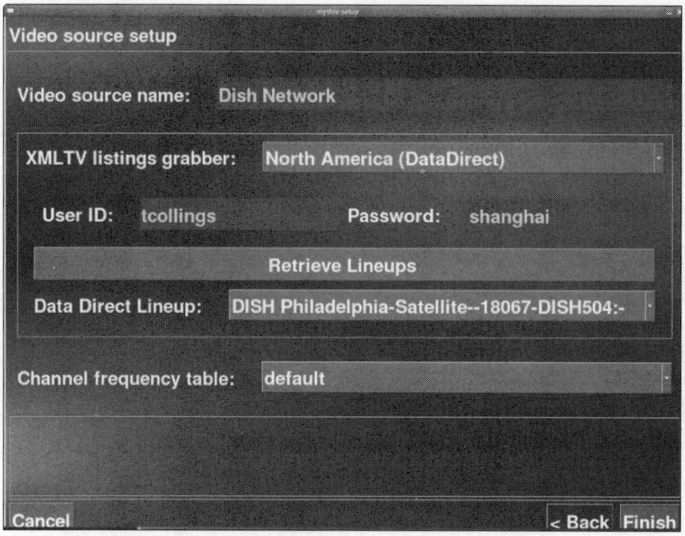

**Figure 6-2:**
The Video
Source
Setup
window for
selecting
your video
source.

If you don't have an account, you need one so that you can retrieve your TV listings. Here's how to set up a Zap2it account:

a. *Go to* `http://labs.zap2it.com`, *and click the New User? Sign Up link.*

b. *Click Accept to the terms of the subscription agreement if you want to use this service.*

c. *Fill in the requested information on the next window (the subscription registration); in the Certificate Code field, enter **ZIYN-DQZO-SBUT**.*

d. *Fill in the survey and then click Subscribe.*

e. *Go to the program information area and select your location and TV service provider. Then customize your channel listings.*

3. **After entering your user ID and password into the appropriate fields, move the highlight to Retrieve Lineups and then press Enter.**

4. **Highlight Finish and then press Enter.**

Your video source is now displayed in the list of video sources. Press Esc to go back to the main settings menu.

## *Input*

In the Input settings, you need to specify the type of input for the capture device. This is one of the video sources. The highlight is on the card you just configured, so press the spacebar or Enter to open the Connect Source to Input window, as shown in Figure 6-3.

**Connect source to input**

| | |
|---|---|
| Capture device: | [ GO7007 : /dev/video0 ] |
| Input: | Composite |
| Video source: | Dish Network |
| Input preference: | 0 |
| External channel change command: | |
| Preset tuner to channel: | |
| Starting channel: | 3 |

Cancel   < Back  Finish

Use the up- or down-arrow keys to move the highlight to the Video Source field and then use the right- or left-arrow keys to select the video source you configured in the preceding section. Press spacebar or Enter to accept your choice. The input connection now appears in the list of connections. Press Esc to go back to the main settings menu.

### Channel editor

You typically don't need to make changes to your channel lineup because these are imported into MythTV from the Zap2it service you signed up for earlier. But you can make any changes you desire. Press the spacebar or Enter to go into the Channels window. Move the highlight over the channel you want to edit and press the spacebar or Enter. After you finish, be sure to press the spacebar or Enter to apply your changes.

To exit the MythTV setup program, press Esc.

### Populating the program guide

You need to fill the MythTV database with your settings and your program guide information. From the command prompt, you start the MythTV back-end server by issuing the following command:

```
$ mythbackend &
```

This starts the backend server and runs it in the background. When your command prompt returns, issue the following command:

```
$ mythfilldatabase
```

This program fills the database with your program guide information from the Zap2it database that you subscribed to in the "Video Sources" section. This process takes a little while, so be patient. After a few minutes, the command prompt returns, and the configuration is almost complete. Next, you need to start the MythTV frontend.

## Configuring the MythTV frontend server

After you've configured the MythTV backend server and populated the program guide with your TV listing information, you're ready to start the MythTV frontend server. You can start the MythTV frontend server by issuing the following command:

```
$ mythfrontend
```

This command starts the frontend server and gives you your interface to the MythTV system. If all has gone well so far, you should see a window similar to the one in Figure 6-4.

Figure 6-4:
The MythTV
main
window
showing
your media
viewing
choices.

This is the MythTV main menu, and from here you can select from the many media options. Eleven choices are available to you from the MythTV main menu. These choices are

- ✔ **TV:** Select this option to see additional choices related to viewing and recording TV.

- ✔ **Music:** Select this option to see additional choices related to selecting and playing music.

- ✔ **Videos:** Choosing this option gives you additional options related to videos stored on your system.

- ✔ **DVD:** Selecting this option gives you control of your DVD player to play or rip DVDs.

- ✔ **Images:** Choosing Images displays any images you have stored on your PC and lets you show slide shows.

- ✔ **Games:** This menu choice is currently not supported by the MythTV program.

- ✔ **Weather:** Choosing Weather displays the current weather conditions in your locality as well as the forecast for several days.

- ✔ **News Feeds:** Choose this option to get news information from the sources you have configured.

- ✔ **Web:** Choose this option to browse the Internet to locations you configured.

- ✔ **Phone:** To use this service, you must be subscribed to an SIP server. If you're using VoIP service, you will know what this is. If not, you can't use this feature.

- ✔ **Setup:** Choosing Setup gives you options for configuring the ten preceding menu choices.

You can usually start using MythTV to watch TV without making any changes to the MythTV frontend setup. But if you want to play music stored on your system or watch videos or view slide shows, you must do a little more configuring. Just choose Setup from the MythTV main menu to open the MythTV frontend Setup menu, as shown in Figure 6-5.

On the MythTV frontend Setup menu are 12 configuration options. The following list shows these options and describes what you can use them to configure:

- ✔ **General:** The configuration settings you can modify here include database configuration settings and audio device settings. Also included are system settings related to starting and stopping the system, automatically running the `mythfilldatabase` program for TV program listings, and system logging.

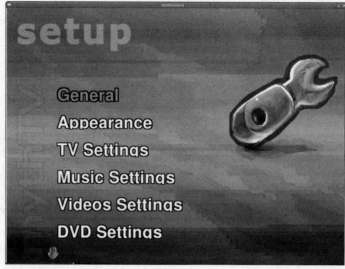

**Figure 6-5:**
The MythTV
frontend
Setup
menu for
configuring
your media
options.

✔ **Appearance:** These settings control how MythTV appears on your display. You can choose from many different themes, as well as change font sizes, languages, and time and date display formats.

✔ **TV Settings:** Choosing this option lets you set parameters related to viewing and recording TV. You can also set your preferences for the program guide display and set recording profiles.

✔ **Music Settings:** In this area, you can set the directory path to the location of your music files. You can also configure the performance of your music player and select music encoding options.

✔ **Video Settings:** In this area, you can set the directory path to the location of your video files. You can also configure the default video player and select video file types and encoding options.

✔ **DVD Settings:** The DVD Setup menu lets you configure your DVD device and set the player settings. You can also configure DVD ripping and transcoding options here.

✔ **Image Settings:** In Image Settings, you can specify the path to your image directory as well as the path to import images from connected devices, such as a CD or digital camera. You can also set the slide show delay here.

✔ **Game Settings:** This menu option is not used by MythTV at this time.

✔ **Weather Settings:** Here you can select the location to display its weather data. You can also choose between imperial and metric unit display.

✔ **News Settings:** In this area, you can choose from a list of news services from which to receive information.

- ✔ **Web Settings:** Here you can create bookmarks for Web sites you want to view. You can also choose which browser to use to view the sites.
- ✔ **Phone Settings:** Choosing this option lets you configure your SIP server connection URL as well as other connection parameters.

# Watching TV

By now you're probably thinking, "I've done a lot of work configuring my hardware and installing and configuring MythTV. When am I going to get to watch some TV?" Well, your wait is over now. Go watch some TV:

1. **From the MythTV frontend main menu, highlight TV and press the spacebar or Enter to open the TV menu.**

   The first option on this menu is TV.

2. **Press the spacebar or Enter while TV is highlighted.**

   Your system displays the default channel, which is typically the first (or lowest) channel number in your program listing. If all has gone well, you see the channel displayed. You can change channels by using the up- and down-arrow keys.

If you're using an external TV tuner box, such as one from your cable company or a satellite provider, you need to change the channel on that device. It is possible to get MythTV to control an external tuner device, but such a configuration is far too complicated to describe in this book. For a complete guide to MythTV, refer to the MythTV Web site at www.mythtv.org.

# Managing Your Recordings

If you want to see what programs are on in your area and at what times, you can view the online schedule. The schedule information is downloaded and placed in your database during the backend server configuration.

## Scheduling your recordings

From the schedule, you can select the programs you want to record and set the recording options. To enter the schedule, move the highlight to Schedule and press the spacebar or Enter; then press the spacebar or Enter on the Guide highlight. You see a listing similar to Figure 6-6.

**Figure 6-6:**
The TV
listings
display in
MythTV.

You use the left, right, up, and down arrows to navigate through the listing. When the highlight is on a program you want to record, press the spacebar or Enter to open a screen where you can set the record options. On this page, you have many options from which to choose. Place the highlight over an option and press the right- or left-arrow key to view additional choices for the selected option. After you make your choices, be sure to click Save These Settings. The main schedule reappears, and the program you selected to record is marked to indicate it is scheduled to be recorded. You can schedule to record as many programs as you like.

## Watching your recordings

After you've recorded some programs, you probably want to watch them. You do this by selecting TV from the MythTV main menu and then selecting Watch Recordings. The Select a Recording to Watch window that appears shows the recorded programs available for viewing. Use the arrow keys to highlight your selection and then press the spacebar or Enter to begin viewing the program.

## Deleting a recording

After you've recorded a few programs, you might want to get rid of some of them. You do this by selecting TV from the MythTV main menu and then clicking Delete Recordings. The Select a Recording to Permanently Erase screen appears, showing the recorded programs available for deleting. Use the arrow keys to highlight your selection and press the spacebar or Enter to delete the recording. You will be prompted to confirm deleting the recording. Choose Yes or No as you desire.

# Managing Your Media

With MythTV, you can watch TV, pause and resume live TV, schedule recordings, and do everything that a typical PVR can do. However, you can do a lot more than a typical PVR will let you do. You can use MythTV as the control center for all the media on your system. You can organize and play all your music files by using the MythTV Music menu. You can play videos stored on your system by using the Video menu choices, and you can organize and display slide shows of all your images by using the Images menu. In this section, I give you a quick look at these items.

## Playing music with MythTV

MythTV gives you the ability to organize and play the music files you have stored on your system; for instance, you can use it to play MP3 files that you've ripped from your CDs. Before you can use the music player, though, you must enter the directory location that contains the music files. Here's how:

1. **From the MythTV main menu, choose Setup⇨Music Settings⇨General Settings.**

2. **Enter the path to the music files in the Directory to Hold Music field.**

3. **Click Next, then Finish, and then press Esc twice to return to the main menu.**

4. **From the main menu, choose Music⇨Select Music.**

5. **Use the arrow keys to highlight the music you want to play and press the spacebar to select it.**

6. **Press Esc when you're finished to return to the Music menu.**

7. **Choose Play Music from the Music menu.**

   Your selected music begins to play.

8. **To stop playing music, press Esc.**

## Playing videos with MythTV

MythTV gives you the ability to organize and play the video files you have stored on your system. Before you can use the video player, you need to enter the directory location that contains the video files. Here's how:

1. **From the MythTV main menu, choose Setup⇨Videos Settings⇨General Settings.**

2. **Enter the path to the video files in the Directory That Holds Videos field.**

3. **Choose Next twice, then Finish, and then press Esc twice to return to the MythTV main menu.**

4. **From the main menu, choose Videos⇨Browse Videos.**

5. **Use the up- and down-arrow keys to find the video you want to play and press the spacebar to select it.**

6. **Press Esc when you're finished to return to the Video menu.**

## Viewing image slide shows with MythTV

MythTV gives you the ability to organize and view slide shows of image files you have stored on your system. Before you can use the image viewer, you need to enter the directory location that contains the image files. Here's how:

1. **From the MythTV main menu, choose Setup⇨Images Settings.**

2. **Enter the path to the image files in the Directory That Holds Images field.**

3. **Choose Finish then press Esc to return to the MythTV main menu.**

4. **Choose Images from the main menu to open the Images page, where you can see your images.**

5. **Use the arrow keys to navigate through the images.**

6. **Press the spacebar or Enter to see a full-size view of the highlighted image. Press Esc to return to the thumbnail view.**

7. **Press the M key to activate the menu on the left side of the screen.**

8. **Use the up or down arrows to highlight your menu choice and press the spacebar or Enter to select it.**

9. **To stop the slide show, press Esc.**

10. **To exit the image viewer, press Esc from the thumbnail viewer page.**

# Chapter 7

# Streaming Music without the Wires

. . . . . . . . . . . . . . . . . . . . . . . . . . . . . . . . . . . . . . . . . . . . . . . . . . . .

## In This Chapter

▶ Selecting the hardware and software

▶ Configuring your system

▶ Choosing your music format

▶ Ripping CDs

▶ Streaming audio

. . . . . . . . . . . . . . . . . . . . . . . . . . . . . . . . . . . . . . . . . . . . . . . . . . . .

*Y*ou could use several methods to stream music from a central server to other locations in your house. In this chapter, you take a look at some of the possibilities for streaming music throughout your house. I show you the solution I chose and how to set it up. Oh, and did I mention that the music is streamed across a wireless connection?

# Selecting the Hardware and Software

The first consideration for wirelessly streaming your audio to different locations in your home is your wireless network. Obviously, you aren't able to stream your audio across a wireless network if you don't have one set up. So be sure that your network is set up and properly configured for wireless access. For more about setting up a wireless network, check out Chapters 3 and 4.

Another consideration is where you want to stream your audio. It is possible to set up a complete streaming solution that would send your music files to anyone who has an Internet connection. But this isn't what you will be doing in this chapter. Here you will find out about streaming audio to your own home network, so the setup will be much easier. There are two sides to set up: the server side and the client side. The *server side* consists of the hardware and software that supplies the music stream to the network. I explain the server side in the "Installing and configuring the media server" section. The *client side* is the hardware device that receives the music stream from the network. I cover the client side in the "Connecting and configuring the D-Link media client" section.

Here's a list of what you need to accomplish your goal:

- A PC running Linux (the media server).
- Media serving software.
- Audio files in the proper format (typically MP3, WMA, or OGG).
- A PC set up as a client, or a dedicated client system. A *dedicated client* is typically a hardware media device such as a D-Link DSM-320 or Netgear MP101.
- A home stereo system.

My media server PC is a system that I built a few years ago. The system specifics are

- AMD Athlon 1800
- 1GB pc133 RAM
- 80GB Seagate Hard Drive
- 10GB Seagate Hard Drive
- DVD/CD burner
- AC 97 Sound card
- 10/100 Ethernet adapter

As you can see, the system doesn't need to be the latest and greatest to perform as a media server. You could probably get good performance by using any recent Pentium class PC with a PIII or greater processor.

The server is running media server software, called TwonkyMedia, that I downloaded from the TwonkyVision Web site. The company makes available a free music server as well as a complete media server that streams videos and photo slide shows. I originally used the free music serving software but upgraded to the full version to take advantage of the streaming video and slide show features. The full version of the media server software cost €15, or about $17 (USD). The Web site where you can download the software is located at `www.twonkyvision.de`.

All my music files are in MP3 format for the greatest compatibility with portable MP3 players. All portable music players can play MP3 files, and some can also play OGG or WMA. I couldn't find a player that would play all three, only MP3 and OGG, or MP3 and WMA. To get the MP3 files, I ripped my CDs to WAV files and then encoded them as MP3 by using a program called Grip. (For more on Grip, check out the section "Ripping CDs and Encoding Music Files with Grip," later in this chapter.)

Always consider copyright issues whenever you're copying CDs. Typically the end user is allowed to make one copy of recorded material as an archival copy. But I'm not a copyright expert, so if you have any questions about the matter, do some searching on the Web for more information.

That's all I have set up for the server side of my streaming music system. Now you need to take a look at the client side, which is even easier to set up.

I decided to go with a dedicated media client that conforms to the Universal Plug and Play (UPnP) standard for streaming media. Any software that also conforms to this standard will work with this device. Some media clients receive only audio, and some clients can receive video and still photos. The price difference between these types of media clients is not that great, so I recommend getting the media client with the additional features.

I chose the D-Link DSM-320 as my media client for two reasons:

✔ It was listed as a supported device by the TwonkyVision Web site for use with their Linux media software. Finding hardware that is clearly supported is always a good idea. You can save yourself a lot of time and aggravation if you pick a device that is known to work with Linux.

✔ It was on sale at my local electronics store. On top of the sale price, the manufacturer offered a rebate, which made the cost only a few dollars more than buying a music-only client. In addition to receiving streaming audio, the D-Link media server can receive MPEG and AVI videos and JPEG, GIF, and PNG slide shows. The cost of the D-Link media server after the rebate was less than $160. The total cost of my media streaming system, not counting the home stereo, was about $175.

If you want to have good-quality sound, you need an amplifier or receiver to connect the audio output from the media client. The easiest solution is to connect the audio to your home stereo system so that the sound can play through your stereo just as though it were playing from a directly attached CD player or other audio source.

# Configuring Your System

To configure your system, you need to download, install, and configure the TwonkyVision media server on the PC that will hold the media files. Then follow the steps required to connect the D-Link media client to the home theater system and configure it to connect to my home network.

## Installing and configuring the media server

Getting the media server running on the Linux PC is relatively easy. But first, you have to download and install it. To do so, follow these steps:

1. **Open your Web browser and go to `www.twonkyvision.de./UPnP/download-trial.html`.**

2. **Click the Linux x86 link to download the file to your PC.**

3. **Extract the contents of the ZIP file.**

4. **Using the `cd` command, change into the folder created during the extraction and run the twonkymedia-trial script.**

   The TwonkyVision media server is now running, and you will use your Web browser to continue to configure the server. You will specify the paths to your files and set performance parameters for the server.

5. **Enter `http://127.0.0.1:9000` in the browser's address bar.**

   The Status page for the TwonkyVision media server, as shown in Figure 7-1, appears. Along the left side of the page is a column of icons; clicking these icons links you to configuration pages, which are respectively named to the icons. Clicking an icon opens the page in the right frame of the main page.

In brief, the following list explains the purpose of these icons, including some detail on the icons that require immediate attention:

- ✔ **Status:** When you log on to the media server Web page, the Status page is the default page displayed. This page provides information about the server, such as the server name, connected clients, content being served, memory usage, and network interfaces used.

- ✔ **Content:** This page is where you can specify the language to use for the server. Even more importantly, though, this page is where you specify the directory locations for your content. This information tells the server where to look — or not to look — for the music, photos, and videos you want to serve.

**Figure 7-1:**
The Status
page for the
Twonky-
Vision
media
server.

In the Content Locations text box, be sure to enter the directories you
want scanned for content. You can enter multiple directory locations
separated by commas. You can safely leave the remaining settings on
this page unchanged, and your server will work properly. Be sure to
click Save Changes when you're done.

If you place all your media in a single directory and then run the server
startup script from that directory, the media server will automatically
scan this directory and all its subdirectories looking for content. For
example, on my system, I created a directory called `mymedia` with three
subdirectories called `music`, `photo`, and `video`. I placed the media
server executable file `twonkymedia-trial` into the `mymedia` folder. I
placed my photos, music, and video files into their respective directories. Then when I start the server from the `mymedia` directory, the
server finds all the media files automatically.

✔ **Radio:** The Radio icon opens a configuration page where you can enable
or disable Internet radio. You can also set a rescan time for the SHOUT-
cast Internet radio site and set a genre filter. Rescan time sets how often
the system should reload the page content.

✔ **Navigation Tree:** On this page, you can set a name for your server. You
can also choose the names for your directories that appear in the navigation tree displayed on the client.

✔ **Tree builder:** This page is where you can refine your navigation tree display. You can specify additional names for your tree, such as Artist, Genre, Albums, and others.

✔ **Network:** On the Network page, you can specify the IP number of the server as well as other settings that affect the media server on your network. Your server will typically work properly without changing any settings on this page.

✔ **Clients:** On the Clients page, you can specify the IP address of specific clients that connect to your server. (On this page, I entered the IP address of the D-Link client I'm using.)

✔ **Performance:** The Performance page is where you can change the streaming buffer size.

Be sure to click Save Changes on any page where you enter information into the text boxes or change any settings. From the Status page, click the Restart Server button to restart the server with any changes you made.

The media server is now configured and ready to serve content. You can move on to setting up the client.

## Connecting and configuring the D-Link media client

You can follow these easy steps to connect your media server to your audio and video devices and your home network. All that is necessary is to enter the proper settings for your network to enable the D-Link unit to connect to your network.

1. **Remove the D-Link unit from the box, and turn it so the rear of the unit is facing you.**

2. **Connect the appropriate cables for your audio and video connections.**

   You can use composite or component video connections and digital coax, digital optical, or composite audio connections. The connection types are labeled on the D-Link unit. Refer to the documentation for your stereo and video components, and use the appropriate connections for your system.

   The unit has an RJ-45 jack, but you won't be using it. You're using wireless, right? So you don't need the RJ-45 jack.

3. **Be sure the antenna is attached to the back of the unit.**

4. **Plug in the power cord, and turn on the D-Link client.**

   A welcome screen appears with the setup wizard.

5. **Press the Enter key on the D-Link remote control.**

6. **Use the down-arrow key to highlight Next and then press Enter.**

7. **The Select Your Network Connection screen appears and displays Wireless as the network type.**

8. **Use the down-arrow key to highlight Next and then press Enter.**

   The next screen shows the SSID for your network.

9. **Use the up- and down-arrow keys on the remote to highlight your SSID and then press Enter.**

   Your current wireless settings are shown (see Figure 7-2).

   You might need to make changes on this page depending on how your network is set up. For example, if you're using WEP, you should enable WEP on this page and enter the appropriate key for your network. To enable WEP, highlight the WEP entry, press Enter on the remote, and use the up- and down-arrow keys to change the setting; then press Enter.

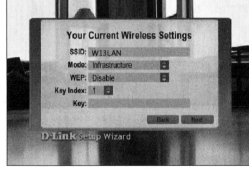

**Figure 7-2:**
Checking
your
wireless
network
settings.

10. **After you make the changes necessary for connecting to your wireless network, highlight Next and press Enter.**

    The next screen displayed is the Your Current Network Settings screen, as shown in Figure 7-3. By default, the system uses DHCP to obtain IP information for your network.

    To see a small help window appear with information about the icon, hover your cursor over the icons.

11. **If you want to use DHCP, highlight Next and press Enter to continue.**

    If you don't have a DHCP server or just want to set your own IP information, you do it on this page:

    *a. Highlight the DHCP entry and press Enter on the remote.*

   b. *Use the arrow keys to select Static IP and then press Enter.*

   c. *Be sure to enter the appropriate IP information for your network into the appropriate fields.*

   d. *Highlight Next and press Enter when you're finished.*

   The Please Select a Media Server screen appears. The last step is to select your media server from the list.

12. **Highlight Next and press Enter.**

   The last screen appears and indicates that the setup process is complete.

13. **Press Done to exit the setup and go to the media server main menu, as shown in Figure 7-4.**

The media client is now configured to connect to your network and should display the main menu shown in Figure 7-5. You can choose Music, Photo, Video, or Online Media to show the content from those areas. In the next section, you discover how to add some music content.

# Choosing Your Music Format

The music format you decide to use is largely determined by the types of formats supported by the media client. Fortunately, the D-Link media client supports a large variety of formats:

- **MP3:** The MP3 format is the most widely used format for distributing audio across the Internet and for playing on portable music players. This is the best choice for most users. Files in MP3 format end with the extension .mp3.

- **WMA:** The WMA format is used by Windows Media player and some other music players. Files in WMA format end with the extension .wma.

- **WAV:** This is the standard file type used by the majority of Windows audio programs. CD music files that are ripped to PC are typically saved as WAV files. Files in WAV format end with the extension .wav.

- **OGG Vorbis:** OGG Vorbis is an open source audio format. Files in OGG Vorbis format end with the extension .ogg.

Another consideration when selecting a music format is whether you will use the files on another media player in addition to your home system. If you will be using a portable music player, choose MP3 or WMA as the music format because these types of players typically can play both formats. On my system, I use the MP3 format and show you how I rip my CDs and create MP3 files.

# Ripping CDs and Encoding Music Files with Grip

A program called Grip allows you to rip CDs to WAV files and encode them as MP3s. You can easily install the Grip program with Yum if you're running Fedora Core, Red Hat Enterprise Linux, or SUSE. If you're using Debian or one of its derivatives, you can use APT to do the install. For example, on my system, I type at a root command prompt:

```
yum install grip
```

Yum searches for any dependencies and installs them as part of the Grip installation. When the command prompt returns, Grip is installed and ready to use. You can run it by entering **grip** at a command prompt or by selecting it from the system menu. On my Fedora Core 4 system, I can choose Applications⇨Sound & Video⇨Grip. No matter how you start the program, the screen shown in Figure 7-5 appears.

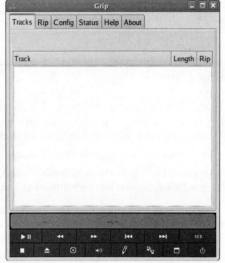

**Figure 7-5:**
The Grip
program
used to rip
and encode
music.

When Grip starts, it's setup by default to encode the ripped files to OGG format. If this is what you want to use as your music format, you don't need to make any changes. In the following steps, I show you how to set up Grip to encode MP3 format music files and then how to start using it:

1. **Click the Config tab from the Grip main screen.**

   Additional tabs appear, including the CD tab screen, as shown in Figure 7-6.

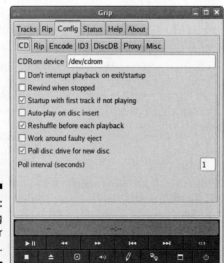

**Figure 7-6:**
Configuring
the CD for
use in Grip.

You typically don't need to make any changes on this screen, but you should check that your CD device is identified correctly.

2. **Click the Rip subtab to open the Rip screen.**

3. **In the Rip File Format text box, enter the path to the directory where you want to place the ripped files.**

   By default, Grip places the files in a directory named OGG in your home directory.

4. **Click the Encode subtab to open the Encode configuration screen.**

5. **Select lame as the encoder. Change the Encode File Extension text box to MP3. Also, change the Encode File Format to point to the directory you want the files to go and change the file extension at the end of the directory path to MP3.**

6. **Click the Tracks tab and put a CD into your CD drive.**

   The CD is read, and a list of tracks appears.

7. **Select the tracks you want to rip by clicking them and then click the main Rip tab.**

8. **Click the Rip+Encode button.**

   The ripping and encoding process begins.

9. **When the entire process is finished, go to the directory that you specified to hold the files.**

   You see the tracks from the CD with MP3 as the file extension.

10. **Move these files to the music directory that you specified as the location of your music files in your media server.**

Instead of moving the files to another location, you can create a link from the directory where your music server looks for the files to the directory that contains them.

# Streaming Your Audio

The steps in this chapter should set you up with a functioning media server and media client. In this section, you check to be sure that everything is working, and then you can try streaming some audio.

Check that your media server is running by running the ps command as follows:

```
ps ax | grep media
```

The system returns information similar to the following:

```
3384 pts/1    Sl      0:00 /mnt/ide2/mymedia/twonkymedia -D
3411 pts/1    S+      0:00 grep media
```

The result of running the ps command shows that the media server is running. You can also check the media server by opening a Web browser and
entering http://127.0.0.1:9000 in the address bar. If the server is running, you see the media server status page.

When you're sure the media server is running, you can go check the client. If
the client is connected to the network and detects the media server, it displays the main menu screen (refer to Figure 7-5).

Use the arrow keys on the remote to highlight Music. Press Enter and navigate the directory tree until you find the files you ripped and encoded.
Highlight a song you want to listen to and press Enter.

Your selection should begin to play through your stereo system. Did you
remember to turn it on? You also see a display that shows the track you
are currently playing.

Congratulations! You now have a streaming music server set up to use at
your home. If you choose to follow my suggestions and use the same D-Link
client, you can also view slide shows of all your photos and watch videos
from the same system.

# Chapter 8

# Having Fun with a Webcam

*W*ebcams are a blast, and they're really useful, too. This chapter shows you how you can use Linux and a webcam to automatically upload new images at timed intervals to your Web site, allowing you to keep an eye on your home when you're away, to make free video calls, and more.

## Sharing the Fun with a Webcam

You can use Linux and a webcam to stream images over the Web. (To *stream* images is to transmit them live.) You can do all kinds of neat stuff with image streams from your webcam.

- ✔ You can set up a babycam near your baby's playpen and broadcast his or her antics to the world.

- ✔ If you're remodeling, you can set up a homecam so that your relatives can watch your progress.

- ✔ You can stream images of your family to your grandmother while you all talk to her on the phone.

- ✔ You can keep an eye on your house while you're out of town.

CamStream is a simple, useful Linux program that makes it easy for you to do all these things, so it's a good starting place for your Linux webcam adventures.

## Installing CamStream

Web streaming software such as CamStream is not usually included as one of the standard applications in most Linux distributions, so you probably need to install it by getting its source code from the author's Web site and compiling it for your computer. Before doing that, you probably want to check that you have a suitable *software driver* — the basic software for your webcam, which enables your webcam to work with Linux software applications.

### Finding your webcam driver

In this chapter, as examples I use popular webcams such as the Logitech QuickCam Pro 4000 and the Logitech Orbit. If you're using a different model of webcam, check the Webcam HOWTO at `www.linux.com/howtos/Webcam-HOWTO/hardware.shtml#MODELS` to see whether your webcam is already supported by your Linux kernel and if not, which driver to use and where to get it.

The *kernel* is the central core of software procedures that coordinates the basic functioning of your computer.

The Webcam HOWTO is a terrific resource that lists dozens of specific webcam models and the name of the Linux kernel module or the driver that supports the webcam. If you can't find the information you want there, the HOWTO has advice on other places to look, and if that doesn't work, you might surf to `www.google.com/linux` and submit a search for `driver` and the name of your webcam — for instance, `"creative labs webcam live! driver"`. This might lead you to a site where you can find and download the Linux driver.

Not all webcams work with Linux, and some webcams have drivers that are still in development and might be buggy, but there's a good chance you'll be able to find a good driver for your webcam. If you're buying a webcam, though, it's worth spending some time first doing a little research to be sure the webcam you purchase has a good Linux driver.

### Using Synaptic to install your driver

If, for example, you plan to use a Logitech QuickCam Pro 4000 webcam with the CamStream software running on Ubuntu Linux, some research on the Web reveals that your webcam works with the Philips webcam pwc driver found on the Web at `www.saillard.org/linux/pwc`. So your next step is to see whether your version of Ubuntu already has the pwc driver installed. The easiest way to do that is probably to use the Synaptic software package management program to see whether the pwc driver is already installed or is in a software repository ready to be installed.

### *Setting up the Synaptic software repositories*

If you're using Ubuntu Linux, you can use the software package manager for Synaptic to get easy access to software beyond what was initially included when you installed your Linux distribution. To do that, you must first set up access to your Linux distribution's software repositories on the Web to get easy access to the webcam driver you want (if it isn't already part of your Linux kernel).

To specify the software repositories you want Synaptic to use, follow these steps:

1. **If you are using Ubuntu with the default desktop (namely, Gnome), from the desktop panel choose System⇨Administration⇨Synaptic Package Manager. If instead you're using the Kubuntu desktop, on the K Menu choose System⇨Package Manager (Synaptic Package Manager).**

   The Run as Root dialog box appears.

2. **Type in the administrator password and click OK.**

   The Synaptic Package Manager window appears.

3. **Choose Settings⇨Repositories.**

   The Software Preferences dialog box appears.

4. **Click Add.**

   The Edit Repository dialog box appears. It has a pop-up menu with four check boxes underneath.

5. **In the Repository pop-up menu, select the top item and then select all four check boxes. Click OK.**

   The dialog box disappears.

6. **In the Software Preferences dialog box, click Add.**

   The Edit Repository dialog box appears again.

7. **From the repository pop-up menu, choose the Ubuntu Security Updates option (the second item down) and then select all four check boxes. Click OK.**

8. **In the Software Preferences dialog box, click Add.**

   The Edit Repository dialog box appears again.

9. **From the Repository pop-up menu, choose Ubuntu Updates (the third item down) and then select all four check boxes. Click OK.**

10. **Click OK in the Software Preferences dialog box.**

    The Software Preferences dialog box disappears.

11. **Choose Edit⇨Reload Package Information.**

    Now, all the Ubuntu software repositories are available to your computer.

## Installing software by using Synaptic

Next, you probably want to install the driver for your webcam. To install software by using Synaptic, you can follow these steps:

1. **If you are using Ubuntu with the default desktop (namely, Gnome), from the desktop panel choose System⇨Administration⇨Synaptic Package Manager. If instead you're using the Kubuntu desktop, on the K Menu choose System⇨Package Manager (Synaptic Package Manager).**

   The Run as Root dialog box appears.

2. **Type in the administrator password and click OK.**

   The Synaptic Package Manager window appears.

3. **Choose Edit⇨Search.**

   The Find dialog box appears. (See Figure 8-1.)

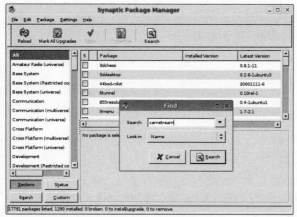

**Figure 8-1:**
You can use Synaptic's Find dialog box to locate software you want to install.

4. **Type in the name of the software you seek (for example, pwc) and click Search.**

   Pwc is the abbreviation for the Philips webcam driver, one of the major drivers for a whole line of webcams, including many from Logitech.

   If software containing the name that you seek is available, it appears in the package list pane of the Synaptic Package Manager window. And if the software is already installed, it has a green mark in the S (Status) column of the list.

   If the software is not available in the software repository, you have the choice of waiting until it is available — this could take an unknown amount of time — or you can download the software from its Web site and follow the installation instructions listed at the site. Ideally, you want to download a version of the software that has been compiled for your particular Linux distribution. If that isn't available, you probably need to download the source code and compile it yourself. Follow the instructions at the Web site. The trick is to make sure you also download and install all the applications that your application needs in order to work.

5. **If the software that you want is available but not installed, select it in the package list pane and choose Package⇨Mark For Installation.**

6. **To install any software packages you marked for installation, choose Edit⇨Apply Marked Changes.**

   A Summary dialog box appears, asking whether you want to apply the changes.

7. **Click the Apply button.**

   The Downloading Package File window appears and disappears, the Applying Changes dialog box appears and disappears, and then the Changes Applied dialog box appears, signifying that the changes you requested have been applied and that the software has been installed.

8. **Click Close in the Changes Applied dialog box.**

### Downloading, compiling, and installing the CamStream software

If you use the Synaptic software package manager to search for the CamStream software (as I describe earlier in this chapter in "Installing software by using Synaptic"), you'll probably find that it isn't in the Ubuntu software repositories. If you use a search engine such as www.google.com, you'll find that you can download the source code for the CamStream software from www.smcc. demon.nl/camstream.

The name of the file you download ends with tar.gz, indicating that it's an archive of files (*tar* stands for tape archive, harking back to the days of yester-year when computer files were usually archived on magnetic tape) and that it has been compressed. (The *gz* stands for GNU Zip, the GNU project's software for file compression.) You need to open the compressed archive and save the archive's files on your computer in their original, uncompressed format. You can use a Linux program such as Ark or FileRoller to do that.

To compile the CamStream source code into a form that your computer can run, you need to open a terminal window and type **cd** and the location of the directory where you saved CamStream — for example, **cd *yourdirectory*/ camstream** — and then press Enter. These actions change your location to the directory you want to work in. Then type **./configure**, press Enter, and watch a bunch of code fly by in the terminal window. (Hopefully, that will finish without leaving any dire comments about not being able to finish the configuration properly, such as a missing driver or a missing application module that you need to find and install.) Then you can type **make**, press Enter, and watch more code fly by (or take a break) as your computer compiles the source code into object code that it can more easily understand. And when that's done, if the compilation finishes successfully, you can type **make install** and watch yet more code go by as the software gets installed into the proper directories on your hard drive.

## Viewing your webcam on your computer with CamStream

If all went well with compiling and installing CamStream on your computer, you now can run it. To run CamStream, follow these steps:

1. **Plug your webcam into the proper port of your computer if you haven't done so already.**

2. **Launch CamStream by choosing it from one of the menus on your Linux desktop, or if you don't find it there, bring up a terminal window (as I describe in Chapter 2), type** camstream, **and press Enter.**

   The CamStreams window appears.

3. **Choose File⇨Open Viewer.**

   The Open Video Device dialog box appears.

4. **Choose your webcam from the Device pop-up menu.**

5. **In the Initial Size pane, choose the size that you want your camera image to display in.**

6. **Click OK.**

   The Open Video Device dialog box disappears, and a viewer window for your camera appears with the live video image from the webcam. Congratulations!

Now that you're getting pictures, you can take screenshots by using any screenshot program and send pictures of your pals, your dogs, yourself, and whomever to your mom.

Next, you might want to adjust the size, brightness, contrast, and other settings of the video image. To fiddle with the video image, do the following steps:

1. **Click the Various Controls button in the CamStream window, as shown in Figure 8-2.**

   The video Settings dialog box appears, as shown in Figure 8-3.

2. **On the Size & Framerate tab, choose the dimensions of the video image and the frames per second (fps) that you desire.**

   Broadcast video is 30 fps. For streaming on the Web, you probably want to choose a slower frame rate, because many people's access to the Internet isn't fast enough to deal with high frame rates.

Various Controls

Show last snapshot

Take snapshot at regular intervals

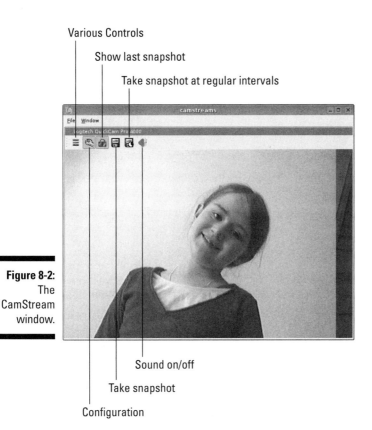

**Figure 8-2:**
The
CamStream
window.

Sound on/off

Take snapshot

Configuration

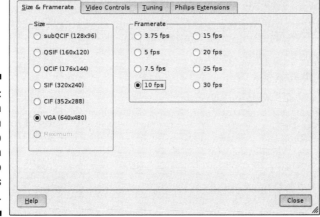

**Figure 8-3:**
You can
fiddle with
your video
image in
the Video
Settings
dialog box.

3. **To adjust Brightness, Contrast, Gamma, and Saturation, click the Video Controls tab and fiddle with the sliders there.**

   - *Gamma* is a curve that depicts how light or dark the gray tones of an image appear.

   - *Saturation* is a measure of the intensity of a hue. A highly saturated image has bright colors, and an image low in saturation is gray with almost no color.

   - *Brightness* defines the amount of white in an image.

   - *Contrast* defines how light the light tones are and how dark the dark tones are.

4. **If you have more than one webcam or TV Tuner card connected to your computer, you can click the Tuning tab and choose the webcam or tuner that you want to view.**

5. **If your camera is a Philips camera, as are a variety of popular Logitech cameras, you can click the Philips Extensions tab to adjust the lighting, noise reduction, and compression of your image.**

## Sending your webcam images to other computers

CamStream generates a series of still images at speeds that you specify and saves them either on your computer's hard drive or sends them via FTP to the hard drive of another computer that you specify.

To send your files to be seen on another computer, follow these steps:

1. **Click the Configuration button in the CamStream window. (Refer to Figure 8-3.)**

   The Snapshot Settings window appears.

2. **Select the radio button for the file format that you desire, such as JPEG, PNG, PPM, or BMP, and then type the name of the file into the Basename text box.**

3. **If you desire, you can select any of these three options:**

   - *Re-Use Filename (Overwrite):* Select this radio button so that every time an image is created, it overwrites the image with the same filename.

   - *Put Timestamp in Filename:* Selecting this radio button makes the time and date part of the filename of each new image.

   - *Number Sequentially:* Select this radio button, and each image will be numbered in sequence.

4. **Type a number in the Maximum Sequence Number text box if you want to modify the default setting.**

   If the computer generates more images than the Maximum Sequence Number, the computer erases the old file and creates a newer one, so you never exceed the limit you specified.

5. **If you want CamStream to save images in the home directory on your hard drive, select the Save To Disk check box at the bottom of the Snapshot Settings dialog box; if you want CamStream to send images to another computer, select the FTP to Server check box.**

   You can select both Save to Disk and FTP To Server if you want. If you choose the FTP route, you'll want to do the following:

   a. *Click the FTP Settings button in the Snapshot Settings dialog box to specify a computer where your images will be sent.*

      The FTP Settings dialog box appears.

   b. *Type in the hostname, username, password, and, optionally, the path of the computer that you want to send your images to, as shown in Figure 8-4.*

      The hostname is the name of the FTP server, such as `ftp.example.com`, or its IP address, such as `192.0.168.55`. The username and password are for the account that you want to log in to. The path specifies where on the hard drive on the server your images will be saved.

      The computer to which you want to send images needs to have FTP server software running so it can accept the images.

   c. *Click OK in the FTP Settings dialog box.*

      The FTP Settings dialog box disappears.

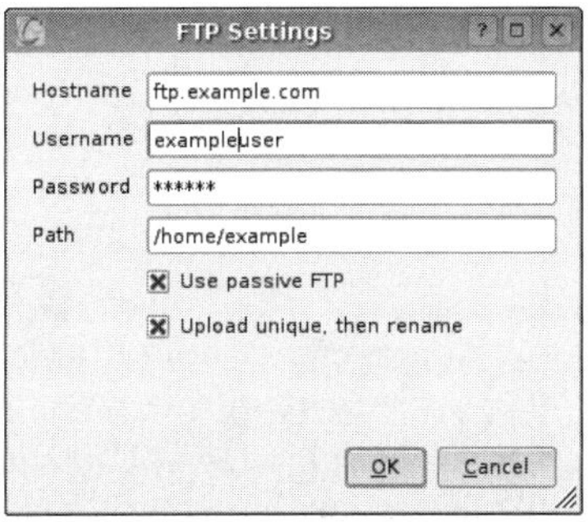

**Figure 8-4:**
You can specify where to transmit your images in Cam-Stream's FTP Settings dialog box.

| FTP Settings | ? □ ✕ |
| --- | --- |
| Hostname | ftp.example.com |
| Username | exampleuser |
| Password | ****** |
| Path | /home/example |
| ☒ Use passive FTP |
| ☒ Upload unique, then rename |
| OK    Cancel |

6. **Click OK in the Snapshot Settings dialog box.**

   The Snapshot Settings dialog box disappears. CamStream starts to send a continuous series of snapshots to your computer or to your FTP server, according to whatever you have specified.

7. **Click the Take Snapshot at Regular Intervals button in the CamStream window.**

   The Timed Snapshot Settings dialog box appears.

8. **Specify the number of seconds or minutes you want between images. Then click OK.**

   The Timed Snapshot Settings dialog box disappears. CamStream sends images to your computer or FTP server at the interval you specified.

You can send images from one computer on your home network to another. For example, you can set up a baby monitor in the nursery and view it in your home office.

### Timestamping your images

To put a timestamp on your stream of images (for security reasons or informational purposes or whatever), click the Configuration button in the CamStream window. Then in the Snapshot Settings window that appears, select the Put Timestamp In Image check box. You can also choose Select Color or Select Font to specify the color and font of the timestamp.

### Seeing your CamStream images on a browser

You can load your CamStream image into your Web browser and click your browser's Refresh or Reload button manually to view a current picture from your webcam if, for example, you want to check on a webcam image of a building site every so often.

If refreshing the Web browser page is too much work, you are just too lazy — okay, there is a way to get a Web page to refresh itself for you. Kind of like a video, except slower or jerkier, at least on our computers. But it works. See the next section.

### Creating a reloading Web page

Here's how to create a Web page that reloads itself with a continuous stream of images updated one after another automatically. In a text editor, create a Web page by using some simple HTML. (*HTML* is Hypertext Markup Language, which is the simple code used to create most Web pages.) You can type this code into your text editor to create a Web page with just a title and an image on it that refreshes itself:

```
<!DOCTYPE HTML PUBLIC "-//W3C//DTD HTML 4.0
        Transitional//EN">
<html>
<head>
<title>CamStream Pix</title>
<meta http-equiv="REFRESH"
        content="1;url=chapter8.html"></head>
<body>
<img src="snapshot.png">
</ body>
</html>
```

Feel free to substitute your own title for `CamStream Pix`. Save the code as a Web page by choosing File➪Save As in your text editor. Give it the name `chapter8.html`.

The part of the HTML code, `1;url=chapter8.html`, specifies that the Web browser should load the Web page named `chapter8.html` in 1 second. If you change this to `5;url=chapter8.html`, the browser will load the page named `chapter8.html` in 5 seconds. Because the page is named `chapter8.html`, the page keeps loading itself again and again, every 1 or 5 seconds or whatever you specify in the page.

An easy way to publish a Web page that constantly shows your webcam images (even if you just want to show them to a few friends or family) is to pay for an inexpensive Web-hosting service. For instance, you can get your own domain name (such as www.*example*.com) from a registrar like www.godaddy.com for $8 or so per year, and for a few dollars a month, godaddy.com will also host your Web site. You upload your version of `chapter8.html` to your site there, and you also have CamStream send its images to your site there via FTP. (Be sure to set up the Snapshot Settings dialog box, as I describe in the section "Sending your webcam images to other computers," earlier in this chapter, so that you are reusing the filename for each new image that CamStream creates.)

Then you and anyone who knows your Web address can view your continuous flow of CamStream images by, for example, surfing to www.*example*.com/chapter8.html — or whatever your Web site is.

# Having Fun with Videoconferencing

Videoconferencing is unreasonably enjoyable. It's fun to see who you're talking to, especially if you're talking to your family or friends. Videoconferencing is also useful. If you're trying to explain something to someone, you can show them diagrams, gesticulate wildly, and make funny faces to keep his or her attention. You can look in on your kids if you have a webcam set up in front of the Nintendo. In business meetings, your body language can help you get your points across.

And with software like Ekiga, videoconferencing is not only fun and useful, it's free. What a great application for your webcam.

## Installing Ekiga

Ekiga recently changed its name from GnomeMeeting and released Ekiga 2.0. The new Ekiga version of GnomeMeeting includes better audio quality and improved camera support. This package is currently available only in its source code. Compiled versions of Ekiga will be available soon for the major Linux distributions, but until that happens, you might want to use GnomeMeeting instead.

Many Linux distributions (including Ubuntu, the Linux distribution we've been mentioning in this chapter) come with GnomeMeeting already installed. And soon, they will undoubtedly come with Ekiga installed. Check your application menus to see whether you have one or the other. If you don't have either, you can look for Ekiga or GnomeMeeting by using a software package manager such as Synaptic. (In Synaptic, choose Edit⇨Search to find it, and then install Ekiga or GnomeMeeting if neither one is already installed, as described earlier in this chapter, in the section "Installing software by using Synaptic.")

## Configuring Ekiga

The first time you run Ekiga, the Configuration Druid window appears so that you can properly set up the program. These basic steps take you through the process:

1. **Go through the Druid, type your name and e-mail address, and click Get an Ekiga.net SIP Account if you'd like to get your own SIP URL so that people can call you for free by using SIP software such as Ekiga.**

2. **Continue to go through the Druid and type your Internet connection type, such as DSL or Local Area Network.**

3. **Click the Detect NAT Type button and read the report on how to configure your NAT router to make calls with Ekiga.**

   If what it says makes sense to you, follow the instructions; if not, you can try Ekiga without following the instructions. If it works, great. If not, you might want to bring up the Configuration Druid again by choosing Edit⇨Configuration Druid and hire some genius who understands what Ekiga is telling you that it requires.

4. **Choose your Audio Manager — usually ALSA is the best choice when it is available.**

5. **Choose your Audio Input and Output devices.**

   Ekiga suggests settings. You can accept the settings or pull down the menu to choose alternative settings.

6. **On the Audio Devices page of the Druid, you can click Test Settings and record yourself saying "1, 2, 3" (or anything else you want to say).**

   You'll hear what you said played back to you so that you know that your audio devices are working.

7. **Choose your Video Manager Software.**

   V4L (Video4Linux) is what you usually want to choose for a webcam.

8. **Choose the Video Input device.**

   Your webcam will show up on the pop-up menu if you installed the driver, as I explain earlier in this chapter, in the section "Using Synaptic to install your driver." The last page of the Configuration Druid summarizes your settings.

9. **Click the Apply button.**

If you want to change your settings, you can always run the Configuration Druid again by choosing Edit⇨Configuration Druid.

## Making calls

You can use Ekiga to make free audio or free video calls to people with hardware or software that supports the H.323 standard, including Microsoft NetMeeting, or the Session Internet Protocol (SIP) which is becoming one of the leading standards for VoIP (Voice over Internet Protocol; in other words, telephony via the Internet). You can also call real phones if you purchase an account that lets you do so.

With Ekiga, you usually call other people by using URLs (Web addresses). There are three kinds of URLs that Ekiga can use. One is `sip:`, which utilizes the increasingly popular SIP standard and is the default for Ekiga. Another is `h323:`, which conforms to the H.323 standard. The other is `callto:`, which Microsoft uses for NetMeeting.

To make a call by using Ekiga, do the following:

**1. Type the URL of the person you're calling into the input box, as shown in Figure 8-5.**

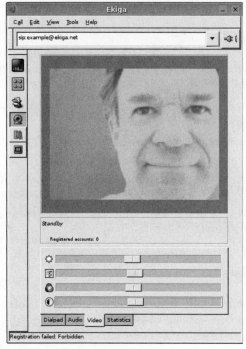

**Figure 8-5:**
To call
someone,
you can
type a URL
directly into
Ekiga's
input box.

**2. Click the Connect button.**

The Connect Button changes to look as if it's connected to a socket, and the status of the call appears at the bottom of the window.

**3. When your call is answered, you have your choice of views. Choose View and in the View menu choose one of the following:**

- *Local Video*

- *Remote Video*

- *Both (Picture-in-Picture)*

- *Both (Side-by-Side)*

- *Both In New Windows*

**4. To end a call, click the Connect button again.**

An easier way to make a call is to use the Ekiga Address Book, which contains the URLs that you retrieve from remote directories as well as URLs that you manually enter yourself. To use the Address Book, follow these steps:

1. **Choose Tools⇨Address Book.**

   The Address Book window appears.

2. **In the left pane, click the Remote Contacts disclosure triangle to show or hide directories of contacts from other locations on the Web or click the Local Contacts disclosure triangle to show or hide directories of contacts you manually enter in the Address Book. Then click the directory of contacts which you want to view.**

   The Remote Contacts directories include by default the Ekiga White Pages directory.

3. **To search for someone, type a full or partial name in the Name Contains text box at the bottom of the Address Book window.**

   The Address Book window fills with the names of people who are listed in the chosen directory and have names that match your search.

4. **Click the Name button at the top of the Name column to sort by Name or click Location to sort by Location, and so on.**

5. **To make a call, double-click the name of the person you want to contact.**

6. **To end a call, click the Connect button.**

Ekiga sounds like a regular phone ringing when a call comes in, so be sure your speakers are hooked up and your computer is on if you're expecting a call.

# Looking Around with Pan and Tilt

Several models of webcams can pan and tilt via remote control. Some of these pan-and-tilters come with stratospheric price tags, but others are more affordable. The Logitech QuickCam Orbit camera is one of the more affordable models. It sells for about $130 and sits like a small head on top of a 9-inch neck. (Logitech claims that raising the camera 9 inches high gets it more to the level of the face of someone sitting at a computer. Sounds good to me.)

Different webcams can pan and tilt different numbers of degrees. For instance, the Logitech QuickCam Orbit webcam can pan 128 degrees and tilt 54 degrees. It also moves silently and quickly. It takes about 1 second for it to move from one extreme side to the other.

Many existing programs let you control the pan and tilt by typing parameters on the command line — but that's a lot of work and definitely not as much fun. One Linux program called OrbitView lets you control the pan and tilt by clicking anywhere on the image, causing the pan and tilt controls to center the image at the point that you clicked. (That's more like it, huh?) OrbitView also lets you control the pan, tilt, and zoom by using the command line, so if you have your heart set on that, you can go for it.

OrbitView is a stable program and works with any camera that uses the pwc driver — which many Logitech cameras use, as well as others. To download OrbitView, go to `http://hcvl.hci.iastate.edu/OrbitView`.

# Putting Your Webcam to Work

When you've got your webcam set up, there are many ways you can put it to work to make your home smarter.

You can use your webcam for home security purposes, for example, by streaming webcam images of your home to a Web page, as described in the earlier section "Sending your webcam images to other computers." You can set up several webcams and stream each of them to a different Web page by using this technique. Or you can plug several wireless webcams into X10 Appliance Modules and use MisterHouse to send X10 signals to turn off all but the one camera you want to see, as I describe in the section on watching your kids from the Internet in Chapter 19.

Then while you're away from home, you can keep an eye on any areas of your home, indoors or out, where you have a webcam. For example, if you've left your kids at home with a babysitter, you can use any Web browser to see how things are going at home.

You can also use one or more webcams to keep an eye on your garden while you're out of town. Then if the weather gets hotter than expected and your plants start to look wilted, you can use the Rain 8 X10 sprinkler control system to give your garden extra water, as I describe in the section on watering your lawn in Chapter 19.

X10.com sells several webcams that are suitable for both indoor and outdoor use — to find them, visit `www.x10.com` and type **"outdoor webcam"** in the Search text box. The wireless XCam2 sells for about $80.

# Chapter 9

# Setting Up a Smart Phone System

*W*elcome to Asterisk, your open source toolkit for telephony applications and a full-featured, call-processing server. Or in plain English, it's like some of the fancy telephone equipment businesses use, but it comes with more features and is easier to set up so people like you and me can use it. You can use Asterisk as a stand-alone system, which is how I show you to use it in this chapter, or as an adjunct to a previously existing PBX or Voice Over IP (VoIP) implementation (something you'll probably begin using within the next few years). You can add telephone applications by using the AGI (Asterisk Gateway Interface). Telephone applications allow you to do all sorts of neat things, such as getting the status of or controlling MisterHouse (software I introduce in Part VI) via your phone or getting weather or other information from the Internet and listening to it over the phone.

Basically, Asterisk is your smart phone system. It has lots of features and supports a lot of hardware. Many of the features you probably wouldn't need in your home unless you have a *really* large family. In fact, there is so much to Asterisk that I can cover only a small fraction of what it's capable of. I'm sorry if that sounds like a cop-out, but it's true. To do Asterisk justice, I would have to devote an entire book to it; instead, I give you the basics in this chapter.

*Note:* In this chapter, I cover enough to get you started with a single extension, voice mail, and the ability to send and receive calls from your phone company. I make most of the configuration decisions because this makes it easier to go through the material. It's one of those unfortunate instances where you need to have experience with the material before you can properly understand and use it. Of course, to get the experience, you have to learn the material. By using my experience, you can get started using Asterisk quicker because I give you a base to expand on.

# *Asterisk 101*

The telephone industry has lots of strange names, terminology, and TLAs (three-letter acronyms). Unfortunately, this causes a lot of confusion, but I need to use those names and TLAs (sorry).

This list explains the names and acronyms I use the most:

- **ATA (analog telephone adapter):** This device takes a telephone and/or the cable coming from the telephone company and allows you to connect it to an IP network and VoIP server (like Asterisk).

- **FXO (Foreign eXchange Office):** The interface that connects to the telephone company's switches. (You plug the cable from the telephone company into the FXO port. Also known as the *line port.*)

- **FXS (Foreign eXchange Station):** The interface that connects to the telephone. (You plug the cable from the telephone into the FSX port. Also known as the *phone port.*)

- **PBX (Private Branch eXchange):** A telephone switch located in a business or home.

- **POTS (plain old telephone service):** Anything to do with non-VoIP home telephone service, such as a *POTS line,* which is the telephone service and cable you get from your local telephone company.

- **PSTN (Public Switched Telephone Network):** The telephone company's telephone network.

- **SIP (Session Initiation Protocol):** One of the protocols that is used in VoIP.

- **Telephony:** The technology used in the telephone industry. *Telephony* is a blanket name for all the stuff that goes into sending a call from your phone to someone else's phone.

- **VoIP (Voice Over IP):** A way of making telephone calls over IP networks such as the Internet.

The setup in this chapter consists of the Asterisk version 1.2 software and the Sipura SPA-3000 hardware. The SPA-3000 is an ATA that allows you to hook up your telephone and your hookup to the PSTN to your local VoIP network (that's what you're building). It really acts like two devices in one box. One of the nice features of the SPA-3000 is that when Asterisk isn't working or the power goes out you can still make and receive calls. This is an important feature that will keep you from getting in trouble with your spouse who might not have your affinity towards modern technology (toys!). I've set up a dial plan that should work for any North American telephony setup (the United States and Canada).

# Dial plans

A *dial plan* is a set of rules that takes a pattern and instructs the device to do something with it. Normally, the phone company does this work, so your phone simply sends everything you dial directly to the telephone company's switch to be processed. With no PBX, you can't do much with the numbers you dial from your home.

To start with, you need to plan out what number pattern you want to dial. I substitute X for a single digit in my dial plan description. For most of North America, you need something like this:

- ✔ 7-digit local dialing (XXX-XXXX)

- ✔ 10-digit local dialing (XXX-XXX-XXXX) to handle overlay plans

- ✔ 11-digit long-distance dialing (1-XXX-XXX-XXXX)

- ✔ Call feature dialing (*XX)

- ✔ Emergency (911 or 311) or information dialing (411)

- ✔ Operator assistance (0)

- ✔ Overseas dialing (01XXX . . .)

- ✔ Long distance dial around (1010XXX . . .)

- ✔ Internal extensions (XXXX)

## Number please?

Allow me to explain how a dial plan works with Asterisk. Normally, you dial a number and the phone company deals with it. It has the dial plan and knows how to properly route your call. If you dial 555-1212, you get your local operator; if you're in an area with 10-digit dialing, you dial something like 732-555-1212. When you add Asterisk, you now need Asterisk to deal with the dial plan. This allows you to have multiple telecom providers and local extensions. You can then set up a dial plan so that a number that starts with 9 (such as 9555-1212) is sent to AT&T local services, a number that starts with 8 (such as 8555-1212) is sent to AT&T Call Vantage, and any number in the 2000 range is a local extension. What Asterisk does is intercept each number you press, and it compares each digit to the dial plan. When it finds a pattern that matches the numbers dialed, it follows the instructions provided in the dial plan. If it finds an exact match, it dials that number immediately. If you dial 911 and you have an exact 911 pattern in your dial plan, it immediately processes the call according to your instructions in the dial plan. If you dial 9112 and use the same patterns, it matches the 911 part and just passes on the 2 to wherever you send the call. This is why you have to select your dial plan carefully.

Some businesses add 4- or 5-digit dialing for calling an extension local to the building. Even though you'll have only one extension, I show you how to use 4-digit dialing for your home setup. Adding new extensions to the `extensions.conf` file will be easy, and they don't have to be phones. Instead, they can be extensions to AGI applications (programs such as weather reports) that I mention earlier. (The `extensions.conf` file is included on this book's CD.)

After deciding what number patterns to dial, you can create a dial plan for the SPA-3000 and Asterisk. The SPA-3000 and Asterisk each have their own format for their dial plan, but the basics of the dial plan are the same. In fact, the SPA-3000 has three (short) dial plans:

- **A dial plan for your telephone on Line 1:** This dial plan decides whether the number is to be sent directly to the PSTN or to Asterisk. The reason for this is that 911 calls should not be handled by Asterisk when the SPA-3000 can send them directly to the PSTN without delay. The rest of the calls are sent to Asterisk.

- **A dial plan for calls being sent to the PSTN:** This one is relatively simple because the decision has already been made to send the call to the PSTN. Either Asterisk has made the decision or the Line 1 dial plan has made the decision (for 911 calling). This dial plan is set up to accept the number and forward it on.

- **A dial plan for a call coming from the PSTN:** All calls from the PSTN are sent directly to Asterisk. The SPA-3000 has many features that you won't be taking advantage of. The dial plan is just one of them, and you'll use only a portion of the power of the dial plan. The reason for this is that Asterisk provides you with much more flexibility, so it's better to allow Asterisk to handle the hard work.

Next, you need to know the rules for creating the dial plan. The SPA-3000 uses a subset of what Asterisk uses, and the two use different layouts but otherwise are quite similar. Here are the general rules that both use:

- Any number dialed not matched by a pattern is ignored. (You get a fast busy warble sound on your phone.)

  A *pattern* is a number, symbol (see the rules below for symbols), group of numbers, and/or a group of symbols that the number you're dialing needs to match.

- You can combine the following rules to make a complex pattern or rule:

  - 0: Match the exact digit (zero in this case, but it can be any digit 0 through 9, *, or #).

  - N: Match a single digit, any digit between 1 through 9.

- Z: Match a single digit, any digit between 2 through 9.

- X: Match a single digit, any digit between 0 though 9.

- XX: Match any 2 digits (but no more than 2 digits).

- XX.: Match any 3 or more digits, any digit 0 through 9, *, or #.

- _: Means match the following pattern as a number, not as a literal string.

- []: Match anything in the list between the brackets (single-digit match).

- [2-6]: Match a single digit in the range of 2 through 6.

- [2-69]: Match a single digit in the range of 2 through 6 or 9.

  ✔ A dash may be used only inside the brackets rule.

  ✔ Do not use spaces in the rules.

The SPA-3000 doesn't use patterns N and Z. Instead, it uses the list ([]) rule. Asterisk keeps its dial plan in a file called extensions.conf in the /etc/asterisk directory. I list a sample later in this chapter. (See Listing 9-6.) The SPA-3000 uses a Web interface to squeeze in its dial plans. Its dial plans are located under the Line 1 tab (shown later in Figure 9-4) and the PSTN tab (also shown later, in Figure 9-6). The _ (underscore) isn't used by the SPA-3000, and its use is rather confusing in Asterisk. VoIP introduces the concept of IP dialing, where the phone number is not a number but rather the name or IP address of the phone to call. The _ tells Asterisk to treat the pattern that proceeds as a number. With IP dialing, the pattern to be matched would be a string, and it needs to be matched exactly. Because you won't be using IP dialing right now, just make sure that your Asterisk extensions patterns all start with an _, except the s extension. I go into further detail about the s extension later in the chapter.

# Context

Asterisk adds the concept of a context in the dialing plan. A *context* is a group of extensions with a name attached to it to make it easy to identify. This allows you to break down the dial plan into sections. Different contexts can be included in (or pulled into) a context by using the include => command. All the extensions of the included context are now part of the context that pulled them in. This allows you to create commonly used extensions and use them in many places, as shown in Listing 9-1.

**Listing 9-1:    The from-pstn Context from /etc/asterisk/extensions.conf**

```
; -[ Calls from the PSTN ]-------------------------------
          --
[from-pstn]
; Timing list for includes is
;    <context>|<time range>|<days of week>|
;            <days of month>|<months>
  include => daytime|8:00-22:59|*|*|*
  include => nighttime|23:00-7:59|*|*|*
```

The `from-pstn` context handles all the incoming calls from the telephone company. It includes two other contexts, `daytime` and `nighttime`. These include statements that also have the conditional arguments (`|8:00-22:59|*|*|*` and `|23:00-7:59|*|*|*`), which are optional. This tells Asterisk to include this context during the time prescribed. Without the conditional arguments, the context is always included. With conditional arguments, you can create contexts that can handle holiday announcements and other neat features.

Both devices (the SPA-3000 is considered two devices) are registered with Asterisk. The `sip.conf` file in the directory `/etc/asterisk` contains the registration information for both Line 1 (where you have the telephone plugged in) and the PSTN (the cable to the telephone company). Under the PSTN registration information is the statement `context = from-pstn`. This is the `from-pstn` context that this device is assigned to. So when a call is received by Asterisk, the call follows the rules provided by the `from-pstn` context. Other devices can use the same context or a different one.

For your setup, there are two main contexts: `from-pstn` and `from-sip`. The context `from-pstn` handles calls from the PSTN, and the calls follow the rules in the context to determine what to do with them. The context `from-sip` handles calls to and from your extensions. Extensions configured in one context are unknown in another context unless they are included in that context by using the `include =>` statement. Listing 9-2 shows just a portion of `extensions.conf`. (I had to trim it to make it fit.) It's a good example of a dial plan (both contexts and extensions).

**Listing 9-2:    The stdexten Macro from /etc/asterisk/extensions.conf**

```
; Some variables
PHONE1 = SIP/2201
VMAIL1 = 2201

[macro-stdexten]
;    ${ARG1} - Extension (could've used ${MACRO_EXTEN} here)
;    ${ARG2} - Device(s) to ring
;
  exten => s,1,Dial(${ARG2},20)
  exten => s,2,Goto(s-${DIALSTATUS},1)
  exten => s-NOANSWER,1,Voicemail(u${ARG1})
  exten => s-NOANSWER,2,Goto(default,s,1)
```

```
exten => s-BUSY,1,Voicemail(b${ARG1})
exten => s-BUSY,2,Goto(default,s,1)

exten => _s-.,1,Goto(s-NOANSWER,1)
exten => a,1,VoicemailMain(${ARG1})

; -[ Calls from the PSTN ]--------------------------------
[from-pstn]
   include => daytime|8:00-22:59|*|*|*
   include => nighttime|23:00-7:59|*|*|*

[daytime]
   exten => s,1,Macro(stdexten,${PHONE1},${RINGS})

[nighttime]
   exten => s,1,Voicemail(u${VMAIL1})
```

Assuming that the SPA-3000 is working, configured, and registered properly, here's what happens when a call arrives:

1. When the SPA-3000 receives a call from the PSTN, it forwards the call, according to its dial plan, to Asterisk.

2. Asterisk sees the call as a phone call from the registered device PSTN, looks at the PSTN SIP entry (in the file sip.conf), and sees that its context is from-pstn.

3. Asterisk then goes to the extensions and finds the context from-pstn.

   In that context, I've added conditional include statements, based on the time of day:

   a. If the time is between 11:00 p.m. and 7:59 a.m., it jumps to the context nighttime, where it then uses the Asterisk command Voicemail to send the call to a voice mail box.

   b. If the time is between 8:00 a.m. and 10:59 p.m., it jumps to the context daytime where it uses the macro macro-stdexten. In the macro, it then dials the extension ${PHONE1}, a variable assigned to SIP/2201. (I explain macros more at the end of this list.)

4. If the dial command returns, the call was not completed; Asterisk then uses the Goto command to jump to the correct status (s-NOANSWER for no answer, s-BUSY for a busy line, or s-. for everything else that doesn't match).

   a. The s-NOANSWER and s-BUSY both send the call to voice mail, and if the user should return from voice mail, the next command instructs Asterisk to send the call to the default context, where more processing can occur.

   b. The s-. extension simply sends the call to the s-NOANSWER extension, where the call gets sent to voice mail. The a extension is used to catch a key press (you can use that to interrupt the voice mail message) and keep the call in voice mail.

The `macro-stdexten` looks like a context, but it isn't. It's an easy way to use the same series of commands in other extensions. This makes it easier to write (and read) extension rules. To call a macro, drop the `macro-` from the name (`macro-x`, just use the `x`). You can pass arguments to a macro, and they will be assigned the variable `${ARGn}`, where the `n` stands for the number in the order they were assigned (for example, `${ARG1}` will contain the first argument, `${ARG2}` will contain the second, and so on).

In the preceding example, there are several variable uses, such as `${ARG1}` and `${PHONE1}`. The `${ARG1}` variable is used inside macros, and the values are assigned by what is passed in the macro call. The `${PHONE1}` variable is a user-assigned variable. In the preceding example, I assign the variable `${PHONE1}` to `SIP/2201`. This is the POTS phone connected to the SPA-3000 Line 1.

The `s` extension is unique in that it matches extensions only when there are none. This ability is useful in macros and in calls from the PSTN where there are no extensions being called. It isn't a catch-all extension. A catch-all extension looks like this: `_.` or `_X.`. Both of these extensions are dangerous to use because when a context is read by Asterisk, it's sorted numerically and not by the order in the file. So the `_.` would show up before the `_2201`, and the `_X.` would show up last. Be careful of your use of the two catch-all extensions. Use of the `_X.` extension is preferred over the `_.` extension. Listing 9-3 shows an example of what I mean.

### Listing 9-3: An Example of a Poorly Selected Dial Plan

```
[from-junk]
   exten => _2201,1,Macro(stdexten,${PHONE1},${RINGS})
   exten => _.,1,Voicemail(u${VMAIL})
   exten => _X.,1,Voicemail(u${VMAIL})
```

Although the preceding dial plan isn't really useful, it is a good example of what will happen when you try to use the catch-all extensions. If you jump into the Asterisk command line interface (see "Installing and compiling Asterisk," later in the chapter) and type **show dialplan from-junk**, you will see the following output:

```
mozart*CLI> show dialplan from-junk
[ Context 'from-junk' created by 'pbx_config' ]
    '_.' =>      1. Voicemail(u${VMAIL})            [pbx_config]
    '_2201' => 1. Macro(stdexten|${PHONE1})          [pbx_config]
    '_X.' =>     1. Voicemail(u${VMAIL})            [pbx_config]

-= 3 extensions (3 priorities) in 1 contexts. =-
mozart*CLI>
```

So what you have is the first extension matching everything with one or more digits, the second matching 2201 exactly, and the third matching two or more digits. As you can see, the order is different, and if you aren't careful, you could be sending everything to voice mail. (Yes, even the extension 2201 matches the first rule!)

# Gathering the Ingredients

Alright, enough of the technical mumbo-jumbo — my head hurts. It's time to configure the hardware and then install the Asterisk software and configure it. The hardware requires a bit of searching on the Internet. I recommend that you use a search engine to find the best price. At the time of this writing, the SPA-3000 was less than $100 (U.S.). The good news is that you can start installing the software without having the hardware. You won't be able to make any calls until you get the hardware, but you will be able to try out the commands.

This list describes what you need, excluding PC requirements (which I discuss in the "How big a PC for Asterisk?" sidebar):

- **Software (found on the CD)**
  - My replacement configuration files
  - Asterisk software, version 1.2 (`asterisk-1.2.0.tar.gz`)
- **Hardware**
  - Sipura SPA-3000 ATA
  - A PC running Linux with an Ethernet interface card
  - A regular, push-button phone
  - PSTN service (the telephone line from your telephone company)
  - Two R-J11 telephone cables
  - An Ethernet cable
  - A home network
- **Optional**
  - A caller ID unit and an extra RJ-11 telephone cable
  - An answering machine and an extra RJ-11 telephone cable

## Stop the presses!

The new Linksys ATA — the SPA-3102 — became available after I wrote this chapter, and by the time you read this, the SPA-3000 may not be available. Normally that would be bad news, but I have the new SPA-3102, and it seems to behave pretty much the same as the SPA-3000 — at least for the needs of this chapter. To find out if there are any changes related to this, visit my Web site (www.linuxha.com/) where I'll post further updates as needed.

You must have a working network to start with. Usually, you set this up at install time. The caller ID and the answering machine are optional. My wife wanted the messages left on the answering machine, so I configured Asterisk to go to voice mail on four rings and my answering machine for three rings. Of course, call after 11 p.m. and you'll get Asterisk and not the answering machine. My wife is happy with that.

The various files on the CD contain the configuration changes I've made to copies of the original Asterisk files. Don't worry about the originals; they'll be renamed with a .bak extension during the install, so you can compare my changes to the original. The files are in the /etc/asterisk directory.

## *Fitting the hardware pieces together*

Figure 9-1 shows the hardware put together properly (remember that the answering machine is optional). Installation instructions are also included with the SPA-3000; both instructions will work properly. The SPA-3000, you'll need to purchase. I suggest using your favorite search engine to find a good price. The telephone must be a push-button phone and not an old-fashioned rotary phone. The SPA-3000 won't recognize the pulses from a rotary phone. (It's strange how many people still say you're going to dial a phone number when you no longer have a dial on the phone.) The home network can be as simple as a Linux server with an Ethernet network interface card connected via an x-over (cross over) Ethernet cable to the Ethernet port of the SPA-3000. Figure 9-1 shows an Ethernet hub or switch being used, which is the preferred method.

The SPA-3000 is a gateway device that connects the PSTN, your phone, and VoIP services (in this case, Asterisk). The SPA-3000's job is to convert a call from your telephone or the PSTN to IP and back. This device does a lot of the hard work for you. Technically, the SPA-3000 doesn't need Asterisk to work, but it's a great interface to use with Asterisk in a home environment. The SPA-3000 has four ports on it: an Ethernet port, an FXO port (telephone company line port), an FXS port (the phone port), and a power port.

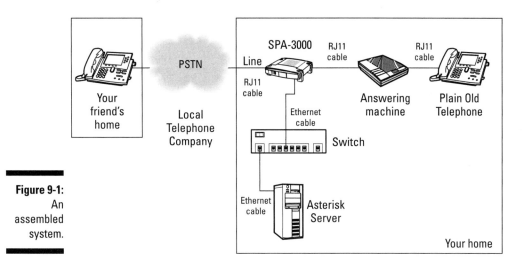

**Figure 9-1:**
An
assembled
system.

The SPA-3000 is an interesting ATA. It has several useful features, the first being that on the loss of power the SPA-3000 will pass PSTN calls to Line 1, and Line 1 calls to the PSTN. This means that you can still make and receive outside calls even when the power is out and your Asterisk server is down. You won't be able to call any of your extensions, but you will be able to call the outside world. In addition to handling the loss of power (and/or the loss of connectivity to your Asterisk server) properly, the SPA-3000 can direct 911 calls directly to the PSTN without going through your Asterisk server. It is very important not to interfere with the 911 services because seconds count in an emergency.

## Configuring the SPA-3000

Before you configure your SPA-3000, you need a couple pieces of information. The first is the IP address of your Linux PC (the one where Asterisk will be running). This is the address to enter as the SPA-3000's gateway address. Normally the gateway address is the address of the device that allows you access to the Internet. But that's not what needs to be configured here as the gateway. The next thing you need is the next available IP address on your network. Remember, no two devices can have the same IP address. When you have this information, you can then begin configuring the SPA-3000 with the following steps:

1. **Pick up the phone and dial four asterisks (\*\*\*\*).**

   Ignore the SIT tones. You should be greeted by someone saying, "Sipura configuration menu." If not, try again.

2. **Configure the SPA-3000 for a static IP address:**

   a. *Dial 111# and then dial the IP address by using the asterisk key (\*) for periods followed by the pound key (#). For example, 192\*168\*1\*10#.*

   b. *Dial 121# and then dial the IP mask. For example, 255\*255\*255\*0#.*

3. **Check your work:**

   a. *Dial 110# to check your IP address.*

   b. *Dial 120# to check your IP mask.*

   If you configured the SPA-3000 incorrectly, go to Step 2 and do it again.

Now that you've got the IP address out of the way, you can use a browser to configure the rest of the settings. Fire up your favorite browser and make sure JavaScript is turned on. I've tried Opera, Konqueror, and Firefox, and they all work fine. Now go to this URL:

```
http://192.168.1.10/admin/advanced
```

## How big a PC for Asterisk?

Many people ask, "How fast a processor, how much RAM, and how big a hard drive does my PC need to run Asterisk?" And the quick answer is: It depends. Some folks are running Asterisk on a Linksys WRT54GS router that has only 8MB of flash storage, 16MB of flash memory, and a 200-MHz processor. That's right — no hard drive. They're using external SIP devices like the SPA-3000 that I describe in the "Fitting the hardware pieces together" section. This setup is serving only a few IP phones and/or ATAs. Other setups require more processor speed and can require more hard drive space and RAM to run all the applications that the user wants. For the setup in this chapter, you need at least a 500 MHz processor, at least 64MB of RAM, and at least a 5GB hard drive. You might be able to run a lesser machine, but I don't go into those details (or how to run and install Asterisk on the WRT54GS). If I'd gone with another starter kit using an X100P PCI board and an IP phone, you would have needed a much more powerful processor. I've run into problems with the X100P board with a 2-GHz processor when the system became busy with other processes, such as MisterHouse. (See Chapter 15 for more on MisterHouse.)

You need to replace the *192.168.1.10* with the IP address you used to configure in the SPA-3000 in Step 2a. This brings up the main Web page with the Info tab selected. This page contains various information such as the IP address, mask, Line 1 status, and PSTN Line Status. You can move to the other tabs by clicking each tab name toward the top of the advanced admin page. The SIP, Provisioning, Regional, User 1, and PSTN User tabs' defaults are fine for your needs, so you don't need to make any changes there. You will need to make changes on the System, Line 1, and PSTN Line tabs; I show you those changes next.

### The System tab

The first tab you need to visit is the System tab, shown in Figure 9-2. Just fill in the Admin Passwd and User Password fields. You can leave these blank if you'd like, but it isn't very secure — anyone who has access to a Web browser on your network will be able to make changes to your configuration. Almost all the other fields will be blank, and that's fine. To save the changes, click the Submit All Changes button at the very bottom of the Web page (although you might need to scroll down to see it).

**Figure 9-2:**
The System
tab.

### The Line 1 tab

On the Line 1 tab, you need to make changes so your telephone can be extension 2201 and talk to the Asterisk server. You must make changes to four sections. At the top of the Line 1 tab, make sure that Line Enable is set to Yes. Then scroll down to the Proxy and Registration section. (See Figure 9-3.) Here, you configure Line 1 to talk to your Asterisk server. Now take care of the following settings:

✔ **Proxy:** *<Asterisk IP Address>*

  Replace *<Asterisk IP Address>* with the IP address of your Asterisk server (your Linux IP address).

✔ **Use Outbound Proxy:** No

✔ **Use OB Proxy in Dialog:** No

✔ **Register:** Yes

✔ **Make Call Without Reg:** No

✔ **Register Expires:** 30

✔ **Ans Call without Registration:** Yes

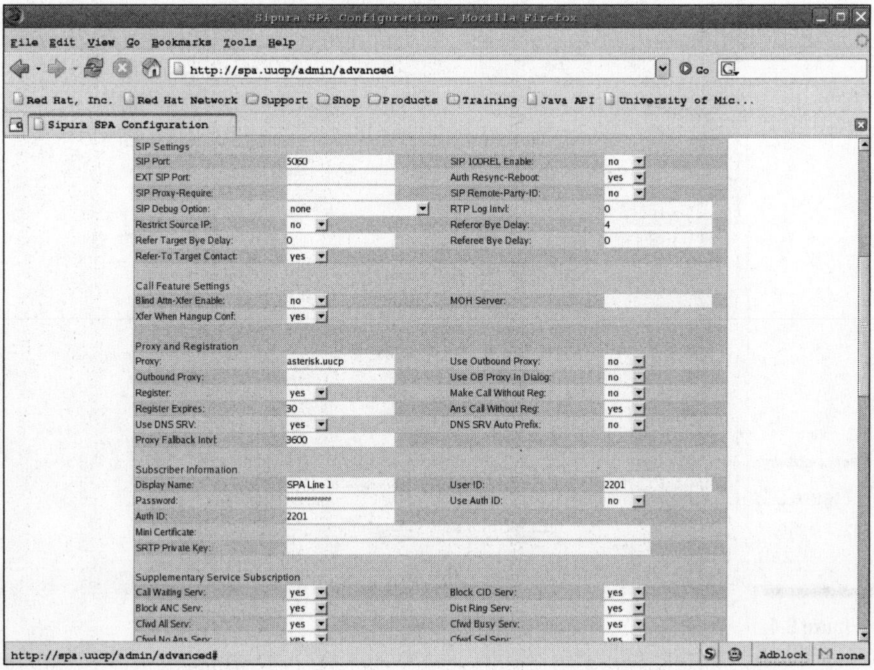

**Figure 9-3:** The Line 1 tab.

You also need to make changes to the Subscriber Information section:

- ✔ **Display Name:** SPA Line 1
- ✔ **User ID:** 2201
- ✔ **Password:** 2201

You can change the Display Name field to what ever you'd like. It's your internal caller ID. You can't change what the telephone company sends because that's in the company's system. Now proceed to the Audio Configuration section and make these changes:

- ✔ **Preferred Codec:** G.711u
- ✔ **Silence Supp Enable:** No
- ✔ **Use Pref Codec Only:** Yes

Now scroll down to the VoIP Fallback to PSTN section and set Auto PSTN Fallback to Yes. This allows you to make phone calls to the PSTN if your Asterisk server gets hosed. You can change the Display Name field (your internal caller ID) to what ever you'd like. And the last part for the Line 1 tab is the dial plan. (See Figure 9-4.)

```
([2-79]11S0<:@gw0>|*xx|0|00|2xxx|[2-9]xxxxxx|1xxxxxxxxxxS0|xxxxxxxxxxxx.)
```

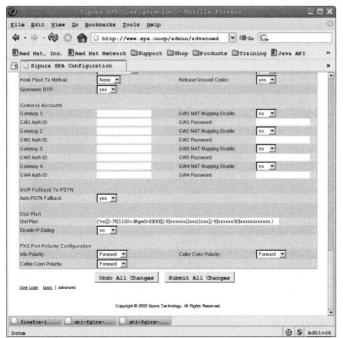

**Figure 9-4:**
Line 1 tab,
Dial Plan
section.

To save the changes, click the Submit All Changes button at the very bottom of the Web page.

Although the rest of the changes are difficult to explain (or would take too long), I explain this dial plan. First, I need to tell you about a couple rules for the SPA-3000's dial plan. The dial plan (everything in parentheses) is broken into sections by the pipe symbol (|). Each section describes an expression that matches a specific number pattern (a telephone number) and describes what to do with it. Here's an explanation of the rules for the SPA-3000's dial plan:

- ✔ (): The entire dial plan.

- ✔ |: An expression separator.

- ✔ 1: The SPA-3000 matches the exact keys. (Valid keys are 1 through 9, 0, *, and #.)

- ✔ x: The SPA-3000 matches any number (0 thru 9).

- ✔ []: The SPA-3000 matches a single digit from a list of digits.

- ✔ [2-9]: The SPA-3000 matches any single digit in a range (always used inside brackets).

- ✔ S0: The SPA-3000 matches the previous expression immediately.

- ✔ <a:b>: The SPA-3000 substitutes the dialed expression *a* with expression *b*.

- ✔ <:@gw0>: The SPA-3000 sends the matching string to the gateway listed.

- ✔ .: The SPA-3000 matches one or more keys no matter what they are.

I've used the substitution command to insert the expression @gw0 (which is the PSTN gateway). This tells the SPA-3000 to send the call to the PSTN port. Also, I've used the brackets, [2-79], to include a list that means match any single number between 2 and 7 or 9. Here's exactly what the dial plan does:

- ✔ [2-79]11S0<:@gw0>: The SPA-3000 sends 211, 311, 411, 511, 611, 711, and 911 directly to the PSTN without delay.

- ✔ *xx: The SPA-3000 sends numbers that start with * and two digits — for example, *69 — to the Asterisk server.

- ✔ 0: The SPA-3000 sends 0 directly to the Asterisk server.

- ✔ 00: The SPA-3000 sends 00 directly to the Asterisk server.

- ✔ 2xxx: The SPA-3000 sends any 4-digit number that starts with 2 directly to the Asterisk server.

- ✔ [2-9]xxxxxx: The SPA-3000 sends any 7-digit number, starting with any number between 2 and 9 inclusive — for example, 5551212 — directly to the Asterisk server.

✔ 1xxx[2-9]xxxxxxS0: The SPA-3000 sends any 11-digit number, starting with 1 and whose 5th digit is between 2 and 9 inclusive — for example, 17325551212 — immediately to the Asterisk server.

✔ xxxxxxxxxxxx.: The SPA-3000 sends any 13-digit, or longer, number to the Asterisk server.

Okay, that was difficult! Dial plans aren't easy, and they take a lot of thought to make them work right. So why didn't I just use x.? Well, the SPA-3000 will send the number pretty soon after matching the 2 (or more) digit sequence. When the sequence reaches Asterisk, Asterisk will try to match a dial plan entry for the exact number of digits it gets sent. This might not be your exact intention.

Sipura has to be given a lot of credit for their product. They've managed to squeeze a lot of power into a Web interface. You can use the SPA-3000 anywhere in the world by adjusting the various parameters in the Web interface. Unfortunately, all that power means complexity. Sipura has a wonderful 87-page manual on its site, and the manual really does explain everything. Unfortunately, you have to understand all the terms and read the entire manual.

### The PSTN Line tab

The PSTN Line tab (see Figure 9-5) configuration is very similar to the Line 1 tab configuration. So you start at the very top and enable the line by setting the Line Enable option to Yes.

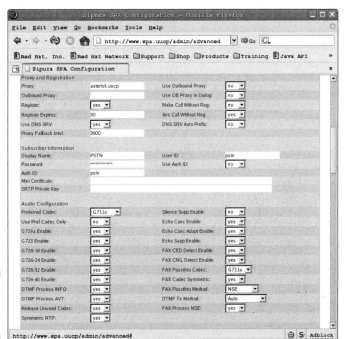

**Figure 9-5:**
The PSTN
Line tab.

Next, jump down to the SIP Settings section. You need to change the port because Line 1 is already using 5060. Set the SIP port as 5061.

Scroll down to the Proxy and Registration section and make the following changes:

- **Proxy:** *<Asterisk IP Address>*

  Replace *<Asterisk IP Address>* with the IP address of your Asterisk server.

- **Use Outbound Proxy:** No
- **Use OB proxy in Dialog:** Yes
- **Register:** Yes
- **Registration Expires:** 30

Next up, scroll down to the Subscriber Information section and make these changes:

- **Display Name:** PSTN
- **User ID:** pstn
- **Password:** pstn
- **User Auth ID:** No

Move down to the Audio Configuration section and enter **G711u** for the Preferred Codec.

Now the dial plan rollercoaster starts up again. (See Figure 9-6.) This time things are a little easier. So scroll down to the Dial Plans section and make the following changes:

- **Dial Plan 1:** (S0<:s@<Asterisk IP Address>>)

  Replace the *<Asterisk IP Address>* with the IP address of your Asterisk server.

- **Dial Plan 8:** ([2-79]11S0|*xx|0|00|2xxx|[2-9]xxxxxx|1xxxxxxxxxxS0| xxxxxxxxxxxx.)

I explain the dial plans, but not until after a few more changes. So scroll down to VoIP-To-PSTN Gateway Setup and make these changes:

- **VoIP-To-PSTN Gateway Enable:** Yes
- **One Stage Dialing:** Yes
- **Line 1 VoIP Caller DP:** 8
- **VoIP Caller Default DP:** 8

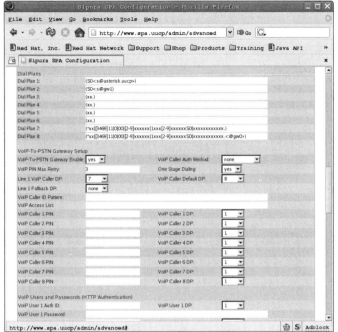

**Figure 9-6:**
The PSTN
Line Dial
Plans.

In the PSTN-To-VoIP Gateway Setup section, make these changes:

✔ **PSTN-To-VoIP Gateway Enable:** Yes

✔ **PSTN Ring Thru Line 1:** No

✔ **PSTN CID For VoIP CID:** Yes

✔ **PSTN Caller Default DP:** 1

To save the changes, click the Submit All Changes button at the very bottom of the Web page.

Okay, now I can explain the dial plans for the PSTN Line. The complicated dial plan (#8) is the plan being used by the VoIP-To-PSTN plan. This one handles the numbers coming from Asterisk to the PSTN and from Line 1 to the PSTN. It's the same as the Line 1 dial plan, so see the preceding section for the explanation. The odd dial plan is #1, which is used for calls from the PSTN to VoIP (to Asterisk). What the dial plan says to the SPA-3000 is to immediately send any call directly to your Asterisk server (in this case, *<Asterisk IP Address>*). This dial plan uses IP addressing instead of an extension or a gateway (gw1, for example, which you can use for other VoIP services).

## How the other half lives: The software

The Asterisk installation instructions are pretty scary-looking to someone who hasn't compiled a large application under Linux. It's intimidating to watch one line after another go scrolling off the screen, not knowing what they mean. (See Figure 9-7.) If you've done a full install of your Linux distribution, you should have no problems with loading the Asterisk package. If you haven't, you need to make sure that you have C compiler and development kit.

```
njc@lha:~                                    _ □ ×

File  Edit  View  Terminal  Tabs  Help
$ tar zxf asterisk-1.2.0.tar.gz
$ cd asterisk-1.2.0
$ make clean
build_tools/make_version_h > include/asterisk/version.h.tmp
if cmp -s include/asterisk/version.h.tmp include/asterisk/version.h ; then echo; else \
        mv include/asterisk/version.h.tmp include/asterisk/version.h ; \
fi
rm -f include/asterisk/version.h.tmp
build_tools/mkdep -pipe  -Wall -Wstrict-prototypes -Wmissing-prototypes -Wmissing-declarations -g  -Iinclude
  -I../include -D_REENTRANT -D_GNU_SOURCE  -O6 -march=i686  -DZAPTEL_OPTIMIZATIONS        -fomit-frame-poin
ter  acl.c aescrypt.c aeskey.c aestab.c alaw.c app.c asterisk.c ast_expr2.c ast_expr2f.c astmm.c autoservice
.c callerid.c cdr.c channel.c chanvars.c cli.c config.c config_old.c db.c devicestate.c dlfcn.c dns.c dnsmgr
.c dsp.c enum.c file.c frame.c fskmodem.c image.c indications.c io.c jitterbuf.c loader.c logger.c manager.c
 md5.c muted.c netsock.c pbx.c plc.c poll.c privacy.c rtp.c say.c sched.c slinfactory.c srv.c strcompat.c td
d.c term.c translate.c ulaw.c utils.c
build_tools/make_version_h > include/asterisk/version.h.tmp
if cmp -s include/asterisk/version.h.tmp include/asterisk/version.h ; then echo; else \
        mv include/asterisk/version.h.tmp include/asterisk/version.h ; \
fi

rm -f include/asterisk/version.h.tmp
        :
        :
        :
make[1]: Leaving directory `/home/njc/stuff/asterisk-1.2/asterisk-1.2.0/db1-ast'
make -C stdtime clean
make[1]: Entering directory `/home/njc/stuff/asterisk-1.2/asterisk-1.2.0/stdtime'
rm -f libtime.a *.o test .depend
make[1]: Leaving directory `/home/njc/stuff/asterisk-1.2/asterisk-1.2.0/stdtime'
$ []
```

**Figure 9-7:**
The Asterisk compile screen.

## Installing and compiling Asterisk

To compile Asterisk, open a shell or terminal and follow these steps:

1. **Type su - and press Enter, after which you will be greeted by a password prompt. Enter the password for root.**

2. **Type cd and press Enter. You will be in root's home directory.**

3. **Type cp /media/disk/chapter09/asterisk.tar.gz . and press Enter.**

   This copies the file to root's home directory.

4. **Type tar zxf asterisk.tar.gz and press Enter to extract the source from the tar archive file.**

5. **Type cd asterisk-1.2.0 and press Enter to change to the directory where the Asterisk source code is.**

6. **Type** make clean **and press Enter to make sure you start with a clean slate and keep odd errors from cropping up.**

   You can ignore any warnings that appear on the screen.

7. **Type** make linux26 **and press Enter to compile the Asterisk program.**

   Lots of messages scroll off the screen. As long as there are no errors, you can safely ignore the messages. See Figure 9-8 for a sample of what shows up on the screen. (I trimmed it because it's several pages long.)

8. **Type** make install **and press Enter. If there were no errors on the previous command, it installs all the asterisk files in the correct places.**

9. **Type** make samples **and press Enter to create the sample configuration files.**

   These are stored in /etc/asterisk.

You must be root to properly run Asterisk.

After the compile and install has finished (warnings can be ignored), you can verify that Asterisk is really working:

1. **Type** asterisk -vvvc **and press Enter at a command prompt.**

   This is a way to test that Asterisk compiled and installed properly. You should see a bunch of messages fly by and then a prompt:

   ```
   hostname*CLI>
   ```

   Don't worry if you don't understand them yet.

2. **Type** help **and press Enter to get a help message (that will scroll off the screen).**

3. **To exit Asterisk's command line prompt, simply type** quit **and press Enter at the prompt.**

Here are a few useful commands:

✔ To properly start Asterisk, you can either let it start when you reboot (via an init.d script that I've set up for you) or by simply typing **asterisk** and pressing Enter. (You'll need to be root.) Asterisk starts up and runs in the background. If all went well, you see nothing but your prompt return.

✔ To get to the Asterisk command line, type **asterisk -r** and press Enter. (Remember this command; it's a popular one.)

✔ To stop Asterisk, type **stop now** and press Enter at the Asterisk command line. This immediately stops Asterisk and drops any calls.

✔ To simply exit the Asterisk command line interface and still allow Asterisk to handle calls, type **quit** and press Enter. For now, I recommend the stop now command. You can restart Asterisk later by typing **asterisk** and pressing Enter.

### Making (necessary) changes to Asterisk

To simplify the installation of Asterisk, I've taken the liberty of providing the bulk of the changes in the file `spa-asterisk.rpm`. Simply type **sh /media/ disk /chapter09/ast_install.sh** and press Enter to install my configuration files.

In the `/etc/asterisk` directory, you can find the original configuration files backed up (as `.bak`) and the new ones installed. This doesn't mean you're going to get away without editing files; it just means you won't have to type in hundreds of lines of configuration information. This is all well and good in that you should be able to start Asterisk and begin using it right away (yeah!), as long as you're in the United States or Canada. For the rest of the world, you need to do some editing to customize it to your needs. For further details about editing these files, visit `www.asteriskdocs.org`.

Speaking of editing, it's now time to change a few things to suit your telephony needs. So open up your favorite Linux editor and edit the file `/etc/asterisk/extensions.conf`. Don't use a Windows editor — it will mess up the line endings, causing you no end of mysterious problems. Search for the following line:

```
AREACODE = 732
```

Change the `732` to match your area code (the first three digits in your telephone number after the 1; for example, the 732 in 1-732-555-1212). Now, you might be fortunate and not have to dial all ten digits to call a local number. If you're one of those lucky few (I'm not), you need to comment out the line of code that deals with adding the area code and uncomment the line before it. First, search for `${AREACODE}`. The code should look like what's shown in Listing 9-4.

### Listing 9-4:  Part of the to-pstn Context from /etc/asterisk/extensions.conf

```
; Remove the comment from the next line and comment
; out the line after if you can still use 7 digit
; dialing.
; exten => _ZXXXXXX,1,Dial(SIP/pstn/${EXTEN})
  exten => _ZXXXXXX,1,Dial(SIP/pstn/1${AREACODE}${EXTEN})
  exten => _ZXXXXXX,2,Goto(s-${DIALSTATUS},1)
;
  exten => _ZXXXXXX-NOANSWER,1,Voicemail(u${VMAIL})
  exten => _ZXXXXXX-NOANSWER,2,Goto(default,s,1)
;
  exten => _ZXXXXXX-BUSY,1,Voicemail(b${VMAIL})
  exten => _ZXXXXXX-BUSY,2,Goto(default,s,1)
```

To comment out a line, simply insert a semicolon (`;`) at the beginning of the line. To uncomment a line, remove the semicolon from the start of a line. When you uncomment a line, I suggest replacing the semicolon with a space to keep the lines tidy. This makes the code easier to read.

### Making (optional) changes to Asterisk

This section is optional. You may skip to the next section. You don't need to make any further changes. I describe how you add another SIP extension.

I've already added the 2201 extension to the extensions file, configured voice mail so 2201 has a mail box, and configured the SIP file so that the SPA-3000's Line 1 is properly recognized, but I explain it here so you will understand what is needed to add a device and extension to Asterisk. That way, you'll be able to add more devices in the future. Now that you have the SPA-3000 properly configured, you'll use that information to add it to the SIP configuration file. Open your editor, edit the file `/etc/asterisk/sip.conf`, and scroll down until you see the section shown in Listing 9-5. (It isn't a very large file.) You probably won't need to make any changes, but if you do, this is a good place to catch mistakes.

**Listing 9-5:    SIP Entry 2201 from /etc/asterisk/sip.conf**

```
[2201]
    username       = 2201
    secret         = 2201
    type           = friend
    host           = dynamic
    port           = 5060
    context        = from-internal
    callerid       = "SPA3000" <2201>
    mailbox        = 2201
    nat            = never
    dtmfmode       = rfc2833
    canreinvite    = yes
    qualify        = yes
    insecure       = yes
    disallow       = all     ; need disallow before can allow
    allow          = ulaw
```

You might want to open a browser to the SPA-3000 and go to the Line 1 tab. (Refer to Figure 9-3.) I jump around a bit so that you can be done with the browser quickly, so pardon my choice of order:

1. **In your browser, scroll down to the Subscriber Information section where you can find the User ID and Password fields.**

    That subscriber information translates into the SIP configuration's username and secret password, respectively. In your editor, you should see a `type` line. This should be set to `friend` for devices such as the SPA-3000 (or any IP phone). This allows you to send calls to Line 1 and receive calls from Line 1 without more configuration in the `sip.conf` file.

2. **In your browser, under the SIP Settings section, (towards the top of the tab), make sure the SIP port is set to 5060.**

This should match the `port` setting under `2001` in the `sip.conf` file. This is the default for most devices, and you didn't change this for the Line 1 settings. (You did change it in the PSTN Line settings.)

You're now done with the browser. From here on, you need only look at the editing and the information in Listing 9-5.

3. **The next important line to check for the entry 2001 (in `sip.conf`) is the `context`.**

   The context `from-internal` is the context you will put your extension information under. It's in the `/etc/asterisk/extensions.conf` file (more on that in a moment). The `context` tells Asterisk where to look for this extensions dial plan.

4. **Next, change the `callerid`, which is used internally only by Asterisk.**

   You can set it up to your liking, but keep the format used above. The mailbox setting should match the username (2201 in this case).

5. **If you have IP phones (hence multiple entries in the `sip.conf` file), you may elect to have those devices use one voice mail box instead of many.**

   For example, each extension can have its mailbox setting like so: `mailbox = 2201`. This sets the mailbox for that extension to just 2201.

6. **Set the `nat` entry to `never` when you use an IP phone on your local network.**

   If you need to set it to `yes`, expect to have a lot of problems and to do a great deal of custom work trying to get it to work.

7. **The `dtmfmode` is a device-specific setting, so you need to match the device's settings (in the device's configuration).**

   For the SPA-3000, it's `rfc2833`.

8. **The `canreinvite` is important. First the device must support this option (which the SPA-3000 does).**

   Setting it to `yes` allows the IP phones to start up a conversation by first sending information to Asterisk. When both phones have been contacted, they can talk to each other without Asterisk playing the part of the middleman. This lowers the workload on the Asterisk server.

9. **(Optional) Set the next two parameters, `qualify` and `insecure`, to `yes`.**

   I do this step because it allows me to see more information when I'm at the Asterisk command line. I recommend setting them to `yes`.

10. **Note the last two lines of Listing 9-5; these lines deal with the _codecs_ (the code used to translate your voice from sound to data) supported by the devices.**

The first line is recommended to always be first (disallow = all). Then list the allowed codecs. I chose to allow only ulaw, which the SPA-3000 supports as G711 (Line 1 tab, Audio section). Although the SPA-3000 can support many different codecs, there are limitations to each. By using the G711 on the SPA-3000, I've kept the Asterisk server from having to do translation from one codec to another (a real CPU killer).

Now that you have an SIP entry, you need an extension. Under the context from-sip, you would add the extension, and it would look like Listing 9-6.

### Listing 9-6:  Extension 2201 from /etc/asterisk/extensions.conf

```
; 2201
   exten => 2201,1,Dial(sip/2201,20,)
   exten => 2201,2,voicemail(u2201)
   exten => 2201,3,Hangup
   exten => 2201,102,voicemail(b2201)
   exten => 2201,103,hangup
```

The extension in Listing 9-6 is 2201. The dial plan works exactly the same way as the previous dial plan in the from-pstn context in Listing 9-4. The difference is that, instead of using the s extension, you actually have an actual extension associated with the dial plan. The interesting parts of this dial plan are the voicemail commands. The first voicemail is when no one answers the phone. The u in front of the extension tells the voicemail command to play the unavailable message. A b tells it to play the busy message.

Voice mail is the easiest part of Asterisk to configure. Simply open the file /etc/asterisk/voicemail.conf with your editor and add a line, at the end of the file, that looks like Listing 9-7.

### Listing 9-7:  A Voice Mail Entry in the /etc/asterisk/voicemail.conf File

```
; Line 1 on the SPA-3000
2201 => 1234,Neil Cherry,asterisk@linuxha.uucp,attach=yes
```

Adjust accordingly with your name, password (the 1234), and correct e-mail address to send a sound file to. The first number is the extension that the voice mail box is for. The second number is the password that you need to enter from a phone to access this mail box. Next is the user ID (a name), and then an e-mail address to send a notification that a message has been received. The last part is an option to attach a copy the message to the e-mail. If you don't want to send an e-mail message when you receive a voice mail message, set attach to no. The ability to send e-mail and attachments is dependent on a working e-mail system.

# Making a Smart Call

When everything is set up and ready to use, you can make some calls. Earlier in the chapter, at the end of the "Installing and compiling Asterisk" section, I had you stop Asterisk from running. You need to restart it because you've made changes to Asterisk. If you're already logged in as `root`, skip to Step 2; otherwise, begin with Step 1 as usual:

1. **Type** su - **and press Enter, and when you're greeted by a prompt, enter the correct password for** `root`.

2. **Type** asterisk **and press Enter.**

   You're greeted by your `root` prompt. It looks like nothing happened, which is okay. Asterisk is running in the background.

3. **Type** asterisk -r **and press Enter.**

   You're greeted by *Hostname*`*CLI>`, where *Hostname* will be the hostname of your machine.

4. **At the Asterisk prompt, type** sip show users **and press Enter.**

   You see output that looks similar to this:

   ```
   mozart*CLI> sip show users
   Username    Secret   Accountcode  Def.Context     ACL  NAT
   2201        2201     2201         from-internal   No   No
   pstn        pstn     pstn         from-sip-pstn   No   No
   ```

   This shows you that you have 2 users (extensions).

5. **Type** sip show peers **and press Enter.**

   ```
   mozart*CLI> sip show peers
   Name/username Host            Dyn Nat ACL Mask             Port  Status
   2201/2201     192.168.24.192  D           255.255.255.255  5060  OK (4 ms)
   pstn/pstn     192.168.24.197  D           255.255.255.255  5061  OK (16 ms)
   ```

   This shows you the status of your two SIP peers. In this case, Asterisk can talk to both and it shows as okay.

6. **Type** show dialplan from-sip **and press Enter.**

   ```
   mozart*CLI> show dialplan from-sip
   [ Context 'from-sip' created by 'pbx_config' ]
       '2201' =>          1. Macro(stdexten|SIP/2201)
                 [pbx_config]
       Include =>         'to-pstn'
                 [pbx_config]
   mozart*CLI>
   -= 1 extensions (1 priorities) in 1 contexts. =-
   mozart*CLI>
   ```

This shows your dialplan for the context from-sip.

7. **Type** show dialplan to-pstn **and press Enter.**

```
mozart*CLI> show dialplan to-pstn
[ Context 'to-pstn' created by 'pbx_config' ]
  '_0' =>             1. Macro(dial-pstn|SIP/${EXTEN}@${PSTN})
          [pbx_config]
  '_00' =>            1. Macro(dial-pstn|SIP/${EXTEN}@${PSTN})
          [pbx_config]
  '_01.' =>           1. Macro(dial-pstn|SIP/${EXTEN}@${PSTN})
          [pbx_config]
  '_1N.' =>           1. Macro(dial-pstn|SIP/${EXTEN}@${PSTN})
          [pbx_config]
  '_2201' =>          1. Macro(dial-extension|${PHONE1})
          [pbx_config]
  '_[2-79]11' =>      1. Macro(dial-pstn|SIP/${EXTEN}@${PSTN})
          [pbx_config]
mozart*CLI>
-= 6 extensions (6 priorities) in 1 contexts. =-
mozart*CLI>
```

The results of Steps 6 and 7 show you what your dial plan looks like inside Asterisk.

Before you start dialing, you have one more thing to check:

1. **Open up your browser and go to**
   **http://192.168.1.10/admin/advanced.**

   Remember that you need to replace the *192.168.1.10* with the IP address you used to configure in the SPA-3000 earlier in this chapter.

   This brings up the main Web page with the Info tab selected. (Refer to Figure 9-2.) Check the status' of Line 1 and the PSTN line. If both are registered, you're ready to dial; if they aren't, you must check the SPA-3000's configuration and Asterisk's configuration files. But first things first — you have to check the status.

2. **Scroll down to the Line 1 Status section and make sure that the Registration State is Registered (which means that Line 1 is ready).**

   If Line 1 is having problems, check the SPA-3000's Line 1 tab. Also check the sip.conf file in /etc/asterisk. For a problem with Line 1, check the lines under the [2201] heading.

3. **Scroll down to the PSTN Line Status section, and again, make sure that the Registration State is Registered.**

   If the PSTN Line is having problems, check the SPA-3000's PSTN Line tab. Also check the sip.conf file in /etc/asterisk. For a problem with PSTN Line, check the lines under the [PSTN] heading. If both show Registered, you're ready to dial.

Now on to the dialing!

1. **Try accessing voice mail by dialing 81.**

   You might need to wait a second or two before it responds. To make it dial immediately, dial the pound sign (#), which might speed things up a bit.

   You should be greeted by a request for your password.

2. **Dial 1234, and you'll be greeted by the voice menu.**

3. **Follow the directions.**

   You should have mail from me.

If you're having problems with dialing, first determine what kind of number you're dialing (as I describe earlier in the chapter). Match that to one of the extensions in your dial plan, like that in Listing 9-6 (the file `extensions.conf` in the directory `/etc/asterisk`). You might need to see whether it correctly matches your dial plan. You should now be able to make a call to the outside world, and the outside world should be able to call you. If you have any questions or problems, check out my Web forums at `www.linuxha.com`; I should be able to help. If you're looking for suggestions, I can provide you with plenty of pointers. On the forums, you can also discuss what features can be added and what other neat things you can do with Asterisk.

# Part IV

# Keeping a Linux Eye on the Sky

The 5<sup>th</sup> Wave                    By Rich Tennant

"Well, that's the third one in as many clicks. I'm sure it's just a coincidence. Still, don't use the 'Launcher' again until I've had a look at it."

# In this part . . .

**N**either rain nor sleet nor snow shall keep Linux from its appointed rounds.

In Part IV, you keep an eye on the live local weather — the *really* local weather, right in your own yard. You find out how to set up your own weather station. You can also keep an eye on Internet weather reports with your browser or your desktop. Your Linux system can even alert you to severe weather, which can help keep you and your loved ones safe.

# Chapter 10

# Letting Linux Watch the Weather For You

A cool project you can do with Linux is set up your own weather station. With your own weather station, you can get the weather conditions from right outside your home. No longer will you be at the whims of the TV weather forecaster. You won't need to go searching for your latest weather data or wait until some particular time to see it. With your own weather station, you can read your weather data anytime you want by just looking at your PC screen. How cool is that? (Well, you can tell *exactly* how cool it is with your weather station!)

## Choosing the Weather Station Hardware and Software

After you decide to set up your own weather station, you have certain issues to consider. For starters, you must decide which hardware and software to use. As always, I recommend that you look for software and hardware that is known to work with Linux and has been used by others. You can save yourself a lot of time and effort if you choose devices and programs that others have used successfully.

Before I chose the hardware for my weather station, I looked at the programs available that ran on Linux. First I decided what program I would use, and then I determined what hardware would work with the program. Then I decided the exact compatible hardware based on best value for the money. I narrowed my search for Linux-based weather station software to two programs:

- **Weather Display, available at `www.weather-display`:** At the Weather Display site is a list of supported hardware and many stations are supported.

- **Oww (One-wire weather), available from `http://oww.sourceforge.net`:** The Oww program is meant to work with one type of weather station: the Dallas Semiconductor 1-Wire system. I researched the Dallas Semiconductor 1-Wire system and discovered that it is reliable, easy to set up, very reasonably priced, and readily available.

  The 1-Wire system is listed as a supported system at the Weather Display site but not for the Linux version of the software. So I couldn't use this type of hardware if I used the Weather Display program. Other hardware listed as supported was more costly than the One Wire system.

The Oww program is designed to work with the Dallas Semiconductor 1-Wire system, so I decided to go with this program for reading the weather data. Now that I had made my choice of the software and the hardware it would use, I could download and install the software and send in my order for the hardware.

I purchased my weather station hardware from AAG Electronica. You can order all the components from its Web site at `www.aagelectronica.com`. The base weather station with a wind vane, *anemometer* (which measures wind speed), and temperature sensor costs $79 plus shipping. I opted to go with additional sensors for barometric pressure, indoor temperature, and humidity. I also bought a rain gauge so I could keep track of rainfall at my location. The total cost for the weather station hardware, including shipping, was $339. It arrived within about a week after I ordered it. You can check out the AAG Electronics site for other sensors or devices that are available for your weather station. The sensors I list here are those frequently used in a weather station.

# Building the Weather Station

Before you can use the weather station, you have to do some assembly of the components and make some electrical connections. I show you how to do so in this section.

Upon opening the box containing the weather station, I discovered the main weather station unit, the wind vane, anemometer cups, a test cable, and serial port adapter. Also included were the additional sensors I ordered to measure pressure, indoor temperature, humidity, and rain. The last item in the package was an aluminum bar for mounting the main unit containing the wind vane, anemometer, and temperature sensor. The box did not contain assembly instructions, but fortunately, the company Web site had instructions available for download.

I decided to completely assemble the weather station inside my house so that I could test the components and be sure everything was working properly. I figured it would be a lot more convenient doing my configuring inside before placing the weather station outside. I downloaded the assembly instructions from `www.aagelectronica.com/PDF%20Docs/` `Assembly%20Instructions.PDF`.

*Note:* On page three of the downloaded assembly instructions, you can ignore the paragraph beginning with Note and the next paragraph. These two paragraphs deal with testing the station by using the Windows weather station software. You'll be using the Oww software, which you will download.

After you've attached the wind vane and anemometer cups to the weather station main unit, the station is ready for testing. I recommend making some kind of temporary mount to hold the station in place while you're making the electrical connections and testing. But before you can do any testing, you need to download the software.

# *Installing the Weather Station Software*

The first step in installing and configuring the Oww weather station software is to download it from `http://oww.sourceforge.net`. Click the penguin icon to go to the download page. If you're running a distribution that uses RPMs, such as Fedora or SUSE, you can download the RPM version of the software. If you aren't using an RPM-based distribution or if you want to build the program from source, download the `tar.gz` version.

Be sure to read the README and INSTALL files in the `oww-0.81.7` directory for information about installing the program. You will often find information in these files that may help you speed up the installation or avoid problems.

1. **To install the RPM version of Oww, enter the following command:**

   ```
   # rpm -Uvh oww-0.81.7-1.i586.rpm
   ```

   If you want to install from the source file first, you must extract the contents of the zipped `tar` by issuing the following command:

   ```
   # tar -xzvf oww-0.81.7.tar.gz
   ```

   A directory called `oww-0.81.7` is created during the extraction and contains the files needed to build the program.

2. **Change into the `oww-0.81.7` directory by entering this command:**

   ```
   # cd oww-0.81.7
   ```

3. **Create the `makefile` for the program build by entering the following command:**

```
# ./configure
```

4. **Make and install the program executable and other files by entering the command**

```
# make;make install
```

When the command prompt returns, the program is installed and ready to run.

After you've installed the software, you're ready to connect the test cable to the weather station and start the Oww program. Proceed as follows:

1. **Plug one end of the test cable into the serial port adapter and then connect the serial port adapter to one of the serial ports on your PC.**

2. **Plug the other end of the test cable into the open RJ-11 connector inside the weather station housing.**

3. **Make sure the user who is running the station program has permission to the serial port to which the weather station is connected.**

   Serial ports are typically identified as `/dev/ttyS0` and `/dev/ttyS1`. This corresponds to Com 1 and Com 2 respectively.

4. **Start the Oww program by entering oww at a command prompt.**

   The program opens two screens: a message screen indicating an error because it didn't find a device and the Oww main screen similar to Figure 10-1. The device error isn't a problem because you haven't configured any devices yet. You do that in the next section.

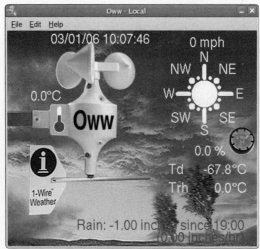

**Figure 10-1:**
The One-wire weather program main screen.

# Configuring the weather station program

When you start the weather station program for the first time, you must configure some parameters. The most important parameter is the serial port to which the weather station is connected. After you specify the serial port, the program should be able to detect the connected devices. Take a closer look at the Oww main screen to find out where to set the serial port and other parameters.

The Oww main screen (refer to Figure 10-1) has three menu choices at the top. These are File, Edit, and Help. From the File menu, the choices are

- ✔ **Auxiliary:** Choosing Auxiliary opens a window that displays a list of the readouts from the connected devices.
- ✔ **Map:** Although this item is listed in the menu, it has no function at this time.
- ✔ **Messages:** Choosing Messages opens the Oww message window that gives status information about the program.
- ✔ **Exit:** Choosing Exit closes the program.

Two choices are available from the Edit menu:

- ✔ **Setup:** This menu choice lets you choose between imperial and metric measurements, set logging parameters, clear station settings, and upload your data to external sites.
- ✔ **Devices:** The Devices dialog box lets you specify the serial port to which the station is connected and configure connected devices.

The Help menu offers only one choice: About. Choosing About gives you information about the program. There is no help actually available by clicking Help.

Immediately below the menu bar is the Oww main graphical display screen, which shows the system date and time. Below the date and time display on the left side is a graphical representation of the weather station showing the anemometer and wind vane. The temperature from the sensor inside the station is displayed here.

To the right of the date and time is the wind speed display. Below the wind speed display is a compass showing 16 compass points to indicate the wind direction. If you have additional sensors such as humidity or pressure, their readings are displayed directly beneath the compass display.

At the very bottom of the screen is the display for the rain gauge, if one is connected. If you have only the main weather station unit, you see only the temperature, wind speed, and wind direction on the Oww main screen.

So now that you know what the Oww main screen is displaying and what the menus let you do, you can set the serial port and try to detect the connected devices:

1. **Choose Edit⇨Devices on the Oww main screen to see the Devices dialog box, as shown in Figure 10-2.**

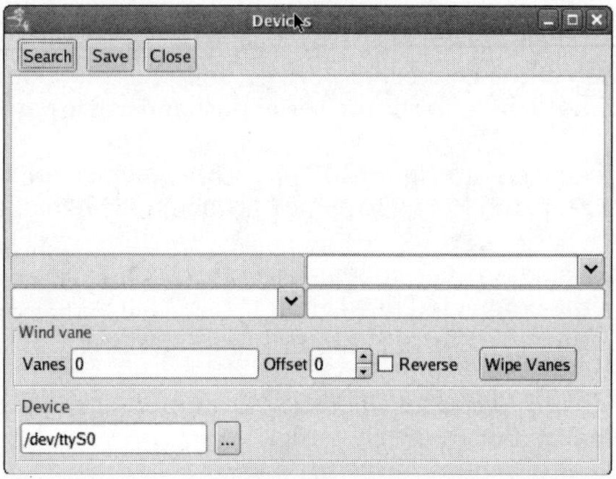

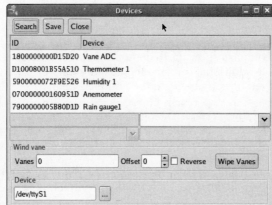

**Figure 10-2:**
Specifying the serial port in the Devices dialog box.

2. **In the Device field at the bottom left of the Devices dialog box, enter the serial port to which the station is connected.**

   On my system, I use `/dev/ttyS1`, so I need to enter this in the Device field.

3. **Click the Search button at the top of the screen.**

   A dialog box similar to Figure 10-3 appears, showing the devices that are detected. If you're using just the main unit without any additional sensors, you see only three devices listed: Vane ADC, Thermometer 1, and Anemometer.

4. **Click Save to save your device settings and then click Close to return to the Oww main screen.**

**Figure 10-3:**
The devices detected by the weather station software.

You should now see the readout from the temperature sensor displayed. You can spin the anemometer cups and turn the wind vane to see whether you also obtain readings from these devices.

If you're seeing readings from the devices you have connected, the weather station is working. If you aren't seeing readings from your devices, double-check your specified serial port and your test cable connections and try again.

## Making the weather station cable

The assembly, testing, and basic configuration of the weather station are nearly complete. Now you need to make and test the cable that you will actually use to connect the weather station when you put it outside.

You can use any four-conductor wire, such as standard telephone wire, to make your cable. You should use a nonterminated wire that you will put your own RJ-11 connector on. The length of the cable will be determined by your mounting location and the distance from your PC. Another good choice for cable is Cat 5 Ethernet cabling. If you decide to use Ethernet cable, you will use only two of the four pairs of wires and will terminate the cable ends with RJ-11 connectors. After you have put the RJ-11 connectors on both ends of the cable, you can use a multimeter to test continuity at each end of the cable. Be sure that you wire the cable straight through with no crossover. This means that pins 1 to 4 should be the same on both ends of the cable.

Even though the weather station uses standard phone-type RJ-11 connectors, you cannot use terminated telephone cable to make the connections. So don't go buy a 25- or 50-foot phone extension cord and think it will work because it won't. Telephone cable is crossover cable, which means that pins 2 and 3 are crossed, so pin 2 on one end of the cable is pin 3 on the other end of the cable and vice versa. This type of cable won't work with the weather station. You must use *straight-through cable* — meaning that pins 2 and 3 are not crossed — for making the connections.

## Configuring additional weather station settings

For the weather station to work properly, you must specify the correct serial port used by the PC. You also have to verify that the devices connected to the serial port are identified and working correctly. There are additional parameters that you can change that affect how the weather data is displayed and monitored. These parameters are available from the Setup menu. In this section, I show you this menu and what you can do with it. Choose Edit➪Setup to open the Oww Setup dialog box, which is shown in Figure 10-4. (Move your mouse cursor over an area to see a help pop-up for that area.)

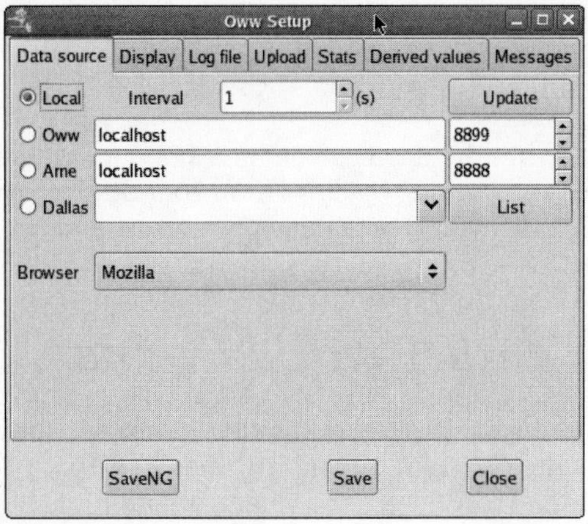

**Figure 10-4:**
The Oww
Setup dialog
box for
changing
system
parameters.

The Oww Setup dialog box features seven tabs from which to select:

✔ **Data Source:** This is the default tab shown when the Setup dialog box opens. On this tab, you can select the source of your weather data.

   • *If the weather station is connected to the PC running Oww,* you should choose Local. (This is the default setting.)

   • *If the weather station is connected to a different PC running Oww,* select Oww and specify the hostname of the PC. You can specify a port number, but in most cases you shouldn't change the default setting.

   • *If the weather station is connected to a PC running Arne Henriksen's MS Windows–based WServer,* choose Arne and specify the hostname of the PC. You can specify a port number, but in most cases you shouldn't change the default setting.

   • *If you upload your readings to a server run by Dallas Semiconductor,* click the List button to get the current list of contributing stations. Select the Dallas radio button, and select one of the stations from the drop-down list. You can also select the update interval and the number of seconds between instrument readings, and you can select which browser to use to view Web data.

✔ **Display:** Settings on the Display tab affect the appearance of the data on the Oww main screen. Figure 10-5 shows the Display tab.

   You can choose to view the data in imperial or metric units. You can also choose an animated display if you want to see the wind vane and anemometer cups moving. And you can select the Use Trh check box to set the thermometer from the humidity sensor as the main thermometer.

✔ **Log File:** On this tab, shown in Figure 10-6, you can specify the location of your logging directory.

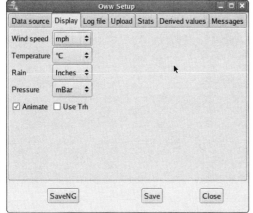

**Figure 10-5:**
The Display tab is where you can change to metric units.

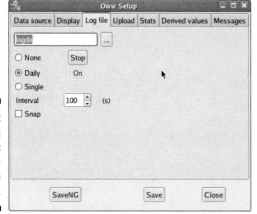

**Figure 10-6:**
Specifying log file types and locations on the Log File tab.

You can also specify the type of logging done by the system. The choices are None, meaning there is no logging; Daily, which writes a log file for each day to the specified location; and Single, which writes a single log file. Select the Snap check box to have the log times snap to clock intervals.

✔ **Upload:** You use the Upload tab, shown in Figure 10-7, to control uploading data to the Web sites listed on the page.

The Interval setting specifies the time in seconds between uploads. If you're interested in uploading your data to any of the listed sites, check their Web pages for instructions on creating an account.

✔ **Stats:** From the Stats tab, shown in Figure 10-8, you can reset the counters used by weather station devices.

You can also choose an interval for resetting the data. Select your choice of Daily, Weekly, or Monthly and enter your desired parameters.

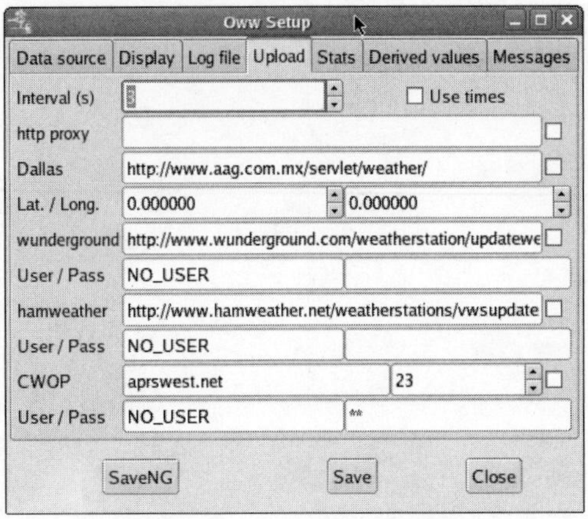

**Figure 10-7:**
The Upload tab for uploading your weather data.

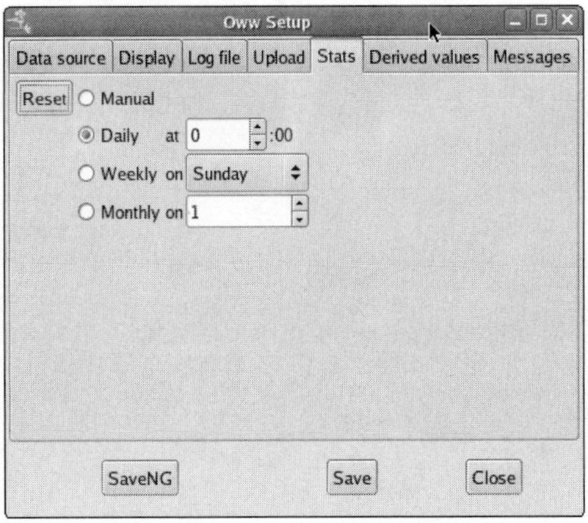

**Figure 10-8:**
Setting the interval to reset the weather station data.

✔ **Derived Values:** You shouldn't need to change any values on this tab.

✔ **Messages:** From the Messages tab, shown in Figure 10-9, you can select the type of messages you want to receive from eight options in the drop-down list. Beginning with none or no messages at the top of the list, the remaining choices give more details. A good choice is the Errors and Warnings listing.

You can also specify the log level for messages and specify a debug file and location. The log level choices are the same as the message type choices and determine the amount of information written to the log file. A debug file contains information about the program if it isn't running properly and is used to help diagnose the cause.

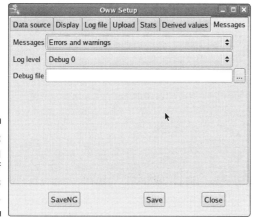

**Figure 10-9:**
Selecting
the types of
messages
to receive.

Any changes you make in the Oww Setup dialog box take affect immediately, except for Data Sources. Whenever you make any changes in the Oww Setup dialog box, however, you should always be sure to click Save. The next time the program starts, it will use the saved values.

# Mounting the Weather Station

After you've made and tested the cable that you're going to use to connect to the weather station when you place it outside, you're ready to do just that. Put the weather station outside and make the connections.

Keep the following considerations in mind when selecting the location for the weather station:

- Be sure that no obstructions are near the weather station.
- Put the weather station above the roof line if possible.
- Be sure there are no power lines that could contact the weather station.
- Be sure the weather station can be securely attached to its mount.
- Consider the cable run to the weather station.

After you've selected a good location for the weather station, you can proceed with mounting it. Be sure it's securely attached to the mounting location. Make sure the cable is properly routed and connected to the weather station. Be absolutely sure that you have made the electrical connections as waterproof as possible. Refer to the weather station assembly and installation instructions (see "Installing the Weather Station Software," earlier in this chapter) for more specific mounting and waterproofing instructions. The downloaded instructions are easy to follow; if you follow the waterproofing recommendations, you're not likely to have any problems with water getting into your weather station.

When you've securely mounted your weather station and connected it to your PC, you're ready to put it to use. Go back to your PC and from a command prompt enter the following command:

```
# oww
```

You are greeted with a display similar to Figure 10-10. Your work is done, and now you will always know the exact weather conditions right outside your door.

**Figure 10-10:**
The Oww program showing the current weather.

# Putting Your Weather Data on the Web

If you so desire, you can put your weather data on the Internet so anyone can see it. You can accomplish this in several ways.

One way is to upload your data to one of the services shown in the Upload tab of the Oww Setup dialog box. (Refer to Figure 10-7.)

Another way is to write some scripts that would take your logged weather data and generate Web pages from it. Fortunately, you won't have to write your own scripts; that has already been done. Actually, the same person who wrote the Oww program has created some scripts to take the weather data and make it available on the Web. If you're interested, take a look at `http://oww.sourceforge.net/plotting.html` for all the details on installing the scripts.

# Chapter 11

# Getting Online Weather Information

In This Chapter

▶ Viewing weather data on your desktop

▶ Getting weather information from your browser

▶ Using MythTV for weather information

*C*hapter 10 covers setting up a weather station at your house so that you always have access to the latest weather data from right outside your door. But suppose you aren't able or just don't want to set up a weather station. You can still get up-to-the-minute weather data about your local area from several different sources. In this chapter, I show you three sources of weather data and how to set them up to provide all the weather data you could want.

## Getting Weather Data on Your Desktop

Many desktops are available for Linux, but the two most common ones are GNOME and KDE. If you're running GNOME as your desktop, be sure to check out the neat Weather applet that's available for installation. Because you can customize the GNOME Weather applet to display any location, you can stay up-to-date on the latest conditions for your area or for any other location that you want to know about. To install and use the Weather applet, do the following:

1. **On the GNOME desktop, put your cursor on the top or bottom panel, right-click, and choose Add to Panel.**

   This opens the Add to Panel dialog box shown in Figure 11-1.

2. **Scroll down the list of applets, click Weather Report to select it, and then click Add to add it to the panel.**

   The Weather applet appears on the panel as a small black box containing a question mark. The question mark indicates that the Weather applet is waiting to be configured.

**Figure 11-1:**
Adding
applets to
the panel in
the GNOME
desktop.

3. **Place the cursor on the Weather applet, right-click, and choose Preferences.**

   The Weather Preferences dialog box appears (see Figure 11-2), with the General tab selected. Here, you can set the update interval, set the display units for the temperature, wind speed, pressure, and visibility, and enable the radar display map.

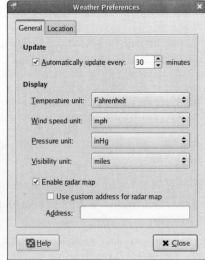

**Figure 11-2:**
Setting the
preferences
for the
Weather
applet.

In the Display area, you see the units of measurement that show the temperature, wind speed, pressure, and visibility.

4. **Click the arrows to the right of the current unit to see the available units. Select your preferred units as desired.**

5. **When you're finished on the General tab, click the Location tab. (See Figure 11-3.)**

**Figure 11-3:**
Selecting
the location
for which to
display
weather
conditions.

6. **Click the arrow next to your continent to expand the list and select other locations.**

In my case, I chose North America, then United States, then Pennsylvania, and finally, Allentown. You should choose the location for which you want to see the weather conditions.

7. **Click Close when you're finished setting preferences.**

The small question mark in the Weather applet changes to an icon that shows the current conditions at the location you chose, and the temperature is displayed next to the icon.

Now that you've set up the Weather applet, you can use it to get information about the specified location. You can always get a general idea of the weather conditions just by looking at the icon and the temperature shown on the panel. But you can get much more information by clicking the icon to open the Details dialog box, as shown in Figure 11-4.

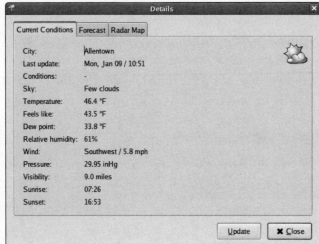

**Figure 11-4:**
Viewing the
weather
details for
the
specified
location.

As shown in Figure 11-4, the Weather applet provides a good deal of weather data for the requested location. In addition to showing the current weather data, you can get a weekly forecast of the upcoming weather for the requested location by clicking the Forecast tab. The Forecast tab of the Details dialog box is shown in Figure 11-5.

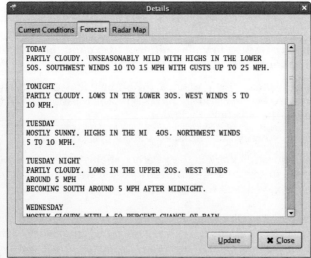

**Figure 11-5:**
The
Weather
applet
displays the
forecast
for the
requested
location.

The Details dialog box also provides a tab that will go to a radar map of the specified location. You can use the radar map, shown in Figure 11-6, to find out what weather might be approaching.

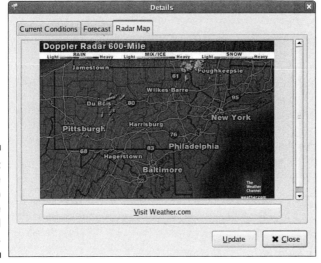

**Figure 11-6:**
Viewing the
radar map
for the
specified
location.

You can click the Visit Weather.com button to go to the Weather Channel Web site, where you can get additional weather information. Clicking this link opens your Web browser (if it isn't already running) and opens the Weather Channel Web Site.

An Update button appears on each of the tabbed screens. Click this button at any time to immediately refresh the weather data regardless of the update interval previously set. When you're finished viewing the Weather applet details, click Close to close the Details dialog box.

# Getting Weather Data from Your Browser

The Firefox Web browser offers an interesting extension that provides weather data to your browser whenever you're using it. It even alerts you to severe weather automatically. The extension is called Forecastfox, and before you can use it, you need to install and configure it. To install Forecastfox, do the following:

1. **Open Firefox.**

2. **From the main menu, choose Tools⇨Extensions.**

   The Extensions dialog box, shown in Figure 11-7, opens.

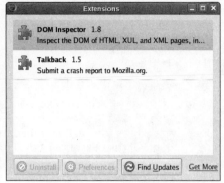

**Figure 11-7:**
The
Extensions
dialog box
for adding
extensions
to Firefox.

3. **Click the Get More link in the lower-right corner of the Extensions dialog box.**

   The Firefox Add-Ons page opens.

4. **Scroll down to find the link for Forecastfox and click it.**

   The Forecastfox information page opens.

5. **Click the Install Now link.**

6. **After the extension is installed, close the browser.**

7. **Re-open the browser.**

   The Forecastfox Options dialog box appears. (See Figure 11-8.)

**Figure 11-8:**
Setting the
options
for the
Forecastfox
browser
extension.

**8. Enter your zip code in the Code field and click Apply.**

If you don't know the zip code, click the Find Code button, enter the city, and click Search. When the city you searched for appears in the list, highlight the name and click OK.

**9. Click Apply.**

Four icons appear on the right side of the browser status bar, as shown in Figure 11-9. Beginning from the left icon, these icons represent a radar map, the current conditions, tomorrow's forecast, and the forecast for the day after tomorrow. You can move the cursor over the icons to see a pop-up displaying information for that icon. For example, if you move the cursor over the icon representing the radar map, a small map pops up to display the current radar map.

**Figure 11-9:**
The
Forecastfox
icons.

You can control how the icons are displayed from the Forecastfox options dialog box (refer to Figure 11-8), where you set the zip code in Step 8 in the preceding numbered list. If you're satisfied with the appearance of Forecastfox, you can leave the settings as they are. But many customization options are available, and I explain them next.

To open the Forecastfox Options dialog box, right-click any of the Forecastfox icons and choose Options from the list. When the Forecastfox Options dialog box appears (refer to Figure 11-8), the General tab is displayed with the settings that can be changed for this page. On the left side of the Forecastfox Options dialog box is a list of additional pages that you can select. Each of the additional pages has settings relevant to the page chosen, as described here:

✔ **General:** On this page, you can create profiles that let you select different options for each profile. On my system, I created named profiles for several different cities and set the display options to cycle through my profiles every few minutes. By doing this, I can see the weather in these cities at different times of the day just by glancing at the lower corner of my browser window. You can also rename or delete a previously created profile.

You also choose the city for which you want to receive weather data by entering the city code. You can enter a zip code for cities in the United States. Click the Find Code button to enter the name of a city, and search for the code for that city. You can enter names of U.S. and international cities in the search box.

You can choose the unit of measurement for the weather data by clicking the button next to your preference. Finally, you can set the display placement for the Forecastfox icons by clicking the arrows on the right side of the Toolbar field and selecting the desired location on your browser.

✔ **Severe Weather:** Clicking this option opens a page where you can enable or disable both the display of the severe weather icon and tooltips. You can also choose to display an icon, an icon and a label, or just a label.

Severe weather alerts are enabled by default, and any time a severe weather alert exists for any of your locations (U.S. only), an alert slider and a red icon with an exclamation point appears in the Forecastfox display.

✔ **Radar:** Selecting Radar gives you the Radar options page. On this page, you can enable or disable the radar and tooltip displays. You can also set the display options as Icon, Label, or Icon and Label.

✔ **Current Conditions:** Selecting Current Conditions gives you the Current Conditions options page. On this page, you can enable or disable the current conditions and tooltip displays. You can also set the display options as Icon, Label, or Icon and Label.

✔ **Today's Forecast:** Selecting this option gives you the Today's Forecast options page. On this page, you can enable or disable the current conditions and tooltip displays. You can set the display options as icon, label, or icon and label. Notice the Switch To area of this page. Here you can choose what to display after 3 p.m. when today's forecast is no longer available.

✔ **Extended Forecast:** Selecting Extended Forecast gives you the Extended Forecast options page. On this page, you can enable or disable the current conditions and tooltip displays. You can also set the display options as Icon, Label, or Icon and Label. An additional option on this page lets you set the number of days past today that you want to receive forecasts. If you change this value from the default, additional icons appear for each number you add.

✔ **Profiles:** Selecting Profiles gives you the Profiles options page. On this page, you can choose to rotate your profiles and set a time in minutes for the rotation. I created several profiles for different cities and opted to rotate them every 5 minutes so I can check the weather in cities I used to live in. Also, on this page, you can import and export your profiles by selecting the option and specifying the directory to find the profile to import or the location to put the profile if you're exporting it.

> ✔ **Links:** When you right-click any of the Forecastfox icons, a menu with links appears. The settings on this page let you decide how the links will open.

In addition to giving you the ability to open the Options dialog, the icons' right-click menus give you more choices, as shown in Figure 11-10. From this menu, you can choose to go to the Forecastfox home page or the Accuweather Web site. You can force Forecastfox to reload the weather data, and you can import or export your profiles if you've created any. If you've created profiles, you can also tell Forecastfox to load a different profile by choosing the Switch to Profile option.

**Figure 11-10:**
The
Forecastfox
right-click
menu
choices.

 I recommend that you experiment with the different settings in the Forecastfox Options dialog box. This is the best way to become familiar with it, and you will quickly discover the effects of applying your choices.

# Using MythTV to Get Weather Data

Your desktop and browser aren't the only sources for weather information. In Chapter 6, I discuss the MythTV program and how to install and configure it for your system. One of MythTV's primary functions is to fulfill your need for a personal video recorder (PVR). But MythTV also has a program called Myth-Weather that you can access by choosing the Weather option from MythTV's main menu choices. In this section, I tell you how you can use MythTV to get your current weather conditions and extended forecast.

## Setting up MythWeather

Make sure that MythTV is running, and you can see the main menu. To properly configure MythWeather to display the weather data for your desired location, proceed as follows:

1. **From the MythTV main menu, choose Setup➪Weather Settings.**

   This opens the Weather Settings dialog box. (See Figure 11-11.) The Weather Units option is selected by default.

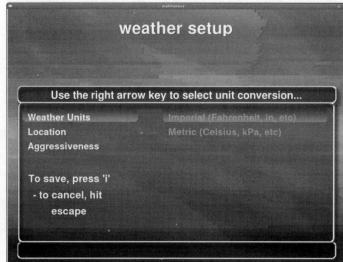

**Figure 11-11:** Configuring the weather settings in Myth-Weather.

2. **Select the units of measurement by using the right-arrow key to move the highlight bar to the right and place the highlight bar over your choice. Then move the highlight bar back to the left.**

3. **Move the highlight bar down to the Location option and use the right-arrow key to move the highlight to the right.**

4. **Use the up- and down-arrow keys to move the highlight to the letter that begins the name of the city you want to use.**

5. **Use the right-arrow key to move the highlight to the right to the cities that begin with the letter you selected.**

6. **Use the down-arrow key to scroll down the list of cities until you find the one you want.**

7. **When you've found and highlighted the city, press the left-arrow key twice to move the highlight back to Location.**

8. **Use the down-arrow key to move the highlight to Aggressiveness.**

9. **Use the right-arrow key to move the highlight to the right.**

10. **Use the up- and down-arrow keys to highlight your connection speed.**

11. **Press the I key to save your changes.**

The MythWeather setup program attempts to connect to www. weather.com to retrieve the weather data for the location you selected. If the system successfully connects, you will see some pages displaying your weather data.

12. **Press Esc twice to return to the MythTV main menu.**

## Viewing your MythWeather information

From the MythTV main menu, you can select the Weather option whenever you want to see the weather for your requested location. After selecting Weather, a display of your current weather conditions appears, similar to the one shown in Figure 11-12.

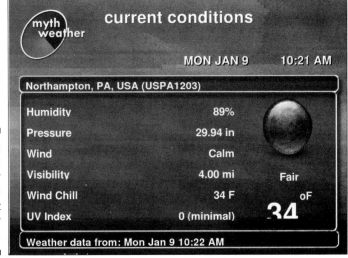

**Figure 11-12:**
Myth
Weather
displays the
current
weather
conditions.

The current conditions are displayed for about 15 seconds, and then the display changes to show the extended forecast. After about 15 seconds, the extended forecast page is replaced by a page displaying today's forecast. Finally, in another 15 seconds, the page of today's forecast is replaced by a live radar map showing the Doppler radar conditions for the selected location.

If you don't want to wait for the pages to change, you can use the left- or right-arrow keys to cycle through the pages as you desire.

When you're finished viewing the weather, press Esc to return to the MythTV main menu.

# Chapter 12

# Staying Comfortable with Thermostat Controls

*H*ave you ever left town and forgot to turn down the heat in your house? Or even worse, did you forget to turn it on, leaving your pipes to possibly freeze? (I did that once and had to call my neighbor to walk over to my house in a snowstorm on Christmas day!) X10 thermostat controls can allow you to change the temperature of your home even when you aren't there. The X10 thermostat is especially nice when you're coming home from a long trip (or even a short trip) and want to warm up your home before you get there.

And don't forget about air conditioning. You can turn off your air conditioning with a keychain remote as you leave the house and use your cell phone or your Internet connection to turn it on so that it's nicely comfortable when you arrive home.

This chapter covers installing and using thermostats that can be operated remotely, by either your computer via the Internet or a remote control device or touch-tone controller. It also takes a look at the Linux DIY Zoning Project, which enables do-it-yourselfers to zone their heating and cooling systems for greatest comfort and cost efficiency.

One requirement of all these systems, of course, is that you do *not* heat your home with a little wood-burning stove.

# *Installing Thermostat Controls*

To heat your home remotely, you'll probably want to install thermostat controls that you can operate by using X10. Using X10 to control your thermostat gives you the power to control your heat in the following ways:

- ✔ **Use remote controllers,** such as the Universal remote or a keychain remote, to raise or lower the temperature if you're within 25 to 50 feet of your thermostat.

- ✔ **Use a free Linux program,** such as MisterHouse, to communicate with your X10 module and raise or lower your temperature by setting a timer or making adjustments via the Internet.

- ✔ **Use a touch-tone controller** to change your heat or cooling setting remotely by phone.

Here are several ways of controlling your heat remotely by using X10:

- ✔ **Install an X10 communicating thermostat.** For about $260, you can change your existing thermostat to a thermostat that communicates with X10. This thermostat is called the X10 Communicating Thermostat TXB16. It can control almost any home HVAC (heating, ventilation, and air conditioning) system, including gas/electric, heat pump, or radiant floors. This model is sold by www.smarthome.com.

- ✔ **Install a system that uses two thermostats and a Universal Module.** Set one thermostat, to your comfort temperature, perhaps 69 degrees, and set the other thermostat to your not-at-home or in-bed-asleep temperature, perhaps 55 degrees. Attach an X10 Universal Module to the 69-degree thermostat so it can be controlled remotely.

- ✔ **Install an X10 Thermostat Set-back Controller.** A *Thermostat Set-back Controller* is a device that sits below your current thermostat and heats up your thermostat, fooling it into believing that your home is warmer than it really is. This is probably the easiest solution for controlling your thermostat remotely because it requires no electrician to install it. Thermostat Set-back Controllers are sold by www.x10.com. They require little energy and can create big savings by keeping your heating bills down.

## *Installing the TXB16 thermostat*

The X10 Communicating Thermostat Model TXB16, by Residential Control Systems, Inc., is probably the most sophisticated solution for keeping control of your temperature wherever you are. It includes

- ✔ A wall display unit (which replaces your existing thermostat)

- ✔ A controller unit (which connects to your HVAC system)

✔ A plug-in TW-523 module (which is a two-way X10 appliance module)

✔ A cable that connects the module to the controller unit

✔ A power supply

The wall display unit has

✔ An LCD temperature display

✔ Buttons to set the temperature manually

✔ A button to check the mode (heat, cool, or off)

✔ A button to start the fan manually

Figure 12-1 shows a diagram of the wall unit and its functions. With the TXB16 thermostat, you can change your temperature setpoints remotely, using standard X10 commands consisting of a house code, unit code, and On or Off signal. *Setpoints* are the temperatures that you set for the heating mode and the cooling mode. You can change either setpoint remotely by using an X10 remote, touch-tone controller, or your computer using an X10 interface, such as the CM11A running X10 compatible software, such as MisterHouse.

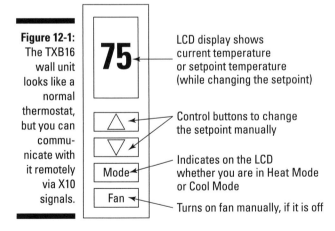

**Figure 12-1:** The TXB16 wall unit looks like a normal thermostat, but you can communicate with it remotely via X10 signals.

75

LCD display shows current temperature or setpoint temperature (while changing the setpoint)

Control buttons to change the setpoint manually

Indicates on the LCD whether you are in Heat Mode or Cool Mode

Turns on fan manually, if it is off

Don't try to wire thermostats yourself unless you are qualified to do so. Hire a professional or get someone who knows exactly what he or she is doing to hook up the thermostats.

If you live in an area that can freeze during the winter, it is required for this thermostat to have a second thermostat installed, as well. The second thermostat could be your existing thermostat, and it needs to be set for at least 40 degrees — maybe more depending on where your pipes are located.

For obvious reasons, the TXB16 thermostat should be installed by someone with HVAC experience. But after it is installed, here's how to set it up and operate it from a remote control:

1. **Turn on Switch #4 on the back of the Control Unit.**

   On the back of the Control Unit are either four or eight switches, depending on which model you have. The first three switches and the fifth, if you have one, are set by your heating contractor, and their on/off states depend on which kind of heating system you have, such as single-stage or two-stage heating.

2. **Plug in a transceiver to control your X10 remote control if it isn't already plugged in.**

   An X10 remote control is available here:

   www.x10-store.com/unlerepu.html

   A transceiver to control it is available here:

   www.x10-store.com/pat01.html

   You can also find them at www.x10.com and www.smarthome.com.

3. **Set your X10 remote control to house code B by doing the following:**

   a. *Press the X10 button on your X10 remote.*

   b. *Press and hold the SETUP button until the LED light remains on, and then release it.*

   c. *Press 2, and then press ENTER.*

   Now your X10 remote should be set to house code B.

4. **To set the temperature on your TXB16, choose the unit code from Table 12-1 that corresponds to the temperature that you want to set and press that number on your remote, followed by either Channel + (for On) or Channel – (for Off), depending on what column your temperature resides in Table 12-1.**

   The temperature changes on the TXB16 thermostat. Or if you press a code for a mode, the mode changes.

| Table 12-1 | TXB16 Thermostat X10 Thermostat Commands | | |
|------------|------------|------|------|
| *House Code* | *Unit Code* | *On* | *Off* |
| B | 1 | 72° | Turn System Off |
| B | 2 | 73° | Heat Mode |
| B | 3 | 74° | Cool Mode |
| B | 4 | 75° | Auto Mode |

| House Code | Unit Code | On | Off |
|---|---|---|---|
| B | 5 | 76° | 40° |
| B | 6 | 77° | 60° |
| B | 7 | 78° | 62° |
| B | 8 | 79° | 63° |
| B | 9 | 80° | 64° |
| B | 10 | 81° | 65° |
| B | 11 | 82° | 66° |
| B | 12 | 83° | 67° |
| B | 13 | 84° | 68° |
| B | 14 | 86° | 69° |
| B | 15 | 88° | 70° |
| B | 16 | 90° | 71° |

Now you can use your X10 remote control to change the temperature of your home when you leave your house, for instance, or before you go to sleep. You can put it on your bedside table for use at night or early in the morning when your snooze alarm goes off.

The X10 codes in Table 12-1 can also be used by Linux X10 applications, such as MisterHouse, to enable you to control your TXB16 thermostat via the Internet. You can also control the thermostat via the phone by using a touch-tone controller.

The TXB16 offers more than just the ability to change the temperature setting remotely. It also offers two-way communication and extended commands. For instance, by using compatible hardware and software, you can read the current temperature of your home from your computer or over the Internet. The TXB16 can also support up to three remote temperature sensors, one of which can tell you the outside temperature. Unfortunately, at present, no Linux software exists to run these features, although if you're a programmer, you might want to consider this an opportunity. However, you can still use Linux software, such as MisterHouse, to send commands to the TXB16 to change the temperature.

Manuals for the TXB16 are available for download from `www.resconsys.com/products/stats/x10.htm`, including the X10 Protocol Manual.

## Installing a two-thermostat X10 control system

Unless you run software that makes full use of the two-way communicating features of the TXB16, which is available for Windows but not available in Linux yet, you might want to set up a simpler and less costly system to remotely control your thermostat — one that would probably work just as well for you.

The idea is to have two thermostats — both independently hooked up to the furnace — so that if either one is on, the furnace kicks in. One thermostat is set to the temperature that you want to keep the house if you aren't at home. The other thermostat is set at your comfort temperature. This thermostat is attached to an X10 Universal Module. The X10 Universal Module allows or disallows the signal from the thermostat with your comfort temperature to start the furnace, depending on whether it is on or off. You can use a Universal remote, a keychain remote, a touch-tone controller, an X10 timer, or your computer to send an X10 signal to the Universal Module to turn it on or off remotely.

The Universal Module is easy to install, although you might want an electrician to do it because you'll probably need an electrician to install an extra thermostat anyway. We do not recommend doing the wiring yourself unless you are qualified to do so. The Universal Module is installed between one thermostat and the wire leading to the HVAC system, as shown in Figure 12-2.

The X10 Universal Module is designed with exposed terminals and to avoid shock hazard is not designed to be connected to wires with more than 30 volts AC or 42 volts DC current.

The Universal Module costs about $18.99 and is available at `www.x10.com/ products/x10_um506.htm`. To install the Universal Module, do the following:

1. **Using a screwdriver, turn the red House Code dial to the same house code as the remote that you want to use to turn it on or off.**

   Conversely, you could choose a house code and program your remote to that house code. Instructions for programming a remote to a house code are listed in Step 3 in the preceding section, "Installing the TXB16 thermostat."

   It might be good to choose a house code other than A, B, M, and P. I give reasons for this in Chapter 13.

2. **Using a screwdriver, turn the black Unit Code dial to an unused unit code for your remote.**

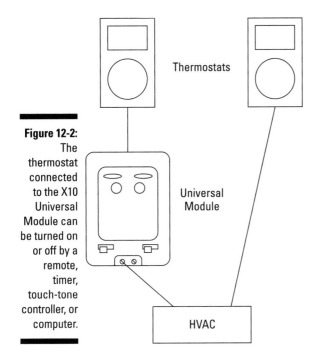

**Figure 12-2:**
The thermostat connected to the X10 Universal Module can be turned on or off by a remote, timer, touch-tone controller, or computer.

Thermostats

Universal Module

HVAC

3. **Set the Momentary/Continuous slider, located at the bottom left of the Universal Module, to the right.**

   This allows continuous contact, which means that an X10 On command, for example, turns the Universal Module continuously on so that the thermostat commands will continuously be available to the HVAC system, until an X10 Off command is received. The reverse is true for the X10 Off command.

4. **Set the slider on the bottom right of the Universal Module to the middle position if you want to hear a beep every time an X10 On or Off command is executed, or set it to the right if you want it to operate silently.**

5. **Connect the low-level current wires to the Universal Module.**

   One wire connects to the thermostat and the other to the HVAC system. Or let an electrician do it if you aren't qualified and absolutely sure of what you're doing.

6. **Plug in the Universal Module.**

7. **Set the Universal Module switch to the off position.**

   It isn't necessary to turn it on for continuous functioning.

If your thermostat goes on or off unpredictably, you might want to see whether any of your neighbors are home-automation enthusiasts.

## Installing a Thermostat Set-back Controller

The Thermostat Set-back Controller is a device like a miniature hotplate that rests on the wall beneath your thermostat and plugs into either an X10 Appliance Module or an X10 Wall Receptacle Module and lets you control the temperature reading of the thermostat remotely in order to control your HVAC system. It uses very little electricity, and when it is on, it continuously raises the perceived temperature of the thermostat about five, ten, or 15 degrees depending on what you initially set it to do. It can be controlled by your computer, an X10 touch-tone controller for telephone remote control, an X10 timer, an X10 Universal remote, a keychain remote, and more. It sells for about $19.99 at www.x10.com.

The Thermostat Set-back Controller works to control your heating and cooling in four ways, as follows:

- ✔ **To turn down your heat,** send an X10 On signal to the Thermostat Set-back Controller.

- ✔ **To turn up your heat remotely,** send an X10 Off signal to the Thermostat Set-back Controller.

- ✔ **To increase your air conditioning,** send an X10 On signal to the Thermostat Set-back Controller.

- ✔ **To decrease your air conditioning,** send an X10 Off signal to the Thermostat Set-back Controller.

To install your Thermostat Set-back Controller, do the following:

1. **Mount your Thermostat Set-back Controller below the thermostat of your home.**

2. **Plug it into either an X10 Appliance Module or the upper outlet of an X10 Wall Receptacle Module (also known as a Super Socket).**

3. **Use a screwdriver to set the house code of the module to the house code of your remote.**

4. **Use a screwdriver to set the unit code of the module to an available unit code for your automation system.**

# *Waking Up to a Warm House*

X10 thermostat systems can operate in the same way as programmable thermostats by using an X10 timer, or you can let your computer do the timing. For more information on automating your X10 modules with your computer, see Chapter 16. The X10 Mini Timer (which looks like a small alarm clock and can function as an alarm clock with a snooze control) sells for about $30 and can time four groups of X10 devices twice a day.

You can program either your computer, running MisterHouse, or your X10 Mini Timer to control your thermostat system in the following ways:

✔ **If you're using a two-thermostat X10 control system,** as I describe previously, with one thermostat connected to a Universal Module, you can send an On signal to your Universal Module set attached to the thermostat with your comfort temperature and start heating up your home half an hour before you need to wake up. And you can send an Off signal half an hour after your expected bedtime, which gives you time to warm up your sheets with your body heat before your room cools down.

✔ **If you're using a Thermostat Set-back Controller** (described in the preceding section), about half an hour before you need to wake up, you can send an Off signal to it to stop fooling the thermostat into thinking the temperature is warmer than it really is and start heating the house. Then you can send an On signal about a half an hour after your bedtime.

✔ **If you are using a TXB16 X10-controlling thermostat,** you can send the X10 code to reset the temperature for the actual degree that you want it to be before you wake up, and you can send a different X10 code for a lower actual temperature after your bedtime.

# *Saving Money with Controlled Heating*

Energy companies say that setting your thermostat back 4 degrees can save $35 to $50 per month in energy bills. So, if you set it back 10 degrees while you aren't at home all day or asleep at home, you can probably save lots of money. With energy prices soaring, micromanaging the heat is a good way to go.

If you have a Universal remote, or even better, a keychain remote, or best of all, a computer that knows your schedule — such as when you plan to be at home and when you need to work or go on a trip — then you can control your furnace or air conditioning by pressing a couple buttons as you leave the house, or you can program your schedule into your computer. And for coming home, unless you have computerized your schedule, you can use a touch-tone controller and send an X10 signal by using the phone to get your home warm again for when you walk in the door.

Some other considerations exist for the X10 thermostats, as well. For instance, if you are going out for a really short time, does it save you money to raise and lower the temperature? If so, how much?

Another way to save money is by zoning your heat. The Linux DIY Zoning Project offers a huge amount of information regarding saving money. This project lives at `http://diy-zoning.sourceforge.net`.

## Saving money by using X10 thermostat systems

It used to be thought that the best way to save money with controlled heating was to set your thermostat at a single temperature, as low as you can stand, and to leave it there throughout the day, unless you are going on vacation. The thinking was that because it takes more energy to increase the temperature of a home than it does to keep it at a constant temperature, it is best not to change the temperature of the home much. Some HVAC contractors, even today, say that it is not a good idea to adjust your thermostat too many times during the day.

But recent research shows that the extra energy to bring a home up to a certain temperature is exactly equal to the amount of energy saved while the home is cooling off. This means that all the energy saved with your home at a constant lower temperature is money in the bank.

However, if you live in a home with lots of thermal mass, such as brick, stucco, logs, earthen walls, concrete, and more, the time that it takes for your home to cool down and heat up might be quite a bit longer than a home without a lot of thermal mass. This means that if your home doesn't cool down quickly, you can't save money by lowering the temperature for shorter intervals than it takes your home to cool down because an equal amount of extra energy is needed to raise the temperature back to where it originally was.

You might want to monitor how long it takes your home to cool so that you know when to make the effort to turn down your heat and when it just doesn't matter.

## Saving money with the Linux DIY Zoning Project

Zoning your home gives you the ability to maintain the heating or cooling of different areas of your home at different temperatures of your choice or at the same uniform temperature. You achieve zoning zen by dividing the home into functional heating zones, placing temperature sensors in each of the zones, and then controlling the heat by using electronic duct dampers, which can open or close remotely, as shown in Figure 12-3. Zones can be groups of rooms or individual rooms. You can create any number of zones in your home.

Before embarking on DIY Zoning, be sure you understand thoroughly all the information that the DIY Zoning Project provides. Zoning your home this way needs to be considered as a labor of love and not a chore. If you're into it, by all means give it a try. Just don't bite off more than you can chew. Find an HVAC professional to guide you through it. Hire him or her for the tough jobs, and let him or her tell you what you can do and shouldn't attempt.

**Figure 12-3:**
Zoned
heating
and air
conditioning
systems use
electronic
dampers to
control the
heat in the
different
zones of the
home.

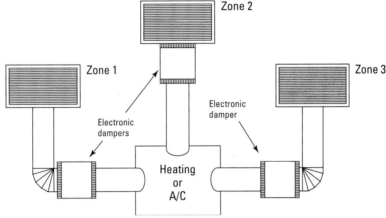

## Saving money with zoning

Zoning your home allows you to save money in the following ways:

- **Maintain a proper temperature balance in your home,** regardless of the time of day and the amount of sunlight heating up the outer walls of your home. This saves money by not wasting heat when you need to increase the heat in rooms that don't need it.

- **Zone your heat so that the areas of your home that you occupy at certain times are warmer than areas that you do not occupy.** This saves money because your furnace needs to work less hard than if it were heating the entire house. For instance, you can supply more heat to the bedrooms at night and less to the living room, kitchen, utility room, and other areas that you don't occupy during those times. Or during the day, you can supply more heat to the living room and less to the bedrooms.

- **Install and use a furnace and air conditioning unit that is less powerful than one needed in an unzoned home** because the demands on them are less. You save money because a smaller furnace and central air conditioner costs less and also takes less energy to run.

### What DIY Zoning can do for you

DIY Zoning is Linux software that can automatically control the opening and closing of the dampers, as well as a multitude of other automated functions to run your zoned HVAC system. It can handle as many zones as you can give it and is compatible with any heating system.

DIY Zoning is also a repository of information on how to zone your heat and air conditioning most easily and effectively. It is found at `http://diy-zoning.sourceforge.net`.

The DIY Zoning software can perform the following functions:

- Maintain temperature control for each zone in your home.
- Schedule temperature changes for your home.
- Enable you to monitor and control the temperature of any zone via the Internet.
- Alert you when your air filter is clogged. (Tells you when it actually *is* clogged, instead of just timing when it *should be* replaced.)
- Warn you if your heating or cooling system is working harder than it should be.
- Send any warnings via e-mail or notify your cell phone or PDA.
- Keep a zone or zones at a single constant temperature, regardless of the temperature in the rest of the home.
- Enable you to shut off the heating or cooling of a zone. This is especially useful for rooms you don't need to air condition.
- Automatically figure out how to optimize savings when you're away — either by turning down the heat or maintaining a constant temperature, depending on how long you're away.

### Pros and cons of doing it yourself

Why zone your heating? And why do it yourself?

*The cons:* First of all, zoning your home yourself is a lot of work. Unless you are an HVAC pro, there is a steep learning curve. Currently, the Linux DIY Zoning Project is for the very capable do-it-yourselfers, although in the future, the project leaders hope to provide a professional package and support.

*Note:* To give you an idea of the philosophy of DIY Zoning and how much work is involved, on their home page is a quote, "An amateur built the Ark. Titanic was built by professionals." This implies that using DIY Zoning advice properly, you can do a better job zoning your heating and cooling systems than an HVAC professional. And it also implies that the learning curve for doing so is as steep as learning to build an ark. (But Noah did it, and so maybe you can, too!)

*The pros:* Properly zoning your heating and cooling offers many benefits. And the costs of having an HVAC professional do it can be large, staggering, or astronomical, depending on the size of your home and your income level. You can do it much cheaper.

Normally, your heating contractor balances your heating system so that you get the same temperature in each room in your home — at that particular time of day that he is working on it. So, if he or she balances the heat in the morning, then when the sun blazes on the western side of your home in the afternoon, the rooms on the west will be much warmer than the rooms on the east. If you zone your home and balance your heating yourself, you can balance it for every moment of the day — not just one particular time of day.

### Using electronic duct dampers and temperature sensors

How do you balance the heating and air conditioning of your home so that it remains in balance all the time? How do you make sure that areas of the home are not hotter or cooler than other areas unless you want them to be? One way is to use automatic dampers, which increase or decrease the amount of heat or cool air entering certain vents. These dampers can be connected to an X10 module, such as the X10 Universal Module and controlled using X10 temperature sensors.

Electronic Duct Dampers are available at www.smarthome.com/3080.html. They cost about $109 to $169.

Temperature sensors that can potentially operate with the DIY Zoning software are available in three styles and different price ranges:

- ✔ **Refined and finished, but needs a Linux driver written for it:** This looks like a wall switch except that instead of the switch there is a small, round, pleasant-looking sensor. These sensors are available at www. smarthome.com/1522.html for about $35 apiece.

- ✔ **Less refined, more clunky, but has a Linux driver:** Temperature sensors are available at www.ibuttonlink.com. The sensor is contained in a small rectangular box a few centimeters long, wide, and deep. It could be placed out of sight, perhaps, in a bookcase. You can buy two cables with sensors attached on each, for $85.

- ✔ **Least refined, do-it-yourself instructions:** If you have a background in electronics, you might want to build your own temperature sensors, as long as they can be placed out of sight. The cost of building them yourself is much less, and if you plan to create lots of zones, you might need lots of them. Instructions for building your own temperature sensors with a Linux driver are found at www.digitemp.com/building.shtml.

And after you've completed the job of zoning your home, maybe there's a career in it for you — if that's the kind of thing you want to do full time.

# Part V

# X10-ding Your Environment with Home Automation

The 5th Wave     By Rich Tennant

"Roger! Check the sewing machine's connection to the PC. I'm getting e-mails stitched across my curtains again."

# In this part . . .

Lights, appliances, and wireless modules are simple building blocks that you can use for many home automation projects. The X10 computer interfaces are the tools that you can use to build those projects. In Part V, I introduce you to some of the hardware to control lights and appliances. You also find out about the software that allows Linux to manage device events. Just don't let all the control go to your head.

# Chapter 13

# Introducing X10 Home Automation

**X**10 is a company that sells X10 power line carrier (PLC) and wireless technology. Until just recently, the X10 company held patents on the X10 technology. Confusing, isn't it? When those patents expired, companies such as Advanced Control Technologies, Inc. (ACT); Leviton; Powerline Control Systems (PCS); Smarthome; and others began making X10-compatible modules (with enhancements). Some modules plug into the wall, replace sockets, work as inline modules (fitting inside electrical boxes), or replace wall switches. The modules I discuss in this chapter are the plug-in wall modules. This allows you to plug an electrical device (a lamp, a TV, or an appliance) into the module and plug the module into the wall. From there, you can control the power to that device. A PC with an X10 interface and control software or an X10 console sends the commands to control the modules. The modules can provide sprinkler, heating, or relay control (to name just a few tricks they do).

In this chapter, I introduce you to some of the many X10-compatible products. (One of the nice things about Linux is that it allows you to extend programs to add functionality you think is missing.) You get to play with the hardware and use the software products under the Linux environment, and I even show you how to use X10 and Linux software to save money by using it to automagically turn on and off the power to your devices (your printer, for example) as necessary. This chapter also covers resolving those little problems that crop up while using X10.

Everyone uses the term *module* to refer to the X10 parts, so I use that term, too. I use the generic term *device* to mean the thing plugged into the X10 modules (which then plugs in the wall outlet just as an extension cord would).

# Introducing X10 Power Line Carrier

You need to know about the X10 power line carrier (PLC) technology (X10 for short). Simply put, X10 uses your home's electrical wiring and the electricity (alternating current, or AC) to carry the X10 commands throughout the house. The software on your Linux PC talks to the X10 interface module. The X10 interface module puts the commands on the electrical wires so that all the wall modules can receive them. The modules listen for commands meant for them. (Each command has an address portion, and each module has an address. I discuss addresses later in this section.) When a command arrives at the correct module, that module performs the requested command (dim, brighten, turn on, or turn off).

X10 communicates at a rate between 50 and 60 bps. Note the lack of the K! Yes, it's that slow; a single X10 command takes about one second to send and be acted on. This means that you can't expect X10 to control fancy blinking holiday lighting displays. Now, one second isn't as bad as it sounds, but it is about at the edge of tolerance of the Spouse Acceptance Factor (SAF). See the nearby sidebar for more about this topic.

I don't go into the technical details of X10. For those who are curious about the actual bits of the X10 technology, Phil Kingery of ACT has written a great series of articles for HomeToys online magazine (at `www.hometoys.com/ articles.htm#X-10%20Technical%20Series%20by%20Phil%20 Kingery`).

So what can you do with X10? This list scratches the surface of what X10 can do:

- ✔ **Send an on or off command.** The simplest devices, such as appliance modules, are capable of handling only on or off commands.

- ✔ **Send a brighten or dim command.** Lamp modules can support dim and brighten commands as well as on and off commands.

- ✔ **Dim or brighten to preset levels.** Some fancier X10 modules, such as those from Smarthome, support preset levels. These modules will either jump to a preset level or ramp to a preset level you program in advance. You can send this specific X10 command as a preset command or by using an extended command. The basic lamp modules can't handle the extended command, but the more expensive modules can.

- ✔ **Send special commands.** When is a dim not a dim? When something like a thermostat receives the dim command. Instead, the thermostat interprets the dim as a command to set back the temperature. Other devices, such as security systems and sprinkler controls, do the same thing.

✔ **Send signals from your computer to an X10 module.** This allows you to control one or more modules. Generally, you can let the X10 software automatically handle the commands that you've preconfigured, but sometimes, you might want to manually type commands, and that's available, too.

✔ **Operate X10 modules manually.** X10 remote control units, console units, and switches allow you to do this. (Manual? Bah! Now, you can't have any of that, can you? Well, maybe you can, just in case.)

For more information about the possibilities of X10, see the later sections, "A (very) short list of X10 modules" and "Cool Things to Do with X10."

The commands that are sent to the modules have an address portion of the command. The X10 modules are listening for this address. The module ignores commands with address portions that do not match a module's address. The module performs commands with address portions that match. X10 modules have two portions of an address: a *house code* and a *unit code*. The house code is made up of a letter between A and P, and the unit code is made up of a number between 1 and 16. For example, a module that is addressed as A1 has a house code of A and a unit code of 1. How you set these codes depends on how you want to set up your module:

✔ **On the simple X10 modules,** you turn two dials to set the address. One dial sets the house code (A through P), and the other sets the unit code (1 through 16). By default, the address of a new module is set to A1.

✔ **On the fancier modules,** you must press a button sequence or send specific X10 commands to set the address of the modules.

Each module must have an address, but multiple modules can have the same address. When a command with the address arrives, only the modules with that address will listen and act upon that command. For more about addresses and codes, see the later section, "Module setup."

## Spouse Acceptance Factor

Though Spouse Acceptance Factor (SAF) sounds like a joke, it isn't. A person (that is, a nut like you and me) interested in using home automation might be willing to tolerate a bit of awkwardness in the beginning for various reasons (like the "Wow, this is cool!" factor), but that person's spouse won't be so tolerant. The spouse just wants it to work and work right the first time. This is a good thing because it makes you think before you do anything. Much of my experimentation lives in my computer room before I move it into the "production" environment. By experimenting first, you might even find that your spouse will come up with the ideas faster than you can.

## *X10 PC interfaces*

One of the first parts of your basic X10 kit is the PC interface. I show you how to put your kit together later in this chapter. The PC interface allows the software on the Linux PC to send and receive X10 commands across your home electricity.

X10 modules and interfaces have transmitters, receivers, and transceivers. *Transmitters* are devices that only send X10 commands (like consoles or wall switches). *Receivers* are devices that only receive X10 commands (like basic appliance and lamp modules). *Transceivers* are devices that can transmit and receive. All of the latest PC interfaces are transceivers. A lot of the newer X10 modules support receiving a command and transmitting a response to a query from your computer for its status.

Many X10 interfaces are available, and some are really old and no longer of real use to anyone — except those people who've been running them for years. Why replace something when it works well? But for your needs, only a few of the interfaces are supported under Linux. Here's a list of most of them (made by the X10 company unless noted otherwise):

- ✔ **CM11A:** X10's RS232 PLC transceiver, which is currently the most popular Linux/X10 interface. The CM11A supports the extended commands, extended data, and newer, preset commands. (These commands are used by the high-end X10 modules.) The CM11A has the capability to have X10 commands and timer events downloaded to an EPROM (Erasable Programmable Read-Only Memory; it's long-term storage), which won't lose the X10 commands if the power is lost). The CM11A can then execute simple X10 commands, such as time of day events, without the assistance of Linux.

- ✔ **CM15A:** The latest candidate is the CM15A, X10's USB PLC and wireless transceiver. It has all the features of the CM11A and then some. As luck would have it, the CM15A came out just as I started working on this book, so very little software was available for this controller when I was writing — but it holds a lot of promise. I expect to see a lot more software available soon.

- ✔ **Powerlinc interface:** The Smarthome interface to the PC. The Powerlinc interface transceiver is made for Smarthome and has an RS232 or a USB interface. Linux software is available for this controller and it supports the extended commands, extended data, and preset commands.

- ✔ **CM17A:** X10's RS232 wireless transmitter.

- ✔ **MR26A:** X10's RS232 wireless receiver. The MR26A (receiver) and the CM17A (transmitter) were released after the CM11A and are useful when used together. They provide the wireless interfaces to send and receive via an RS232 port.

✔ **CM19A:** X10's USB wireless transceiver. The CM19A can be used to replace the MR26A and the CM17A. Unfortunately, however, so far very little Linux software is available for the CM19A.

✔ **TW523:** X10's two-way, powerline interface, the oldest interface. Generally, it's not meant to be controlled directly by a PC. Instead, it's typically used with devices, such as a Rain-8 (sprinkler controller), or as an interface to other end devices. It can't receive extended commands, extended data, or the newer preset commands.

✔ **CP290:** One of the oldest PC interfaces, the CP290 is X10's RS232 PLC transmitter. It's a transmit-only device and is no longer available (except on eBay). I mention it simply as a warning; some people are tempted to purchase it because of its cheap price. If you do, you'll quickly be surprised at its lack of features.

The CM11A's outlet, on the front, is just a pass-through electrical outlet. It isn't controlled by X10, and no amount of commands can turn it off and on. It's intended for use by the PC's power cord. Of course, some PC power supplies and monitors are X10 *black holes* (signals go in and never come back out). So using the CM11A's outlet for those devices might not be a wise idea.

The CM15A is similar to the CM11A, but it's beefier than the CM11A. In addition to all the CM11A's features, it has a wireless interface, more memory for macros and events, and several new features that I don't have space to go into here. (The new features are for running X10 commands in standalone mode.) But you can see why I think this will be more popular with Linux in the future (hint: PLC and wireless X10 in one interface).

If you intend to run your Linux system 24/7, let Linux do all the fancy work; it's much more flexible and powerful than the standalone CM11A . Linux can be triggered to run other programs and can use the programs to trigger X10 events, something the CM11A and the CM15A can't do.

If you intend to use the CM11A without Linux (that is, standalone), disconnect the serial cable from the CM11A case. Don't just disconnect it from the PC; the hanging cable (disconnecting the serial cable from the PC) causes strange problems for the CM11A. (The CM15A doesn't have these problems.)

## A (very short) list of X10 modules

The list of X10 modules to choose from is quite long — it would probably put Santa's Naughty and Nice list to shame. And the list of vendors who make X10 modules is almost as lengthy. In addition to X10 (the company), you have ACT, Leviton, PCS, RadioShack, Smarthome, and others. They make all sorts of X10 products, and I can't do them justice here in the confined space of these pages. To find out more about these companies' products, visit their Web sites. (I include URLs in the appendix and links on the CD.) Here is a very short list of X10 modules available:

- ✔ **AM466:** Standard X10 three-prong appliance module that handles simple on and off commands only.

- ✔ **AM486:** Standard X10 two-prong appliance module that handles only simple on and off commands.

- ✔ **LM465:** Standard X10 two-prong lamp module; this module handles simple on, off, dim, and brighten commands.

- ✔ **AM14A:** Two-prong, two-way appliance module. In addition to the normal on and off commands, this module can respond to status requests and supports extended commands.

- ✔ **LM14A:** X10 two-prong, two-way lamp module. In addition to the normal lamp module support, this module can respond to status requests and supports extended commands.

- ✔ **ApplianceLinc three-prong module:** This is similar to the AM466 but is made for Smarthome.com.

- ✔ **ApplianceLinc three-prong, two-way module:** Similar to the AM486, this one is also made for Smarthome.com.

- ✔ **LampLinc three-prong dimmer:** Similar to the LM14A, this is made for Smarthome.com and has extra support for the older, preset, dim/bright commands.

- ✔ **LampLinc three-prong, two-way dimmer:** Similar to the LM14A, made for Smarthome.com. It has a three-prong outlet and extra support for the older, preset, dim/bright commands.

- ✔ **LampLinc Plus two-way dimmer:** This is similar to the LampLinc three-print, two-way dimmer but also support status requests.

- ✔ **Relay modules:** These are used to directly control low-voltage devices, and they have support for basic on and off commands.

The term *two-way* means that the module supports two-way communications; as well as receiving X10 commands, it can transmit a response to X10 commands (such as a status poll, which can tell you the module's dim level). Some other modules can only receive X10 commands, while others are transmit-only devices such as wall switches.

## Purchasing X10 devices

You really need to do your homework before you start buying too many X10 devices. Some are cheap; others look the same and cost more but are of better

quality. But you can find many more devices than you'd expect. You can purchase some directly from X10 (watch out for the pop-up advertising that X10's
notorious for) or places like Smarthome.com. I buy from Smarthome.com
often, and most of the X10 devices (if not all) are available from its online site.
Though I don't mention X10 wireless in this chapter (I mention only a few
wireless interfaces), the X10 company's wireless X10 technology works in conjunction with the X10 company's PLC technology. Here's a list of various non-
wireless X10 devices:

- **WS467:** This X10 wall switch can receive an X10 command for off, on, dim, or brighten as well as be manually controlled (like a normal switch).

- **Mini Controller:** This eight-unit desktop controller has buttons to send on, off, dim, and brighten commands to one house code and eight unit codes (for example, A1 though A8, just one command at a time).

- **Maxi Controller:** This 16-unit desktop controller has buttons to send on, off, dim, and brighten commands to one house code and eight unit codes (for example, A1 though A16, just one command at a time).

- **Rain8:** This X10 sprinkler system controller controls up to eight sprin-kler zones by issuing X10 commands.

- **TempLinc:** This sends an X10 command based on temperature highs or lows. You can also poll the device and find out the current temperature.

- **TXB16 X10 HVAC System:** This is an X10-controllable HVAC thermostat that allows you to send X10 commands to set your home's temperature.

- **Universal Module:** This controls a single, low-voltage device with X10 (receives on or off commands).

- **Eight Relay Controller Latched:** This controls multiple low-voltage devices with X10.

- **TC184W:** This is an eight-button, wall-mounted, transmitter controller. This module can send out preprogrammed X10 commands and can per-form *scenes* (lots of commands with one button push); *toggle* (push a button once to send an on command, push the button again to send an off command); or even send more complex commands. This is one of my favorite X10 switches!

- **Siren:** The X10 security siren responds to X10 signals by turning on a loud siren and turning on all the lamp modules for a preset house code.

# Building a Starter Kit

In the previous sections of this chapter, I give you a general idea of what
equipment and technology is available. So in this section, I move on to
showing you how to put together an X10 kit to work with Linux. Here's what
you need to build a starter kit:

- CM11A, X10's RS232 power line carrier (PLC) transceiver (the PC's interface module).

- An X10 appliance module (preferred) or lamp module (a module to control the device's power).

- A working RS232 or USB serial port on your computer. (The PC interface will need to plug into this.)

- Heyu2 software (the X10 home automation and command line software).

So why did I choose the preceding combination? Well, I want to start you out with something useful that can do something right away after installation. Plenty of other programs (as my Web site can testify to) can interface to X10 controllers, but Heyu is one of the better software packages for Linux, X10, and new users. Bear in mind that the only controller that Heyu supports is the CM11A, which is a very popular X10 controller. The lamp and appliance modules are just a good starting point and are available at local RadioShack stores, so they're easy to find and cheap to purchase (which is X10's biggest selling point).

## The software: Compiling Heyu

I've tested Heyu with my 2.6 kernel under Gentoo and my 2.4 kernel under Fedora FC2 , and it works fine.

To compile Heyu at the shell prompt, just follow these steps. (Further details are available on the CD.)

1. **If you aren't already logged in as a user (you probably shouldn't log in as root), log in.**

2. **When prompted for your password, enter it.**

   If you're logging into X, you'll get your default desktop. If you're logging into a console (or via telnet), you'll get a shell.

3. **If you aren't using a GUI, open a terminal command line window.**

4. **In the terminal window or shell, type** su – **(that's a hyphen, and yes, you need it) and press Enter. When prompted for a password, enter your root password.**

   Normally you shouldn't be logged in as root unless you're doing system administration work. Software installation is one of those duties.

5. **If you haven't already done so, insert the CD into your CD drive. If Linux doesn't automount the drive, type** mkdir –p /media/disk ; mount /dev/hdc /media/disk **and press Enter.**

6. **Type** cd **and press Enter.**

   This takes you back to root's home directory.

7. **Next, untar the file by typing** tar zxf heyu-2.0beta.5.tgz **and pressing Enter.**

8. **Change directory to where Heyu's files are by typing** cd heyu-2.0beta.5 **and pressing Enter.**

9. **Configure Heyu for your system by typing** ./Configure **and pressing Enter.**

   You should see the configuration routine busy working its magic.

10. **Compile all the files by typing** make **and press Enter.**

    Again you'll see lots of information about what make is doing. You may see a few warnings, too, but you can ignore them.

11. **Install all the files by typing** make install **and pressing Enter.**

12. **Copy the Heyu configuration file by typing** cp /media/disk/chapter13/x10config /etc/heyu/x10.conf **and pressing Enter.**

    This is the location of the default configuration file for Heyu.

13. **With your favorite editor, edit the /etc/heyu/x10.conf file by changing the line that starts with TTY to the serial port you intend to use.**

    If the TTY line begins with a # (hash symbol), remove the # because it comments out the line (meaning the program ignores the line). I defaulted the TTY line to /dev/ttyS0, the first serial port (the only serial port on my computer; you might have additional choices on your computer).

14. **Find and change the lines that start with the LATITUDE and LONGITUDE settings. (Remove the # if the line starts with it.)**

    Go to www.heavens-above.com/countries.asp to find the latitude and longitude settings of where you live.

15. **When you're done with your changes, save the file.**

    Heyu has all sorts of bells and whistles, including scheduling, scripting, and downloadable macros.

    To find out more about these features, simply type **man *subject***, where ***subject*** is one of the following: **heyu, x10config, x10sched,** or **x10scripts.**

## *The hardware*

After you have Heyu compiled and installed correctly (see the preceding section), the next step is to hook up the hardware:

1. **Hook your CM11A and serial cable to your serial port (the one you configured Heyu for in Step 13 of the preceding numbered step list).**

   I used /dev/ttyS0. It's the only serial port on the back of my computer.

2. **Take your lamp module or appliance module and set its house code and unit code.**

   The factory default is A1, which is fine for testing, but I recommend using something else. I describe how to set up the modules in the next section.

If you've gotten to this point with no errors, you're ready to go. (Cool!)

## Module setup

X10 modules are pretty easy to install: Just set the house and unit codes (turn each dial until they're set), plug in the appliance, and plug the module into the wall. The module is pretty much ready to use. Some vendors use a push-button interface to set the device (such as some Smarthome modules) or use specially sequenced X10 commands to set the modules (such as ACT). The easiest way to find out how to set your module is to check the user's manual.

Planning how to make the best use of the entire range of house and unit codes isn't difficult. Some people use one or two house codes (A through P) and all the unit codes (1 through 16). Others, like myself, assign each house code to a room or space around the house. I keep all the assignments in a file so I know what's where. See Table 13-1 for an example of my current setup.

| Table 13-1 | My X10 House Code Assignments | | |
|---|---|---|---|
| *House Code* | *Room Description* | *House Code* | *Room Description* |
| A | Testing | I | Master bathroom |
| B | Study | J | Bedroom #1 |
| C | Computer room | K | Bedroom #2 |
| D | Washroom | L | Master bedroom |
| E | Bathroom (downstairs) | M | Garage |
| F | Living room | N | Back yard |
| G | Dining room | O | Front yard |
| H | Kitchen | P | Miscellaneous usage |

X10 modules have an address, the house code and unit code, that needs to be set. By default, the house code is set to A, and the unit code is set to 1. This is fine for testing, but for actual use, I recommend changing it. You can even have multiple modules on the same house and unit code. The fun really begins when a nearby neighbor is also using X10 and is using the same addresses as you are. Although this usually isn't a problem because the transceiver's signal isn't that strong, sometime conflicts occur. It isn't so bad if you're friends with your neighbor and you can agree to a compromise. If you have grumpy old Mr. Wilson for a neighbor, though, you need a whole house blocker, and it's probably a good idea to let a certified electrician install it.

Here are some rules for X10 house and unit codes:

- ✔ Try to avoid using the house codes A, B, M, and P initially. The house code A is the default setting. Anyone in your neighborhood might just leave the module set to the default, not knowing others might also be using it. House codes B and P are just one click away and the next most likely house codes to be used. Use them for testing or for less-important, automation tasks. House code M is a bit odd. When some X10 devices lose their little electronic minds, they send out a continuous stream of M13 or M All Units Off commands, or they think they see those commands. By not using M, or at least not M13, you avoid confusion when debugging a problem on the M house code. Because you have nothing on M, you know it's an X10 device that's lost it's mind.

- ✔ You can set different modules to the same house and unit code. This allows many devices to be turned on or off, dimmed, or brightened at the same time.

- ✔ You can set different types of modules, such as lamp and appliance modules, to the same house and unit code. A dim command sent to an appliance module will be ignored, but the lamp module will respond to the command.

# Cool Things to Do with X10

In the previous section, "Building a Starter Kit," I take you through the processes of setting up your interface, your module, and the software. After you complete those steps, the next thing you do is start having fun — that is, actually using X10. To name just a few things to do with X10, you can set up an egg timer, time things to turn on around sunrise and sunset, and allow your printer's power to be controlled by X10. (Sound good? I hope so because that's what I've got for you in this section.)

The most basic Heyu commands are on and off. Now, although typing commands at the command line can be useful, flipping a switch to turn things on and off is a lot easier. Unless, of course, you're miles away from your home and you're turning things off and on. (Of course, this lowers your SAF! For more about this phenomenon, check out the "Spouse Acceptance Factor" sidebar in this chapter.) To send a command by using X10, simply type the following at the command line:

```
heyu command housecodeunitcode
```

Just replace *command* with the command, such as on or off, and replace *housecodeunitcode* with the house and unit codes, such as a1.

The egg timer and CUPS (Common UNIX Printing System) backend scripts both use an appliance module. You might be able to substitute a lamp module for the egg timer, but don't use the printer with a lamp module.

Never use lamp modules on any device with a *wall wart* (a power supply that converts AC to DC) or which has active electronics (such as TVs, computers, or stereos). These devices aren't made to handle being dimmed, and using a lamp module can damage the devices (sometimes very slowly). Lamp modules should be used only with things that are dimmable. Plain light bulbs (not the low-voltage type) and some fluorescent bulbs are dimmable (they state such on the package).

## Egg timer

This little program came about because I have an EPROM erasure that needs about 5 minutes to erase an EPROM (yes, I still have a need of EPROMs). I hated sitting there waiting for the 5 minutes to pass, so I created a script called et. No, not that E.T.! This et is short for egg timer. Basically, you type et 5, and the command turns on an X10 appliance module, waits 5 minutes, and turns it off again. I have egg timer set as an alias (the address of the X10 module to be controlled) in my x10.conf file. Listing 13-1 shows the script, which really isn't too complicated (most of it is comments).

### Listing 13-1:   The Egg Timer Script

```
#!/bin/bash
# Egg Timer

# Help message
if [ $# -ne 1 ]; then
    echo "Usage $0 TIME"
    echo
    echo "Start the egg timer X10 module and turn"
```

```
        echo "it off TIME minutes later Where TIME"
        echo "can be an integer or a decimal (to"
        echo "get minutes and seconds)"
        echo "Example"
        echo "        ${0} 1.5"
        echo "This will turn on the egg timer X10"
        echo "module and then turn it off 1 minute"
        echo "and 30 seconds later (90 seconds)"

        exit 1
fi

Arg1=${1}
Arg1=${Arg1:="0"} # if there is no argument set it to 0

# bc is the binary calculator

# Perform simply math on it (${Arg1} times 60).
Time=`echo "${Arg1}*60"| bc | cut -d . -f1`

# Turn on the eggtimer X10 module
# The eggtimer alias must be defined in the X10.conf
# file
heyu on eggtimer

# Put the next command into the background so we don't #
#       have to wait for it to complete, it will go off
#       in
# ${Time} seconds
(sleep ${Time}; heyu off eggtimer) &

echo "The Egg timer will go off in ${Time} seconds."
```

You don't have to type this in. It's on the CD in `/media/disk/chapter13/`
`eggtimer` called `et`. For these steps, I'm assuming that you're still logged in
and the CD is still mounted. (If not, follow Steps 1 through 4 in the section
"The software: Compiling Heyu," earlier in this chapter.) To install `et`, follow
these steps:

1. **Type** cp /media/disk/chapter13/eggtimer /usr/bin/et **and press Enter.**

   If your CD automounts to a different mount point, adjust the path
   (/media/disk/) accordingly.

2. **Type** chmod 755 /usr/bin/et **and press Enter.**

You're now ready to use the `et` command. The script takes the first argument
(the number of minutes to run), does some math, turns on the egg timer, and
sends a set of commands into the background that turns off the egg timer in
`${Time}` minutes. While that's waiting to turn off the egg timer, you can continue with other things. Now you're beginning to automate!

## Sunrise, Sunset

The CD contains a set of sunrise and sunset programs and scripts. For these steps, I'm assuming that you're still logged in and the CD is still mounted. (If not, follow Steps 1 through 4 in the section, "The software: Compiling Heyu," earlier in this chapter.) To install the sunrise/sunset application, follow these steps:

1. **Type** cp /media/disk/chapter13/sun* /usr/bin/ **and press Enter. This will install all of the scripts in the directory /usr/bin/**

2. **Now you need to make the scripts executable, so type** chmod 755 /usr/bin/sun*.sh **and press Enter.**

   (To find out what 755 really means, type **man chmod** and read through the man page.)

3. **Type** cd **and press Enter.**

   This takes you back to root's home directory.

4. **Next, untar the file by typing** tar zxf /media/disk/chapter13/today.tgz **and pressing Enter.**

5. **Change directory to where the today files are by typing** cd today **and pressing Enter.**

6. **Edit the** Make **(use you favorite editor) and change the strings** Summer **and** Winter **to your time zones (the settings are currently EDT and EST respectively).**

   To find your time zone, visit www.time.gov and click on your location.

7. **When you're done with your changes, save the file.**

8. **Compile and install the programs by typing** make sun **and pressing Enter.**

9. **Create a directory to store the sound files by typing** mkdir -p /usr/share/sounds **and pressing Enter.**

   Don't worry if you get an error that the directory already exists.

10. **Copy the sound files to the sound directory by typing** cp /media/disk/chapter13/*.wav /usr/share/sounds/ **and pressing Enter.**

    You may add any optional commands to the scripts /usr//bin/sunrise.sh (commands that run at sunrise) and /usr//bin/sunset.sh (commands that run at sunset). You can add your commands just after the line # add your commands below.

The key script is the sun script. It's small and uses the `at` command to run other scripts around the time of sunrise or sunset. Here it is:

```
:
#

BINPATH="/usr/local/bin"
# Returns the sunrise time, ex: 05:27
SUNSET=`${BINPATH}/sunset`
# Returns the sunset time, ex: 20:23
SUNRISE=`${BINPATH}/sunrise`

# Run the script at sunrise (its time changes daily)
at ${SUNRISE} -m -v -f ${BINPATH}/sunrise.sh
# Run the script at sunset (its time changes daily)
at ${SUNSET} -m -v -f ${BINPATH}/sunset.sh
```

The `at` command is a program that schedules commands or *scripts* (groups of commands) to be executed at a specific time in the future. The superuser (`root`) is permitted by default to use this command. To permit yourself and other users to use the `at` command, edit the `/etc/at.allow` file. For further information on `at`, go to a shell prompt and type **man at**.

The `at` command is a very useful command. Basically, it sets up a command you want to run at a specific time — in this case, sunrise and sunset. At sunrise, the shell script `sunrise.sh` gets run (put the commands you want run at sunrise in `sunrise.sh`), and at sunset, the shell script `sunset.sh` gets run (put the commands you want run at sunset in `sunset.sh`).

The sunrise and sunset scripts both can contain other UNIX commands (anything you want). You don't have to limit them to just Heyu. Included in the `sunrise.sh` script is the command for playing *Reveille,* and the `sunset.sh` script contains the command for playing *Taps.* To use either command (Reveille or Taps), simply uncomment it (remove the hash symbol (#) from the start of the line). Both sound files can be found in `/usr/share/sounds` after you install the sunrise/sunset package.

To make sunrise/sunset complete, you need to add the sun script to the `crontab` file and run it at a minute after midnight (12:01 a.m. or 00:01 military time) every day. First, make sure you're logged in as a user and not as `root`. At the command line, type **crontab -e** and add the following line to the bottom of the file:

```
# Figure out Sunrise/Sunset times and schedule at
# those times
1 0 * * * /usr/bin/sun.sh
```

The first two lines are just comments; adding descriptive comments is always a good idea. The third line is formatted as minute, hour, day of the month, month, day of the week, and finally the command and its arguments. The asterisks match any time (such as any day of the month, as shown in the preceding example). You use the script sun.sh to calculate the times of sunset and sunrise. The script then uses the at command to schedule the sunset.sh and sunrise.sh scripts to run. I run them at 12:01 a.m. because it's the earliest I can calculate the sunrise and sunset for a given day.

You use the cron program to schedule commands and *scripts* (groups of commands) to be executed at specific times and dates, at regular intervals. These commands can be run on the minute, hour, day of the month, month, day of the week, or any combination of those options. To add commands to cron, you use the crontab command to put you into the editor to edit your crontab file. For further information on cron and crontab, get to a shell prompt and type **man cron** or **man crontab**. To schedule commands once but at a specific time, use the at command. (Type **man at** for further infomation.)

## X10-powered printer

The setup I have for printing uses CUPS (Common UNIX Printer System). I have my HP682C remotely connected to an HP Jetdirect EX print server. The reason for this setup is so my wife and I can share one printer from many computers. (Don't ask how many; it's too many.) I use Samba to share the printers with Windows and CUPS to share with the rest of my Linux computers and Samba. We can print from any computer in the house, and the pages come out in one place. Great, huh?

Although sharing one printer is a good idea, leaving it on all the time is a huge waste of energy. So here's an idea: Team up X10 with CUPS and turn on the printer only when you need it. (I found this answer after a great deal of research.) By adding a backend program, I can send a print job and the backend script turns on the printer before the print job gets sent to the printer. When the print job is done, the backend script turns off the printer.

### Things you're going to need

To take advantage of X10 and printing, you need a few things. The good news is that most of the items you probably already have. Here's what you need for this section:

- ✔ CUPS software
- ✔ A printer installed and running under CUPS
- ✔ My X10 backend script
- ✔ An X10 appliance module

The installed and working printer is important. You need the name of the printer so that you can modify the correct information to add the X10 control of the printer. If you can't remember the name of your printer, type (at the command line) **lpstat –a**. This lists the available printers. To make this script work, you need to modify the CUPS printer configuration file. Not-so-coincidentally, I tell you how to do that in the following section.

### The UNIX way

For these steps, I'm again assuming that you're still logged in and the CD is still mounted. If not, follow Steps 1 through 4 of the section "The software: Compiling Heyu," earlier in this chapter. At times, doing something via the command line is easier than point and click via a GUI. I think this is one of them. So, to the command line, Batman!

1. **Copy the new backend file to the CUPS backend directory by typing** cp /media/disk/chapter13/x10backend.pl /usr/lib/cups/backend/x10 **and pressing Enter.**

2. **Copy the script to turn off the printer by typing** cp /media/disk/chapter13/x10off.sh /usr/lib/cups/backend/ **and pressing Enter.**

3. **Make the scripts executable by typing** chmod a+x /usr/lib/cups/backend/x10* **and then pressing Enter.**

4. **Open your favorite editor and edit the** /etc/cups/printers.conf **file. Find the printer you currently have working under CUPS and prepend the** DeviceURI **line with** x10://.

   Say your printer is named bw. In your editor, you scroll down the <Printer bw> entry, and a few lines down, you find the DeviceURI line. Perhaps it looks like DeviceURI parallel:/dev/lp0. Your entry may differ slightly, but don't worry — the instructions are still the same. To add the X10 control to the device, you change the line to read DeviceURI x10://parallel:/dev/lp0.

   You should see a section that looks something like this:

```
<DefaultPrinter bw>
Info HP Deskjet 682C on HP JetDirect EX
Location Computer room HP Deskjet 682C
DeviceURI x10://parallel:/dev/lp0
State Idle
Accepting Yes
JobSheets none none
QuotaPeriod 0
PageLimit 0
KLimit 0
</Printer>
```

5. **Don't forget to save the file.**

6. **Set up your X10 module to a convenient address. (See the earlier section, "Module setup.")**

    You may have already done this earlier in the chapter.

7. **Insert the electrical plug for your printer into the outlet on the X10 appliance module and plug the module into the wall.**

8. **Edit `/etc/heyu/x10.conf` to add the alias `printer` with the module's settings.**

    For example, `ALIAS printer C5 StdAM`.

9. **Test run Heyu with your new alias: Type** heyu off printer **and press Enter.**

    The printer should now run. You might need to first turn on the printer (type **heyu on printer** and press Enter) before you can turn it off. Then leave it off.

10. **Restart CUPS by typing** /etc/init.d/cups restart **and pressing Enter.**

11. **Test your changes by typing** lp –d *bw* /media/disk/chapter13/blank **and pressing Enter. Replace** *bw* **with the name of your printer. If the printer you modified is the default printer (it will be if you only have one printer installed), you can type** lp /media/disk/chapter13/blank.

You should now see the power come on for your printer, and the print job should come out as it normally would. The test page is blank to save ink. Had this not been a test, the actual print job would have printed as it normally does. If the printer doesn't turn on or the printer job doesn't print, check the `/var/log/cups/error_log` for errors (towards the bottom of the file). If that doesn't help, drop by the forums (`www.linuxha.com/FD/php2/`) and post a question.

# Troubleshooting X10 Problems

If I had started this chapter with the troubleshooting information, you would have run for the hills and never used X10 for anything. After reading this section, you might wonder why anyone even uses X10. The reason I use it is that it's the best thing around for the price. If you're controlling holiday light displays, missing a single command isn't a big deal. To be safe, just send it twice. With a little work, you can get X10 to behave most of the time — and those times when it won't behave, well, I have enough information here to resolve those problems.

# Common problems

By *common,* I don't mean that you'll run into these problems often. I'm just saying that if you have a problem, it's likely one of these:

- **Phase problem:** In the United States, the majority of homes have a split-phased power system. This means that two 120V AC lines are brought in from the power company, and each phase is separate. The two phases are distributed to the fuse panel and then to each half of the house. If you're using X10 and half the house appears to be dead, you might need an X10 phase coupler or amplified phase coupler. If your home is more than 2,500 square feet, you need the amplified phase coupler. My home is only 1,800 square feet, but I found that I need an amplified phase coupler. You can purchase a phase coupler from online stores like Smarthome.com.

- **Signal attenuation:** This is also known as a *black hole* or *signal sucker* — signal goes in but doesn't come out. As the X10 signal travels through your home, the signal becomes weaker. This is because various signal sucking devices suck the life out of the helpless signal. Some devices are worse than others. TVs, entertainment systems, computers, and peripherals are notorious X10 black holes. The solution is to put these devices on a filter such as a plug-in noise filter. You can purchase filters from the same place you purchase your modules.

- **UPS or battery backup power supplies:** Three problems occur with power supplies. The first is putting an X10 module behind a UPS (uninterruptible power supply). This doesn't work because the UPS filters out any *noise* (anything that's not 120V AC), and X10 looks like noise. The solution here is not to put X10 behind the UPS. The second problem is the UPS can be a black hole. A properly rated filter will take care of this problem. The third issue is trying to use a UPS to replace the AC during a power loss. This won't work on most UPS's because the UPS only approximates the shape of the AC. It's close enough to provide temporary power for computer equipment but not good enough for X10.

- **Baby monitors:** Wireless baby monitors and intercoms that use the AC both cause problems with X10. The only solution is not to use the monitor or the intercom.

- **Whole house blockers:** Sometimes X10 signals can enter your home from a neighbor's home. A *whole house blocker* stops your X10 signals — that use your home's electrical wiring — from leaving your home and outside X10 signals from entering your home. You can purchase a whole house blocker from online stores like Smarthome.com. In all my time using X10, I haven't run into anyone else using X10 whose house is on the same power transformer as mine. But if I did, I might need a whole house blocker to keep my neighbor's signals from entering my home. A whole house blocker does nothing to stop *wireless* X10 signals from exiting or enter your home because wireless X10 doesn't use your home's electrical system.

✔ **Stuck CM11A:** This problem drives me nuts from time to time. The power in my area isn't the greatest, so we occasionally have brownouts or full blackouts. When power is restored, my CM11A usually doesn't quite work correctly. The fix is to use something that will send an X10 signal on the AC. When the CM11A sees the signal, it's unstuck. My favorite device to unstick the CM11A is my X10 Powerhouse Remote and RR501 (X10 wireless). Alternatively, you can just use a minicontroller (X10 PLC).

✔ **Local control:** Some appliance modules support a feature called *local control*. What this does is allow the user to manually turn the device on, then off, and then on again. How does this work? It permits a small amount of current to pass through the module to the device. However, sometimes local control causes problems for things such as routers and firewalls. One solution is to add an extension cord and plug in the device and a small 7-watt nightlight with tape over the sensor. Another solution is to open up the module and clip a diode. More information can be found at Ido Bartana's Web page: www.geocities.com/ido_bartana. There, you can find instructions, warnings, and pictures on how to perform the modification.

✔ **Dimmers and X10:** Cheap wall switch dimmers are electrically very noisy and cause all sorts of problems with X10. Sometimes, X10 fails to work when the dimmer is in use. Other times, it causes the X10 module to heat up, which shortens the lifespan of the X10 module. Solution: Try another dimmer switch.

Watch your ratings! Each X10 device has an electrical rating on it stating how much power it can handle. Amp, horsepower, and watt are units of power, and each household device (such as a lamp, a TV, or a fan) has a power rating on a label found on the device. So why the different ratings? Well, each appliance has a different starting and running power characteristic. Your home wiring, fuses, and switches can handle this just fine, but the X10 module's electronics have a tougher time. The best way to keep from damaging the module's electronics is to not exceed the ratings. A RadioShack Heavy Duty Appliance Module (61-2684B) can handle

✔ Resistive load (a heater) 15A (amp)

✔ Motor load 1/3 HP (horsepower)

✔ Incandescent lamp 500W (watt)

✔ TV 400W

# Isolating a problem

If you intend to use X10 for anything more than holiday lights, I recommend that you get an ELK ESM1-X10 Signal Meter. (See Figure 13-1.) This inexpensive device can easily save you lots of time. The meter displays the X10 signal strength and has an LED that indicates that the signal is good. This will keep you from having to turn off the circuit breakers.

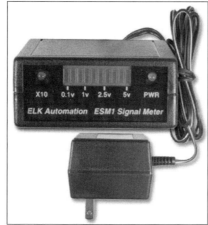

**Figure 13-1:**
ELK ESM1-
X10 Signal
Meter.

If you're doing serious X10 work, get the ACT AT004 Multi-Tester. This baby is expensive, but it can send any X10 signal, adjust the power output, and do many more complicated functions. I had a chance to use it while testing some new ACT switches and found it to be a great tool. By the way, I love the ACT switches — they have neat features, offer excellent reliability, and they're well worth the extra money.

If you don't have an ESM1, you can test each circuit by performing the following steps:

1. **Turn off each circuit in order, one at a time, at the circuit breaker. Don't turn off the circuit you have your CM11A or X10 module on.**

2. **Test the X10 device to see whether the problem goes away and that the device works properly. To test, just send an X10 command to the address of the module in question.**

3. **If the device doesn't start working, turn the circuit back on and continue to the next circuit (the next switch in the circuit breaker box).**

4. **When you find the troublesome circuit, turn it back on and start unplugging the devices in the circuit, one at a time, until you find the troublemaker.**

Generally, start with TVs, entertainment systems, computers, and so forth — the devices that have active electronics. When you find the troublemaker, put a plug-in noise filter on it, and that should solve the problem.

If you have the EMS1, you don't need to turn off the circuits. Start by plugging the ESM1 into the same circuit as the CM11A. Then, at the command line, run this shell script (it's on the CD and it's called debug_x10):

```
#/bin/bash
#
while `true`    # Loop forever
do
   heyu on m13  # You are not using M13 right?!
done
```

This sends a nice continuous stream of X10 packets into the circuit. A good signal is close to 5v; the minimum valid X10 signal is 100mv. Anything less is not a good signal. Simply move the ESM1 around to each circuit until you find a weak or nonexistent signal. Then start unplugging devices on the circuit until you have a good signal. When you find the troublemaker, put a plug-in noise filter on it, and that should solve the problem. Oh, and remember to plug everything back in to help keep you out of trouble with your spouse.

# Chapter 14

# Going Wireless with X10

*W*elcome to X10 wireless, X10's other half. If you've read Chapter 13, you'll be familiar with some of the concepts used in X10. If not, don't worry — I explain enough to give you a firm basis for using X10 wireless. In the preceding chapter, I discuss using the X10 PLC (power line carrier) technology over your home's AC electrical system. The X10 PLC modules and controllers need to be plugged in to take advantage of X10 to control devices plugged into the modules (such as lamps). See Figure 14-1 for a typical home setup with X10 wireless.

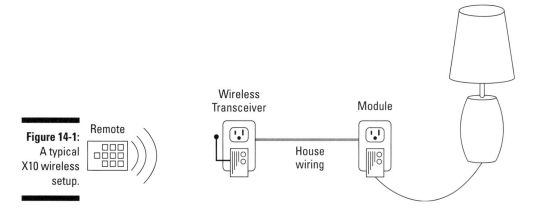

**Figure 14-1:** A typical X10 wireless setup.

Wireless X10 extends your reach by using wireless controllers. X10 has controllers that look like a TV remote, a wall switch, keychain fob, or even a credit card. These controllers are mated to a wireless transceiver, which you plug into a wall, and they're used to convert the signals sent wirelessly to the power line signals. This allows you to control a number of other X10 devices that are on the same unit code. These remotes have a range of about 25 to 50 feet from remote to transceiver. Distances depend on obstacles such as walls and floors.

X10 wireless isn't secure! Anyone with an X10 wireless remote that's set to the same house code as your transceiver can send commands to your X10 network. (To see what I mean, see the "X10 wireless is not secure!" sidebar elsewhere in this chapter.) This might not be too much of a problem if the other person using the remote isn't within 30 to 40 feet of the receiver. As long as you're aware of this, it's still okay to use X10 wireless in your home. Just don't put your security system on it.

# Getting Familiar with the X10 Interfaces

You use X10 modules to control the appliances plugged into the module. Each module has an X10 address that is made up of a house code (A through P) and a unit code (1 through 16). You set the X10 address by turning the dials found on the front of the module. Modules don't need to have unique addresses. This can be very useful when you want a group of appliances (such as lamps) to execute the same command at the same time. I recommend that each room be given a house code and that you use the unit codes as needed. See Chapter 13 for more about the X10 addresses.

X10 commands are made up of the address and the command to initiate. You can send these commands via a table-top remote (you press a button and the command is sent) or a computer interface (you use a program to control the interface). Although the remote is nice to have, the computer interface gives you the power of automation. Appliances that you normally turn on each day at a specific time can be automated on the computer. It becomes a set-it-and-forget-it type of setup.

X10 has quite a list of modules, remotes, and interfaces for you to work with. Here are some of the devices that are available for use with X10 wireless:

- X10 wireless computer interfaces:
    - **CM17A:** X10's RS232 wireless transmitter
    - **MR26A:** X10's RS232 wireless receiver
    - **CM19A:** X10's USB wireless transceiver
    - **CM15A:** X10's USB PLC and wireless transceiver
- Wireless modules
    - **TM751:** X10's wireless appliance module and receiver
    - **RR501:** X10's wireless appliance module and 2-way transceiver

✔ Wireless remotes

- **UR19A:** Wireless remote
- **KR19A (SlimFire):** Wireless keychain remote
- **KR22A:** Wireless credit card remote

✔ Wireless kits

- **CK18A:** X10's wireless kit

X10 is now supporting the CM15A and has discontinued the CM17A, MR26A, and CM19A controllers (computer interfaces). The CM15A is too new to have software available for Linux. (The Linux community doesn't have the details to program the new device yet.) But not to worry! There are plenty of places on the Internet where you can purchase these devices. And the X10 devices are very popular with online auctions. I did a search and found several CM17As still available, and I expect that they will be available for quite a while to come. If you can, try to get the CM18A kit because it's usually a better deal than the CM17A alone. The kit comes with the CM17A Firecracker, Palmpad Remote, a lamp module, and a TM751 wireless transceiver.

The CM17A is an X10 wireless transmitter that isn't limited to a single house code (as are the wireless remotes). It can send to all 16 house codes and all 16 unit codes (for a total of 256 unique X10 addresses). The TM751 transceiver has a built-in module for controlling appliances. This module can be controlled only by wireless signals. If you'd like a wireless transceiver that can accept both the power line and wireless commands, the RR501 transceiver is probably a better choice than the TM751. Both the TM751 and the RR501 translate the wireless command to a PLC command so that other modules can also be controlled. Both transceivers are limited to a single house code. This means that if the CM17A transmits an X10 command for J1 (house code J, unit code 1), a wireless transceiver with a house code set for A won't translate the command for J onto the power line. But it can translate any X10 command with an A house code.

# Gathering the Tools

In this chapter, I show you how to use the CM17A, a wireless X10 computer interface, to send X10 commands from your computer to X10 transceivers and modules. You have a choice of issuing an X10 command from either the command line (using the BottleRocket command, `br`) or a Web interface provided by your Web server and BlueLava. BlueLava acts as a frontend to the BottleRocket command. You will be able to access the Web interface from other browsers, not just those on your Linux computer. Here's a list of what you need:

- ✔ Software
  - httpd, Apache Web server (included with most distributions)
  - Perl (included with most distributions)
  - GCC compiler
  - BlueLava (on this book's CD, `bluelava-0.4.3a.tar.gz`)
  - BottleRocket (on this book's CD, `bottlerocket-0.04c.tar.gz`)
- ✔ Hardware
  - An available serial port
  - Firecracker (X10 CM17A); costs about $17 on auction sites
  - X10 wireless module (X10 RR501, PAT01, or TM751); costs about $15–$25 at auction sites
- ✔ Optional
  - Additional X10 modules; they cost about $10–$50 at `www.smarthome.com`
  - Palmpad wireless remote; costs about $20 from X10
  - A keychain remote; costs about $20 from X10
  - A credit card remote; costs about $20 from X10

## Software

httpd is the Apache Web server that comes with most distributions. It's version 2.0, but if you're running a system with Apache 1.2, it should work. The Perl programming language also comes with most distributions. I'm using Perl version 5.8, but BlueLava should work with Perl version 5.6. All the recent distributions of Linux use Perl 5.8. I'm not sure about using Perl 6.0 (it's too new), so I don't recommend it at this time. The BottleRocket software package needs to be compiled, and any version of the GNU C compiler should work.

BlueLava is the Web frontend, the software you'll access with your Web browser. BlueLava was created by Bruce A. Locke and is now maintained by Ian Wilkinson. BottleRocket is the Firecracker software. BottleRocket sends the X10 commands to the CM17A; Tymm Twillman created it, but I now maintain it.

## Hardware

You need an unused serial port. There is one limitation on the kind of serial port you may use: It must support control of the RS232 leads (DTR and RTS specifically). Some USB adapters, such as those that support connectivity to PDAs, don't support control of the RS232 leads. I don't know of any other serial ports that have a problem with controlling the RS232 leads.

After you've decided on the port, just plug in the CM17A and make a note of the serial port. It's usually something like `/dev/ttyS0` for COM1 or `/dev/ttyS1` for COM2. If you want, you can use a serial cable to move it away from the back of the computer. This might help with the distance the signal can travel because the metal computer case can block the X10 signal.

# Setting Up the X10 Wireless Network

It's time to get busy with configuration, compilation, and installation (and I said it without inhalation) of the Apache (httpd), BlueLava, BottleRocket, and the CM17A — Firecracker and X10 wireless module.

## Setting up the X10 transceiver

Now would be a good time to set up the X10 transceiver, which is a simple process that involves setting the dials to the X10 address. The X10 transceiver has two dials: The top one is the unit code (1 through 16), and the bottom one is the house code (A through P). To change the unit and house code, you turn the appropriate dial to set the X10 address. By default, the address of a new module is set to A1.

The house code is very important because it's the house code that the wireless module will translate into a power line command. The house and unit code are the X10 address that the wireless module will listen to for commands, but the module will translate only X10 commands with the same house code. If you want to change it to something other than the default, you can. If you have a wireless remote, however, remember that the X10 house code that it transmits, as part of the X10 command, must also match that of the wireless transceiver so that it will translate or respond to the wireless commands. In other words, if you change the house code of the transceiver, you must also adjust the house code of the wireless remote so that they match.

The CM17A doesn't need to be set up for an X10 house code because it can send to any X10 address. As long as there is a wireless transceiver listening on that address, the command will be acted upon or passed to the power line.

# Starting the Apache http server (httpd)

If you have Fedora 4 and you've installed everything, you need to perform only a few commands to get httpd started. Other Linux distributions will require different amounts of work but will be similar to the instructions found here. If you don't have Apache installed on your system, you need to install it. Follow the directions for Apache at its home page: www.apache.org. Apache serves up the BlueLava Web pages. BlueLava, in turn, calls on BottleRocket to issue the X10 commands to the Firecracker, which sends the wireless X10 signal to the wireless receiver to turn on/off the device attached to the module. In Fedora, it's very easy to turn on the Web server — just follow these steps:

1. **Type** su - **and press Enter to switch user (su) to the** root **user. When you're prompted for** root**'s password, enter it.**

2. **Type** cd /etc/init.d **and press Enter.**

   This command puts you in the directory with the startup scripts.

3. **Type** chkconfig –list httpd **and press Enter.**

   This command checks to see what level the program will be run at. If you get and error here, you might not have Apache installed. This is what you should get back:

   ```
   # chkconfig --list httpd
   httpd           0:off  1:off  2:off  3:off  4:off  5:off  6:off
   ```

4. **Type** chkconfig –level 345 httpd on **and press Enter.**

   This turns the Web server on at levels 2, 3, 4, and 5. Next time you reboot, the Web server will automatically start on its own.

5. **Type** chkconfig –list httpd **and press Enter to double-check your work.**

   The output should look like this:

   ```
   # chkconfig --list httpd
   httpd           0:off  1:off  2:on  3:on  4:on  5:on  6:off
   ```

6. **Type** ./httpd start **and press Enter to start the Web server.**

   You see something like this:

   ```
   # httpd start
   Starting httpd:                                    [  OK  ]
   ```

If you use the chkconfig and set the levels that Apache will run at, you don't have to worry about restarting Apache each time you reboot Linux. It will come up automatically. You needed to start it only this one time because it wasn't told to start when you last rebooted. You now have your own private Web server on your machine. To see the Apache documentation, open your Linux Web browser and enter the following in your browser's address bar:

```
file:///var/www/manual/index.html.en
```

This is the English-language Web page, but Web pages are available in other languages, also. Just see the language links on the page.

# Installing BlueLava

Now that you've started the Apache http server (it must be running before BlueLava can be used), it's time to install BlueLava. To install it, follow these steps:

1. **Take the CD from the back of this book and insert it into your CD-ROM drive.**

2. **In your terminal window, type** cd /var/www/cgi-bin **and press Enter.**

   This is the default directory for Apache (httpd).

3. **Type** sudo tar jxvf /bluelava-0.4.4.tgz **and press Enter. When prompted for a password, type the user** root's **password.**

   This step installs BlueLava. Don't be surprised by the information that appears on the screen (unless it's an error); it's just there to let you know it's doing something.

4. **Type** cp -f /media/cdrom/chapter15/bluelava.conf.Fedora bluelava/ bluelava.conf **and press Enter.**

   This step installs the default `config` file for BlueLava. This step saves you from having to do manual editing of the `bluelava.conf` file.

# Installing BottleRocket

After you've installed the BlueLava application, you're almost ready to use it. The last software package to install is the BottleRocket. You have to configure, compile, and install BottleRocket. As scary as that sounds, it's actually just a few easy steps:

1. **With the book's CD still in the CD-ROM, type** cd **and press Enter at a command line.**

   BottleRocket is also included on the CD. Typing **cd** takes you back to your home directory.

2. **Type** tar zxvf /media/cdrom/chapter15/bottlerocket-0.4c.tar.gz **and press Enter.**

3. **Type** cd bottlerocket-0.04c **and press Enter.**

4. **Type** cp Makefile Makefile.bak **and press Enter.**

5. **Type** sed -e 's/ttyS0/*SomethingElse*/g' <Makefile.bak >Makefile **and press Enter.**

   Just change *SomethingElse* to the serial port you connected the CM17A to (see the "Hardware" section earlier in this chapter). If it's /dev/ttyS0, you can use just the ttyS0.

6. **Type** ./configure **and press Enter.**

7. **Type** sudo make install **and press Enter.**

## Configuring BlueLava

Before you can use your X10 wireless network, you have one last stage in the setup process to complete: You have to configure BlueLava. So open up your favorite browser and enter this link into the address bar:

```
http://127.0.0.1/bluelava/bluelava.cgi
```

There's no need to replace the IP address with another because this one is correct. BlueLava permits you to configure it only from this address. You can use BlueLava from your server's IP address, but to configure it, you must use the preceding link. After you open the link, the BlueLava greeting screen appears.

Although you shouldn't need to make any changes to the config file, it's a good idea to inspect the settings to make sure they're correct. Click the link titled BlueLava Settings (Figure 14-2) and make sure that the backend that is selected is BottleRocket and that the backend setting is set to /usr/local/bin/br. For now, leave the rest of the settings as they are. If you make any changes, make sure that you save them.

When you're satisfied with the setting and you've saved any changes, you can proceed to the room setup. Here, you can add rooms and devices to be accessed via the BlueLava Web interface. Click the Room Setup link and follow these steps:

1. **Add a room under the Room Name input box and call it whatever you like.**

   In Figure 14-3, you can see that I've already added CR (computer room) and Living Room.

2. **Save your entry by clicking the Save Rooms button.**

   Now you can add a unit (an X10 module).

3. **Examine the house and unit dials on the front of the X10 wireless transceiver to find the X10 address of the transceiver.**

   The default setting is A1.

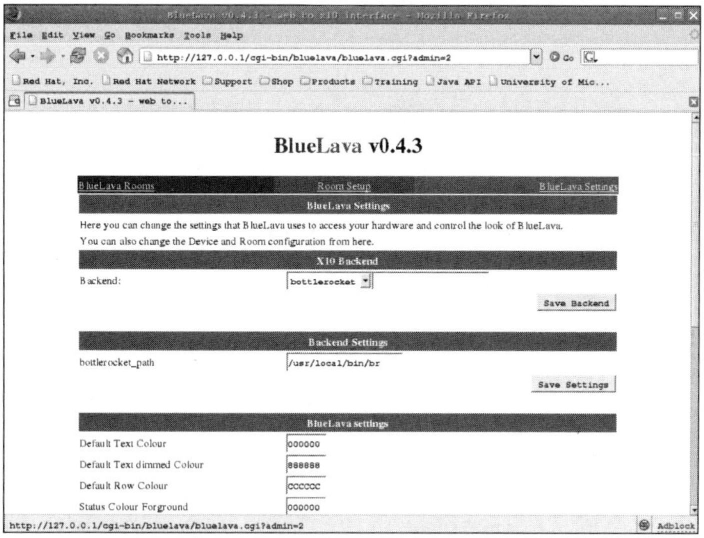

**Figure 14-2:**
The
BlueLava
admin
screen.

4. **Enter the X10 address of the X10 wireless module into the Unit Code input box.**

5. **Choose a Type from the drop-down menu next to your Unit Code entry.**

A transceiver can only be an appliance, so select Appliance. If you're entering other modules, select the one that is appropriate for your module.

**Figure 14-3:**
The
BlueLava
rooms
screen.

## X10 wireless is not secure!

Anyone with an X10 wireless remote that's set to the same house code as your transceiver can send commands to your X10 network. To give you an idea of what can happen, here's a nice story: While working on this chapter, I needed to fix a problem I was having with the X10. I'd turn something on and it would go on and then off a second later. I must have spent an eternity trying to figure out what X10 device was sending the contradicting commands. (Yeah, I have more than a few X10 devices.) After a while, I notice a giggling coming from another room that happens to coincide with the device change state. Then I noticed that one of my remotes was missing from its place beside the phone. My wife was having some fun at my expense (and my sanity). Ha, ha, honey, you've now been mentioned in the book. I hope you're happy.

6. **Enter a short description of the device, something that makes sense to you (like "test device").**

7. **Select the room you added at the start of these steps.**

8. **Now that everything is entered, click the Save Units button to save your work.**

## Using your wireless X10 network

When you're ready to start using BlueLava to control your modules, click the BlueLava Rooms link to access the links to turn on and off X10 modules. At this time, you can control only the one module (unless you purchased more modules). To turn on the module, click the On link for that device (the X10 module). To turn it off, click the Off link. If you have a lamp module and you've added it, try the dim and brighten commands. Those commands are ignored by the appliance modules. Remember that lamp modules can be used only with incandescent lamps.

As you add modules, make sure that the house code matches that of the X10 wireless transceiver. If you want to access other house codes, you need to purchase more wireless transceivers and set them to the desired house code.

# Part VI

# Controlling and Securing Your Automation Network

## In this part . . .

MisterHouse might not slice and dice and puree, but it does just about everything else. Part VI covers MisterHouse, an open source home automation program written in Perl. By adding your own Perl code, you can customize MisterHouse to your heart's content. But that's not all! In this part, you also find out how MisterHouse can extend your control of X10; you discover how to use the Web interface; and, with a bit of Linux security, you gain access to MisterHouse from any location that has an Internet connection.

# Chapter 15

# Controlling Your House with MisterHouse

A sk any geek what one thing he or she wants most to computerize; I guarantee that his or her home is right there at the top of the list. I've dreamed of automating my home since 1978. My first setup included a Heathkit X10 interface and my Atari 800. X10 wasn't really useful, though, until 1998, when Bruce Winter wrote MisterHouse (MH), an open source home automation program written in Perl. MH was originally written to control just X10 under Linux. Now MH runs on Linux, Mac, and even (yuck) Windows. Kidding aside, that is one major accomplishment — one program, many operating systems! There are now several hundred contributors to MH. Each contributor adds modules, writes documentation, fixes bugs, and does other assorted tasks.

Bruce still actively maintains MH, and there is a very active developer mail list. One of the things that makes MH troublesome to use is that it has a steep learning curve. There is so much that you can do with it that you can become overwhelmed and have no idea where to start. So that's why I wrote this chapter! I can't show you everything there is to know about MH, but I do show you how to install and configure it and then add a few features — enough to get you started and feeling comfortable with MH.

## Introducing X10 and MisterHouse

I remember my first setup — a Heathkit X10 interface and my Atari 800. I wasn't really allowed to control much because I was in my parents' home, but it whetted my appetite for home automation (HA). Later, when I moved into an apartment, I had an AT&T UNIX personal computer and a RadioShack CP290. It was great because I could turn things on and off by using `cron` and various other UNIX commands. UNIX gave me a lot more flexibility. The apartment I was living in was small, and X10 was still very difficult to use. My wife was not happy with X10's performance, so I still wasn't doing very much with it.

Several years later, my wife and I moved into a house. At last! Now was my chance to finally control the world — err, start automating my home (yeah, that's it!). At that time, Linux was an up-and-coming operating system, and my UNIX PC was on its last legs. My friend Donald gave

me a CM11A kit for Christmas, and I started using X10 again. It was at this time that I also created a Web page. I collected links, software, and information to help other nonWindows users get support for HA. Since then, I've run all sorts of software to automate my home. Many fine programs are available, but none quite fit my needs perfectly.

When MH first came out, I wasn't too keen on the idea of a program written in Perl. I thought it would be slow and resource intensive because it's interpreted just like BASIC was in my old Atari 800. My machine was a slow 133MHz Pentium processor with lots of RAM. MH worked well on the machine — only the speech processing would not run. As I used MH more and more, it grew on me because it's both flexible and extensible. I describe how exactly in the "Introducing MisterHouse" section of this chapter.

# Introducing MisterHouse

Over the years, a number of contributors to MH have added support for all sorts of interesting devices that allow you to manage, monitor, and control things around the house. The one thing MH has going for it is its flexibility and extensibility. Initially, the only home automation (HA) protocol that MH understood was X10, which has a reputation for unreliability because it's an *open loop protocol* — where a command is sent and no acknowledgement is returned. You have no idea whether the command did anything, and you can't find out, either. A *closed loop protocol* requires some kind of feedback. If you send out a command, you can get an acknowledgement (the command executed okay); get a negative acknowledgement (oops, something's wrong, try again); or get no acknowledgement (wow, something's really wrong). Two new HA protocols — both closed loop — are now available, and they are being worked into MH:

- Insteon (www.insteon.net)
- UPB (www.pulseworx.com), which stands for Universal Powerline Bus

I've recently added Insteon support to MH. Insteon is similar to X10 but much better because it fixes a lot of things that were weak in the X10 protocol. Another gentleman is writing an interface to UPB (such as Insteon), and others have added support to use Internet tablets (such as the Nokia 770 and 3Com Audrey). Today, I use MH to control my X10 and Insteon modules, get my weather station information, get my favorite comics, and do a whole lot more!

## The MisterHouse interfaces

When you first start MH from the command line, MH presents you with a choice of two different user interfaces. If everything you need is loaded on your machine, the Tk interface (see Figure 15-1 later in the chapter) will display on your screen. I don't use Tk much, so I don't discuss it much, other than to introduce it to you. You can turn off the Tk interface by using the -tk 0 option or by making a change in the mh.private.ini file (more on that in a moment). This is especially useful when you have MH start up at boot (like I do) and you aren't logged in. This allows MH to run as a *daemon,* a program that runs in the background doing its work, usually unnoticed by you and the rest of the world. (Daemons are not malicious programs that try to hide their presence. Actually, they're rather helpful programs that automatically run at startup while allowing you to do other things.)

To access MH in this configuration, you simply enter into your browser's address bar: http://127.0.0.1:8080/ (but not now). Most people prefer the browser interface to MH (shown later in Figure 15-2) because it's fairly flexible, easy to use, and pleasant to look at. Because you need to configure MH, you will be using the browser interface. I recommend you leave JavaScript on because it provides useful features when using MH.

Command input comes from a number of interfaces. MH can also accept commands via instant messaging (AOL, MSN, Yahoo!, and Jabber), via e-mail, via SMS, and even via a telnet interface. You have to use a secure application to log in to MH over the Internet, and I get into ways of doing that in Chapter 18.

## So what can MisterHouse do?

MH can manage, monitor, and control information and devices in your home — in short, MH can interface to just about anything. Only your willingness to do it, your imagination, and perhaps, in rare cases, your soldering skills are your limits. Don't worry; you aren't required to solder, but if you can, be aware that a few people have created some really neat things that you can build. Sometimes they sell these neat things in kits, and you can assemble the thing yourself. Sometimes people sell ready-made kits. A good example is Dave Houston's BX24-AHT (discontinued) and his roZetta board, which is a work in progress.

Dave's boards can handle things like barometric pressure, X10, wireless X10, receiving most radio frequency (RF), converting RF to IR, receiving IR, interfacing to the CM11A, and the Ocelot (another HA controller). All this is connected to one serial port (no wasted serial ports here) and controlled by MH. Basically, if you can imagine it, there are people who can figure out a way to interface to it.

So here is a quick review of what MH can access and/or control:

- ✔ **X10, Insteon, UPB, and EIB (European Installation Bus).** MH supports a variety of HA protocols and hardware (interfaces and modules).

- ✔ **Maxim One-wire devices, analog and digital I/O boards.** MH supports various sensors and I/O (input/output) for monitoring and control.

- ✔ **Other home automation systems, such as the HCS_C, HCS II, and Elk M1.** If you already have a security or an HA system, MH can interface to that system, providing further features that the original system didn't have or that were too expensive to add.

- ✔ **Automate home systems.** With MH, you can automate your home security system, telephone system, and heating/air conditioning systems.

- ✔ **Have your computer talk to you with text to speech (Festival).** By using a program called Festival, you can have MH speak to you. This is very useful for when people call your home. For example, if you have caller ID, you can set up MH to speak only the names of people who are on your okay list. Of course, you might agree with my wife that it's a bit nerve wracking to have the computer begin speaking when no one is around.

- ✔ **Monitor the weather.** By getting information from weather stations, MH can then parse the information and make decisions based on that information. A very good example is watering your lawn. I have a Rain8 X10 Irrigation Controller. I set up a schedule with MH, and it can get the weather report from the national weather service, see whether it's going to rain, and keep the sprinkler from running that day.

- ✔ **Calculate sunrise, sunset, and phases of the moon.** MH can help you turn lights on and off at sunrise or sunset. And tracking the phase of the moon can let you know when all the loonies are out on the road. There's just something about a full moon and crazy drivers. . . .

- ✔ **Play MP3s.** You can use MH to create a jukebox to listen to your MP3s.

- ✔ **Organizer and PDA interface.** MH has software to interface to your PDA (such as the Palm Pilot). MisterHouse has support for calendar, reminders, and phone book applications.

- ✔ **Download information from the Internet.** I enjoy getting my morning comics, but MH can also get breaking news, stock information, particular TV listings, top-ten lists, and more.

✔ **Automate kitchen appliances.** Using Insteon, UPB, or X10, you can program MH so you can schedule your tea machine to turn on before you wake up. (Sorry, my wife and I are not coffee drinkers.) Anyway, tea takes a bit of time to steep, so having it ready when I get up is a time saver. Although some coffee and tea machines already use timers to turn on, there are none that I know of that you can schedule to also make sure it's off when you leave. No more worrying about whether you left the machine on or not. It's off! You can also use the Web interface to tell MH not to start the tea machine at its normal time because you've decided to sleep in late.

✔ **Reboot routers.** You can use MH to reboot routers that no longer respond. Over the years, I've had a few firewall routers that were no longer supported by the manufacturer, yet they still ran quite well. Somewhere along the line, they develop a problem that won't be fixed, and they stop working until they're rebooted. You usually have to live with it until you can get a replacement. By using MH to ping the router, you can tell when it's working, and when it doesn't respond, you can use Insteon or X10 with MH to turn the router off and on again.

✔ **Regulate your Internet use.** You can extend this a little bit further by using MH to turn off your Internet connectivity at a certain time of day. This helps assure that bedtime is bedtime! You can also use MH to gather the statistics of how much traffic you're sending and receiving on an hourly, daily, weekly, and monthly basis. You can even make graphs of the data. These statistics are useful to know, especially when ISPs are keeping an eye on bandwidth hogs. (Thankfully, I'm not a bandwidth hog.)

You aren't limited to the HA protocols and hardware (Insteon, UPB, and EIB). MH can also use digital and analog I/O (input/output, interfaces you can monitor and control). However, I don't recommend it for the tea machine because a bird's nest of wires will probably scare anyone but the foolhardy from touching the tea machine. A nice Insteon module will work well for controlling small appliances.

# Installing MisterHouse

The good news is that MH is very easy to install. The problem is that after you have MH installed, you have to decide what you want to do. Like a kid in a candy store, you're probably going to want to do it all. I suggest that you tackle one topic at a time, starting with X10. After MH is installed and you've taken care of the initial configuration, you can begin playing with MH. From there, just take it one step at a time. But first things first — you have to get the thing installed before you can do anything else. So this section covers two topics: the logging in as `root` (for this chapter only) and the actual installation.

## Logging in as root

In this chapter, you need to be root whenever you're in a terminal window or at the command line interface. To find out whether you're root, simply type **id**. It should return a long string that starts with uid=0(root). This means you are root. If you don't get this in the return string or you're uncertain, simply type **su -** and press Enter. The command might ask you for a password, and you need to enter the user root's password. You should then get a prompt that looks something like this:

```
[ root@localhost ~]#
```

The prompt should end with #, which usually means you're logged in as root.

*Being root is powerful juju!* Being root means you have power to make changes to the entire system — or put another way, if you make a mistake, it could be permanent. Normally, you don't want to be root for anything other than system administration and installing. MH falls under that work. In this case, you'll be root for the entire chapter instead of being root for quick installs. So as you type in your commands, be wary of the directory you're in and be careful about what you type. Remember: If you want to browse the Internet, compose mail, or play games, do it as a normal user. Be root only when you have to be root.

## The installation

Before you can do anything fun with MH, you have to first install it. Here's what you need to start with:

- ✔ **Your favorite Linux distribution:** The Linux distribution is pretty obvious. I don't think you need the entire development environment, but my setup does have everything.

- ✔ **Perl 5.8 and a variety of modules:** Don't use Perl 6.0 because MH is not written for it, and I don't know whether MH will work properly with it. Most modern Linux distributions are still using Perl 5.8, so that version shouldn't be a problem.

- ✔ **A Web browser such as Firefox, Opera, or Konqueror:** MH is pretty flexible, and as long as you're using a modern graphical browser (sorry, Lynx won't cut it), you've met this requirement.

- ✔ **An X10 CM11A PC interface controller:** You need the CM11A for X10 control, an X10 module, and a device to be controlled. By the time this book is published, MH will also have support for Insteon and UPB. Currently, MH has support for controllers, but they require a much more difficult install.

## More MisterHouse to come!

I can't help you set up everything MH can do. Really, I'm sorry about that, but doing so would take a couple books all by itself. In this chapter, I can only introduce you to MH and help you install it, configure it, and add a few features for you to get comfortable with. I introduce you to enough topics to point you in the correct direction, and this introduction will make MH usable

home automation. The good news is that I include a couple more chapters on MH stuff:

- ✔ Chapter 16: Controlling X10 from MisterHouse
- ✔ Chapter 18: Remotely Accessing Your Mister-House Controls

✔ **At least one X10 module:** An appliance or lamp module is okay as long as the device you're plugging in works with the module. Remember that lamp modules are for lamps.

✔ **A device to plug into the X10 module:** Normally, I just use an extra lamp. I have a spare that a neighbor had tossed in the trash. This keeps my spouse happy and costs down. Waste not, want not.

✔ **Your favorite Linux text editor (optional):** Your favorite editor is pretty obvious. The vi editor is fine. I use emacs because I've used it since 1978. It isn't an easy editor to use, but it's very powerful. Most likely, you're running X11 (the graphical login) so gedit or kedit are fine. Whatever you do, don't edit the file with a DOS or Windows editor. (Yes, people still do.) Those editors tend to mess up the file.

MH can be installed anywhere on your system, but I recommend installing it like a package in /opt. In the past, I've actually installed MH in the directory /usr/local/; but I'm an old-school UNIX user, and some habits die hard. All new Linux distributions have the directory /opt. But not all have /usr/ local/, so the choice is probably a good one. If you decide to install it elsewhere, you'll need to make adjustments in various files to correct the PATH variable and to point the various options to the correct places so that MH can find everything. To install MH, make sure you're logged in as root, and then type these commands in a terminal window:

1. **Type** cd /opt **and press Enter.**

2. **Type** useradd -d /opt/mh -c MisterHouse -p MH mh **and press Enter.**

3. **Type** tar xzvf /media/disk/MisterHouse/misterhouse.tar.gz **and press Enter.**

4. **Type** mv misterhouse-*/* mh **and press Enter.**

5. **Type** mkdir mh/code/local **and press Enter.**

6. **Type** cp mh/bin/mh.ini mh/bin/mh.private.ini **and press Enter.**

7. **Type** cp /media/disk/MisterHouse/local/* mh/code/local/ **and press Enter.**

8. **Type** chown -R mh:mh mh **and press Enter.**

9. **Type** cp /media/cdrom/MisterHouse/mh.rc /etc/rc.d/init.d/mh **and press Enter.**

10. **Type** chkconfig –add mh **and press Enter.**

11. **Type** chkconfig -level 345 mh on **and press Enter.**

12. **Type** rm -rf misterhouse-* **and press Enter.**

That wasn't so bad was it? Here's a summary of what you just did:

In Step 2, you added the user, mh, with a home directory in /opt/mh/ and with a password of MH — which is a really bad password choice. Change it to something else, something more secure. This is the password used to log in as the user mh under Linux. It isn't the password for using MH via the Web interface. MH defaults to not asking for a password.

Next (Steps 3 and 4), you installed the MH package and put it into the /opt/mh directory.

Then, in Step 5, you created the user code directory /opt/mh/code/ local/ for local Perl code (code you add that is specific to this machine).

In Step 6 and 7, you copied some user files into the local directory. (I describe these a bit later in this chapter.)

Next (Step 8), you changed the owner and group on all the files and directories under /opt/mh to user mh. This allows the user mh to make changes to the various files.

In Steps 9 through 11, you installed the startup script and set it up to run at run levels 3, 4, and 5 (terminal and graphical modes 4 and 5).

Finally, in Step 12, you cleaned up the unneeded directory misterhouse-*. On your next reboot, MH will start automatically.

## Preparing MisterHouse for Setup

Now that MH is installed, be sure to have a look around before you start making changes (which I discuss in the next section, "Setting Up MisterHouse"). Don't worry that you haven't told it where to find the CM11A or anything else. MH will run without any trouble. Perhaps a few error messages will show up, but it won't crash — it just won't turn the lights on and off yet.

Besides, to keep your `mh.log` file from filling up with information that you might not really need to see, you must turn off a few options before you get started.

1. **Start MH by running the following commands:**

```
export mh_parms=~mh/bin/mh.ini
perl /opt/mh/bin/mh
```

If `Tk.pm` is not installed, you see an error telling you that the Perl module (`Tk.pm`) is not installed. If you don't need to use the Tk interface, don't worry about it. Another error that you might see is one that the GD module is not installed. Neither error will stop MH from running. The Tk error will keep the Tk interface from displaying, and the GD error will prevent you from creating custom buttons for the Web interface (which you won't be doing right now). You definitely want to install the GD module, which I explain in a moment. Meanwhile, if you have the Tk module, you will be greeted by a new Tk window, which looks like Figure 15-1. There is nothing there to help configure MH, but this is a good test to see whether it installed properly. Of course, if you received the Tk error message while MH was starting up, you won't see the Tk interface.

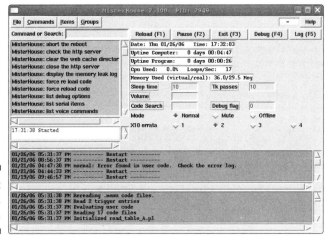

**Figure 15-1:**
MisterHouse,
Tk interface.

2. **Start up your browser under Linux and enter the following URL in the address bar:**

```
http://127.0.0.1:8080/
```

The browser window looks similar to Figure 15-2.

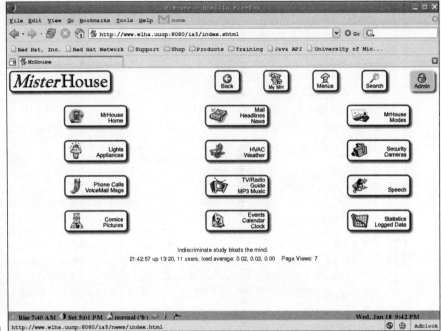

**Figure 15-2:**
MisterHouse,
main Web
page
interface.

You navigate the MH Web interface by using the various links provided. These links are usually displayed as buttons. When I speak of a button, I describe it this way: [*button text*]. The *button text* will be whatever is written on the button. When I want you to descend multiple buttons (they're really just links), I describe the buttons to follow, like so:

```
Main Web page
  -> [MrHouse Home]
    -> [Browse MrHouse]
      -> [Force Reload]
```

This means that you start at the main Web page by entering the URL http://127.0.0.1:8080/ or by clicking the upper-left icon titled MisterHouse. Then click the [MrHouse] button, click the [Browse MrHouse] button, and finally, click the [Force Reload] button. From there, I continue with the description of what needs to be done for that section of the chapter.

The Web interface is pretty and busy, and it works on screen resolutions down to 640 x 480 pixels (the old VGA standard).

3. **To get to most of the MH setup screens, use the [MrHouse Home] button.**

This is where you find the links to the setup pages. The Web interface allows you to activate, access, set up, and configure MH. Also through the Web interface, you can access custom Web pages via the [My MH] button, the X10 interface via the [Lights Appliances] button, and other topics by the appropriate buttons. (You probably can see why I prefer the Web interface to the Tk interface.)

4. **To stop MH, return to the terminal window and press Ctrl+C, or from the Tk window, press the F3 key.**

   This step aborts the Perl program running and returns control back to you at the command prompt.

   Now is the time to add any Perl modules that were missing.

5. **If you think you might want to start MH into the Tk interface some-time in the future and you received the Perl error in Step 1, type the following command:**

   ```
   perl -MCPAN -e"install Tk"
   ```

6. **If you're going to create custom Web pages or you might install some-one else's sample code to generate Web pages, definitely install GD by typing in the following:**

   ```
   perl -MCPAN -e"install GD"
   ```

   The GD module is an important module. It allows to you to create new buttons for MH's Web interface, especially custom interfaces.

7. **Under Linux (and most UNIX systems), MH must have the Time::HiRes Perl module, which you add by typing:**

   ```
   perl -MCPAN -e"install Time::HiRes"
   ```

   This module provides an interface to the Linux libraries for various time functions.

8. **Install the Perl module for the audio mixer interface by typing:**

   ```
   perl -MCPAN -e"install Audio::Mixer"
   ```

   This allows you to control the volume of your sound card. You don't want MH to announce David Letterman's Top Ten list when you're asleep, do you?

Don't worry if at any point you get a *blah::blah is up-to-date* mes-sage. This message just means that the module is already installed, and it's the most recent version. Remember that any time you get an error from MH that a module is missing (sometimes this will stop MH from running, but other times it won't), you can just install the missing module by using the cpan com-mand (just type **cpan**) or the Perl command above. The cpan command has built-in help. You could have used `cpan` instead of the previous commands, but these were quicker because I knew exactly which Perl modules were missing.

# Setting Up MisterHouse

Now it's time to set up MH. This process involves three steps:

1. Start MH as if it started at boot.
2. Modify the parameters.
3. Restart MH.

I go through each step in much detail throughout the rest of this section.

## Starting MisterHouse

You need to start MH as if it were automatically started at boot. Linux supplies you with an easy way to do this without having to reboot the entire computer. You simply type the following command:

```
service mh start
```

Now that it's started, you can use your browser to access MH. Enter this URL into your browser's address bar:

```
http://127.0.0.1:8080/
```

You should see the same page that you saw the previous time you connected to MH. (Refer to Figure 15-2.) Click the following buttons, starting at the main screen:

```
Main Web page
-> [MrHouse Home]
   -> [Setup MrHouse]
      -> [INI Editor]
```

You should now see the MisterHouse `mh.ini editor` Web page. (See Figure 15-3.)

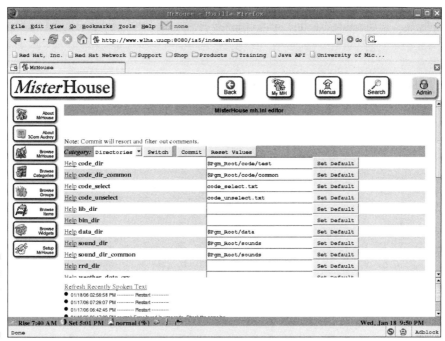

**Figure 15-3:**
Mister-
House, INI
Editor.

You will be using this editor to edit various categories. You can also manually edit the `mh.private.ini` file located in the `~mh/bin/` directory. I give you the information to be changed to reduce the confusion. To select a category to edit, click the drop-down menu, choose the category, and then click the Switch button to go to the category. If you choose to use your favorite editor, you can do a search on the category name. The categories will be in the same order on the Web interface and in the `mh.private.ini` file in your editor. Inside the `mh.private.ini` file, it will look something like this:

```
# Category = Directories
@ Point to the directory that has the user code files in
@ it
@ Notes:
@  - $Pgm_Root is the directory that mh is installed in
@    (e.g. x:\misterhouse\mh\)
@  - code_dir_common points files that would likely
@    be common to all mh uses.
@  - code_dir can be a comma delimited set of paths.
code_dir         = $Pgm_Root/code/test
```

You can then find the parameters to change beneath that category (the `code_dir` line, for example).

If you're using the Web interface, you don't need to add the = sign when making changes. Just change the parameters and when all the changes for a given category are made, click the [Commit] button to save your changes. Then you will then need to click the [Setup MrHouse] and [INI Editor] buttons to get back to the INI editor. You can then choose the next category from the pull-down menu and click the [Switch] button to move to the next category. Keep doing this until you've made all the changes.

## Modifying the parameters

Any entries that I haven't listed here should be left alone. The following sections tell you about the categories and parameters to change.

### Directory

This is the directory where you will put your user code. Your user code is the custom code that you write to make MH do what you want it to do. You can have many directories; just separate each directory with a comma. For now I suggest just one directory.

```
code_dir = $Pgm_Root/code/local
```

### Web

Use the Web parameter when generating URLs that point to your server (for example, get_tv_grid). If you set this to your MH/Linux box's IP address, you should be able to access your Web pages from anywhere, assuming that you have your firewall properly set up to permit that. (I cover that in Chapter 18.) The web_refresh configuration entry is sort of a screen saver. You use the configuration to display photos in the browser when your keyboard has been idle for five minutes. I've found this very annoying, so I turn it off. If you don't mind this pseudo screen saver, leave the default setting alone.

```
http_port   = 8080
http_server = 192.168.0.1
web_refresh = (Leave this field blank to turn it off)
```

The default entry for web_refresh is <meta http-equiv='Refresh' content="600;url=/misc/photos.shtml:>. (Enter it as one line.)

### Location

The latitude and longitude setting tell MH when sunrise and sunset are for where you live. The other settings are used for Internet weather functions. The lines that start with the hash symbol (#) are comments; you don't enter those. The line with the URL is the suggested URL to help you find out your latitude and longitude.

```
#
country  = US
city     = Bronx
state    = NY
zip_code = 10010

# Use http://www.heavens-above.com/countries.asp
latitude  = 40.850
longitude = -73.867
time_zone = -5
```

### Server

If you're just starting with MH, you won't need XAP or XPL support, and you can just change the 1 values to 0. This will decrease the messages found in your mh.log file. If you intend to use either right away, don't make these changes. If you're unsure, set them to 0.

```
xap_disable=1
xpl_disable=1
```

### Serial

The serial setting is very important because it tells MH where to send the X10 commands. MH is able to keep running even if the setting is incorrect, but that doesn't do you much good if you're left in the dark. ;-)

```
cm11_port=/dev/ttyS0
```

### Misc

The Misc category covers various settings that don't quite fit in other areas. The no_log configuration entry is useful for reducing the information that goes into the log file. Because the "saved state" log entry really doesn't tell you anything, you can turn it off. The next entry is the tk entry. Because you'll be starting MH as a daemon, you need to disable the Tk window. MH will start before the graphical X interface. If you leave tk = 1, MH won't properly start. If you aren't going to start MH at boot, you can leave the value as 1. For the remainder of this chapter, I assume the tk is 0.

```
no_log = save_state
tk = 0
```

# Restarting MisterHouse

Although the preceding sections require a large number of changes, they get you through the initial configuration. If you're using your favorite editor, you could have made changes to the mh.ini settings, but that isn't a good idea.

Make changes only to your `mh.private.ini` file. When you need to upgrade to later versions of MH, the `mh.ini` file gets overwritten and the `mh.private.ini` does not. This allows you to upgrade MH and not destroy all your default settings. If you'd like to remove the configuration information from your `mh.private.ini`, you will use the default settings in the `mh.ini` file. If you have multiple configuration entries, you must use the last matching entry in the `mh.private.ini` file.

Now that everything is configured, you can restart MH. You might be interested in the `mh.ini` file, which contains all the parameters and various comments. The contents are both interesting and informative. It can be found in the `~/mh/bin/` directory. The initial `mh.private.ini` file is a copy of the original `mh.ini` file, but the Web interface tends to remove all the comments. Now is a good time to connect the CM11A to the serial port you assigned the parameter to. You need to restart MH. To restart, just type the following command:

```
service mh restart
```

This command properly stops MH and restarts it. To find out whether MH is running properly, type in the following command:

```
service mh status
```

To find out whether there were any problems with MH, you can check the log file located here: `/var/log/mh.log`. Just type this command:

```
less /var/log/mh.log
```

What you will see probably won't make a lot of sense at first, but you can see that MH is very busy.

# Using MisterHouse to Retrieve Your Favorite Comics

Now that you have MH up and running, you can do something useful and fun with it — like accessing your daily dose of comic strips! That's right, comic strips. Chapter 16 deals with doing X10 with MH, so now you can focus on something fun. To enable MH to pull down the daily comics, just follow these steps:

1. **Enable the code by clicking the large MisterHouse icon or typing this URL (you might want to bookmark this) in your browser's address bar:**

```
http://127.0.0.1:8080/
```

**2. From the main Web page, follow these links:**

```
Main Web page
-> [MrHouse Home]
  -> [Setup MrHouse]
    -> [Common Code Activation]
```

The Select Common Code Web page (see Figure 15-4) appears. Now, remember that the temptation to turn all the code files on is powerful, but you must resist! Receiving too much of a good thing too quickly is not a good thing.

Figure 15-4:
MisterHouse,
the Select
Common
Code page.

**3. For now, just click the Entertainment link.**

You should see a comic_strips.pl link somewhere on the Web page. Next to it is a link marked EDIT.

**4. Click EDIT.**

If you've disabled JavaScript, you'll get a File Not Found error. If that happens, enable JavaScript, go back to the comic_strips.pl link, and try the EDIT link again. If you have JavaScript enabled, a pop-up window appears. (See Figure 15-5.)

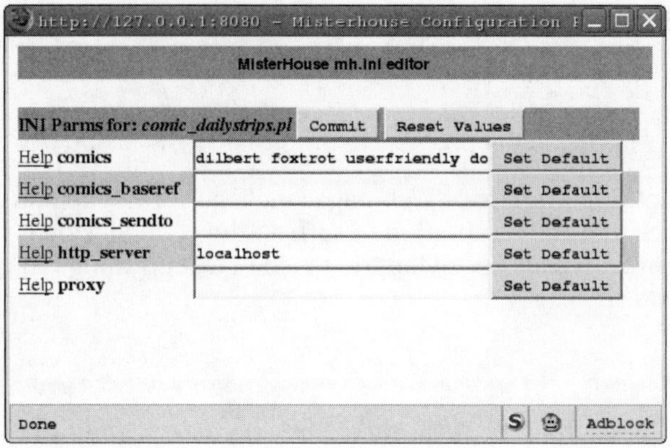

**Figure 15-5:**
MisterHouse
pop-up
window.

The pop-up window shows the default options. MH is set up to pull down the daily comics from Dilbert, Foxtrot, Userfriendly, Doonesbury, and Speedbump. For most users, the default setting will be fine.

5. **Change any that you want to and save your changes by clicking the Commit button; otherwise, just close the window.**

   To find out what comic strips are available, just visit the file: ~mh/web/comics/dailystrips/strips.def.

The lines that start with the word *strip* are the lines with the comic strip names. Listing 15-1 has a sample of *Dilbert*. Don't get greedy and try to download them all; they do eat your bandwidth and take a long time to download.

### Listing 15-1:   Comic Strips

```
strip dilbert
        name Dilbert
        artist Scott Adams
        homepage http://www.dilbert.com/comics/dilbert/
        baseurl http://www.dilbert.com
        type search
        searchpattern <IMG
           SRC="(/comics/dilbert/archive/images/.+?\.(gif|
           jpg))"
        provides latest
end
```

6. **On the Select Common Code page, click the box next to the comic_strips.pl link (see Figure 15-6), and a check mark will appear.**

**Figure 15-6:**
The
MisterHouse
comic_
strips.pl
select link.

**7. Click the Process Selected Files button. (Refer to Figure 15-6.)**

This enables the comic strip's Perl script under MH.

You see a page that summarizes the changes. Now MH is ready to get the comics. At about 4 a.m., MH goes out to access the Internet and pull down the comics. So when you get up in the morning, you should have a Web page with five comic strips on it. To get to this Web page, return to the main Web page:

```
Main Web page
 -> [MrHouse Home]
  -> [Comics Pictures]
```

You can visit that page now and find one sample comic that was installed with MH.

# A Maze of Twisty Little Passages

An old and fun text adventure game had a section where you ventured into a maze of twisty little passages, all different. At first, the maze was annoying because finding your way around was difficult. However, after you'd figured it out, you could breeze through the maze with no problem. MH is somewhat like that; it takes time to get to the point where you know what MH is capable of, but after getting past that point, you can go on to more complex things.

This chapter gives you a step up on MH's steep learning curve, but fortunately or unfortunately, it only scratches the surface. There is still code that gets information from the Internet, such as earthquake information, updated news, top-ten lists, and the daily comics. You can access local OS commands, so why write something that's already written for you? Instead, just parse the output. MH can get your e-mail and sort it for you. You can have MH speak to you. There's IM, SMS, a guide for your TV, and the Asterisk PBX. You can find lots of stuff out there on the Web to play with — here are two specific sources:

✔ **Weeder Technologies boards (`www.weedtech.com`):** If you're an electronics nut, these boards are useful for analog or digital data acquisition and control.

✔ **Maxim iButtons (`www.ibutton.com`):** This site offers temperature sensors and security pads.

Here is one more Web page I'd like you to visit. You get to it from the main Web menu:

```
Main Web page
-> [MrHouse Home]
  -> [Setup MrHouse]
    -> [Common Code Activation]
```

Here you can find more code to activate.

Be sure that you turn on only one thing at a time. I suggest that you click the file links and read through the comments because MH programmers have a habit of putting the instructions in the comments of the file. Well, good luck, and enjoy MH and remember that a few more chapters are directly related to MisterHouse. So visit them first.

# Chapter 16

# Controlling X10 from MisterHouse

. . . . . . . . . . . . . . . . . . . . . . . . . . . . . . . . . . . . . . . . . . . . . . .

## In This Chapter

▶ Setting up MisterHouse tables

▶ Sending and receiving X10 commands

▶ Writing some code

. . . . . . . . . . . . . . . . . . . . . . . . . . . . . . . . . . . . . . . . . . . . . . .

*I*n this chapter, I show you how to take control of X10 from MisterHouse. The chapter takes you through the whole process, from initially setting up X10 to working with MH to creating MH tables for organizing X10 data to writing code that controls the devices and processes data.

*Note:* Before jumping into this chapter, I recommend that you take a look at Chapter 14 (which introduces you to some of X10's common problems and various methods for finding and resolving those problems) and Chapter 15 (which takes you through the process of installing MH). Also be sure to read the first section of this chapter because it highlights the prerequisites for the rest of the chapter.

## Getting What You Need

What better place to start than with the prerequisites? To use this chapter, you must have

- ✔ MisterHouse installed and working (see Chapter 15)
- ✔ X10 CM11A
- ✔ X10 modules to control
- ✔ Electrical devices for X10 to control
- ✔ Your favorite Linux text editor
- ✔ Working knowledge of Perl
- ✔ A good book on Perl

You can, of course, read this chapter if you don't have MisterHouse (MH) installed, and reading before you install is a good idea. If you don't have MH installed, however, you won't be able to put any of this code into practice because it depends heavily on the code inside. If you haven't installed MH, make sure that you at least understand the material in Chapter 15.

Now, I have a few things to say about Perl showing up in the prerequisites list. I would like to say that no programming is required. Unfortunately, most of the really powerful home automation (HA) programs require a little programming knowledge, and MH is one of the most powerful HA programs around. (At least I don't make you break out your soldering iron.) I'm confident that you can follow the examples I provide and have some fun doing it. Eventually, you'll get to a problem that even the examples supplied with MH (in the ~mh/code/examples/ directory) won't be able to cover, and some further Perl knowledge and a good book will help you succeed. What you won't need is a degree in programming!

Day in and day out, I expect MH to run with no user intervention. When I come home after sunset, I expect my front porch and garage lights to be on; after midnight, I expect the garage light to be off; and before sunrise, I expect the front porch lights to turn off. Other lights and appliances are also controlled by MH, but the outside lights are the most noticeable, and with MH they work dependably. This wasn't always the case, but the problem wasn't MH's fault — X10 can be finicky to work with. For instance, a black hole (where X10 signals disappear) might be stopping the signal, or perhaps X10 is taking a long time to do something. In most cases, X10 takes about 1 second to respond to a command signal, which can seem like a long time when you're expecting an instant response. Many people in the home automation community have come up with all sorts of ways to get X10 to behave.

To get X10 to behave the way I want it to, I use a couple devices that aren't always necessary but are certainly useful to have:

- **Noise filters:** These eliminate black holes or electrically noisy appliances.
- **A Smarthome 3-pin SignaLinc coupler-repeater.** This plugs into my electric dryer to fix the problem of only half my house getting X10 signals. (It didn't require an electrician to install.)

By starting with a clean, noise-free electrical environment, X10 becomes more dependable. Now, armed with this knowledge, you can get MH to do some HA by using X10 for you and your family.

# Setting Up X10 for MisterHouse

Make sure that you have all the necessary pieces (see the preceding section) and then follow these steps to set up X10 for MH:

1. **Use the Web browser interface to assign the `mh.private.ini` parameter:**

   ```
   cm11_port=/dev/ttyS0
   ```

   If you've been through Chapter 15 as I recommend, you've probably already completed this step.

   The `/dev/ttyS0` parameter is the first serial port on your computer (COM1 for Windows users). If you have the device connected to the second serial port, use `cm11_port=/dev/ttyS1`. It doesn't matter which serial port you use for the device as long as you correctly identify the port in the `mh.private.ini` file.

2. **Break out your X10 module(s) and set them up the way you want them.**

   See Chapter 14 for details. I have assigned each room to a house code. It's just a debugging technique I use, but it does help. If you have too many rooms, you can let multiple rooms share codes. Too few rooms, just use fewer codes.

   For your first tests, I recommend setting up at least one X10 module right next to your computer where you can easily see it. I like to use a small table lamp that I've made sure is turned on and that has a working bulb. If you have X10 modules that don't have the code wheels, follow the manufacturer's instructions for properly setting up the module.

3. **Make sure you have control of all X10 consoles in the house so that no one can play with it while you're debugging a problem.**

   Nothing will drive you crazier than working on a problem while someone is playing with other X10 controls. My wife drove me nuts for 10 minutes while I was debugging an X10 problem (very funny, honey). The problem was that she had the console, ARGH!

# Linux and serial p

Not all serial ports are created equal. The serial ports on your motherboard use chips that are in the 16550A family and are well known (programming wise). They directly interrupt the CPU, and some software prefers to use that kind of serial port. Fortunately, MH and the CM11A software aren't concerned with which serial port they use. The CM11A will work with USB dongles, motherboard serial ports, add-on serial port cards, or even intelligent multi-port cards (the kind that have their own CPU for handling the serial data). But if you plan to use the serial IR transceiver (Chapter 19), you need a motherboard serial port or a serial port card that uses one of the 16550A family chips. The good news is that there are USB IR transceivers that are supported. The bad news (for me at least) is that I don't have one — I have one of the IR transceivers that requires the use of one of the special serial ports. So choose your serial ports wisely. I have an intelligent 8-port serial card (Dallas Onewire, CM11A, Insteon controller, weather station, CM17A, IR transceiver, MR26A, chip burner), and I find that I'm running out of serial ports.

# Creating MisterHouse Tables

MH has a rather nice feature called *tables*. MH tables are nice in that they provide an easy way of declaring objects (Items) and defining various parts of the object. A not-so-nice aspect of tables, as you can guess from the words "declaring objects," is that they require you to do a bit of programming. *Objects* are like variables that hold a great deal of information. For X10, you need to define the following parameters:

- ✔ **The module type:** There are eight types of X10 modules that MH supports. To start with, you need to worry only about the appliance (X10A) and the lamp (X10I) modules because those are the two modules you'll use the most.

- ✔ **The X10 address:** The X10 address (which I first discuss in Chapter 13) is the address you set on the X10 module's code wheel. It consists of a house code and a unit number. House codes run from A–P, but unit codes are a little more complicated. In MH, you can use the unit code 1–16 or 1–9 and A–G. A–G replaces 10–16. This allows MH to use a single letter to replace a two-digit number. It's easier for the programmers to deal with the single character code rather than the two-digit code. The two-digit code is also the preferred method, so I recommend using it.

- ✔ **The Item's name:** The Item name is the name you will use in your code. You can call the item whatever you want, but it is best for the name to reflect the location or function of the X10 Item. So if you name an Item Desk_Lamp, in your Perl code, you will reference the object by calling $Desk_Lamp (note the $ in front of the name). The name must be unique, and be sure to avoid using two names that are identical except for the case of the letters. That will cause you no end of confusion when you need to debug something.

- ✔ **The groups to which the item belongs:** The groups parameter is used in at least two ways. You can have X10 commands act upon the entire group (on, off, or whatever) by using the group name, and MH uses the group name when you visit the [Lights Appliances] button on the main page (see Figure 16-1).

- ✔ **Other (name chosen by you):** Use this parameter to specify the type of interface used by the device. It's a way of telling MH to use this interface with this object instead of the CM11A.

When you install MH (I show you how in Chapter 15), you copy several files into the ~mh/code/local directory. One of these files, x10.mht, is a MisterHouse table that contains the definitions for a few X10 Items. The file can also contain the definitions for other Items besides X10, but I discuss only the X10 Items here.

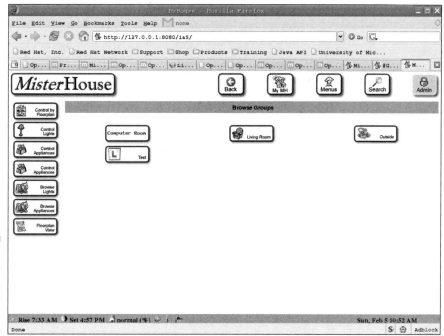

**Figure 16-1:**
The Browse
Groups
page for
MisterHouse.

Now that the x10.mht file exists, you can add a few X10 Items to it, which you do through the Item editor. A file must exist (although it can be empty) before MH can edit it within the Web interface. To edit the MH table file, follow these steps:

1. **Access the Item editor by going to the main Web page and selecting these buttons:**

```
Main screen
-> [Mr. House]
   -> [Setup Mr. House]
      -> [Edit Items]
```

You should now be greeted by the Items menu (see Figure 16-2). If you had more than one .mht file in the directory, you would have a choice of which file to edit. Because you have only one, it will be the one that is displayed. Unfortunately, I had to create two Items for you so MH would start properly, but I'd like you to create at least one. If you have other X10 modules, now would be a good time to add them.

To create an X10 Item, you need to know the module type, the X10 address you want to assign to the module, the name of the object, and what group or groups you want to assign it to. These are the parameters that you must define for the X10 item.

**2. Set the module type.**

If you don't know the module type, just use the X10A because it supports the on and off commands that almost all X10 modules support. If you don't like the entry or you've made a mistake, you can always delete it.

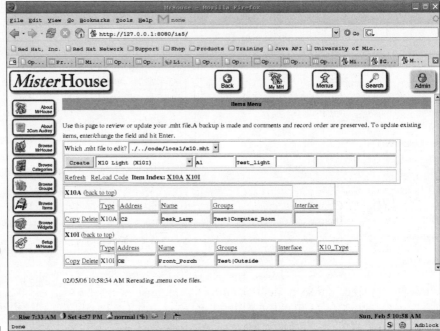

**Figure 16-2:**
The MisterHouse Items Editor.

**3. Enter the device address into the X10 address box.**

I explain the device address earlier in this section.

**4. Enter the name that you want to use to identify the device.**

For example, if this device will control the living room light, you could use living_room as the name.

**5. Assign the object to a group.**

You can define multiple group names by separating the group names with a pipe (|). I've put these X10 devices in the group Test and their respective rooms. The group is used by MH when you click the [Lights Appliances] button on the main interface. There, you can reference the group and find the appropriate device.

The last parameter is Interface, which you don't use here.

Here are the entries in the x10.mht text file in the ~mh/code/local directory:

```
# Type      Address    Name          Groups
X10A,       C2,        Desk_Lamp,    Test|Computer_Room,
X10I.       OE.        Front Porch.  Test|Outside.
X10I,       B1,        Table_Lamp,   Test|Living_Room,
```

The first line is a comment; any line that starts with a # is a comment. Any line that starts with #@ is used as documentation by MH. The next two lines have already been entered for you. The last line is the one I'd like to enter via the Items menu you now have in your Web browser. Don't worry if you make a mistake entering the information — you can correct it. You can even choose to edit the file with you favorite text editor. If you do, just copy the information as you see it here and save the file. To enter it via the Items Menu Web page, enter all the data on the last line in the preceding code, and then use the drop-down menu and select the X10 Light (X10I) option for X10I. Fill in the next three boxes with the rest of the data from the last line in the preceding code and leave the last box empty. That's the Interface field, and you don't need it for these entries. When you've filled in the data and you're satisfied with it, click the Create button. To make the changes active, you need to click the Reload link.

6. **Change any of the parameters that you don't like — except for the Item name.**

   Remember that the first two Items are already used in code. (I just needed to provide examples for you to follow.) I don't recommend deleting the first two entries at this time because I've used them in code that is installed in the user's code directory (~mh/code/local/). But anything that you've added in Step 5 can be changed or deleted with no problem because there is no code currently using those Item names.

7. **Save any changes by clicking the Create button; then click the Reload link to make the changes active.**

8. **Look at the new file that was created from the MH Tables file (x10.mht).**

   You can find it here: ~mh/code/local/x10.mhp. The table in Step 5 saved you from having to type all that in. Don't edit the .mhp files — they are created by MH using the information in the corresponding .mht file and will be overwritten.

# Sending and Receiving X10 Commands

Before you can send commands to X10 devices, you must first turn on the X10 devices. (After you turn on those devices, you can write code that will enable you to monitor the X10 devices and automate their functions, but first things first.) To turn on an X10 device — for example, the desk lamp — just use this code (to turn on other devices, you would substitute Desk_Lamp with Table_Lamp or whatever):

```
set $Desk_Lamp 'on';
```

There, that was simple! Well, I have to tell you that it's never that simple. Yes, that code will turn on the desk lamp, but there's always a catch, and in this case, there are two:

✔ **Before you can use a variable or object, you must declare it.** The good news is that you've declared the X10 Desk_Lamp in the preceding section in the x10.mht file. If you need another variable but not an Item, this is how you declare a variable:

```
my $variable_name;
```

The good news is that the desk lamp Item is already defined for you. The .mht file and MH has already done that for you. Although Perl might let you get away with not defining a variable or an Item before you use it, MH won't.

✔ **The MH program is basically a big loop, and every time MH finishes executing one loop it starts all over again.** On a very fast machine, you can execute the same command several times per second. Remember that an X10 command takes about 1 second to complete. If you send a whole bunch of X10 commands every second for as long as MH runs, you won't be able to send any other X10 commands. So you need a way of telling MH that you want the X10 device to do something only when a particular event happens. MH has plenty of built-in functions to do just that.

To see all the available built-in functions and their descriptions, just plug this URL into your browser:

```
http://127.0.0.1:8080/
```

and then follow these buttons:

```
Main web page
-> [Mr. House]
  -> [Local Documents]
    -> [Docs]
```

There, you can find a complete list of all the functions, options, variables, objects, and methods directly available to your code. Here are a few functions that might be of interest to you for use in this chapter:

✔ new_second: True only on the *n*th second. I discuss this function in the upcoming "x10.pl" section.

✔ new_minute: True only on the *n*th minute.

✔ new_hour: True only on the *n*th hour.

> ✔ `time_now`: True for the 1 pass that matches the specified time. I discuss
> this function in the upcoming "x10_II.pl" section.
>
> ✔ `state_now`: True only for one pass after object state is set. I discuss
> this in the following section, "Creating X10 macros."

The `state_now` function is very important to X10. You use it to do something when an X10 device changes. That physical X10 device doesn't even
have to really exist. You can use this to your advantage to create macros,
which I discuss next.

## Creating X10 macros

In the living room of my home next to my wife's comfy chair on the table
beneath the lamp, there sits an X10 console. This console is capable of controlling 16 X10 devices. It can send `on`, `off`, `bright`, or `dim` commands for
each X10 device. With a little creative code, MH can use those commands to
do all sorts of different things. I have MH programmed to respond to those
commands and do different things based on the time of day. The code required
to do this is a bit complicated, and you won't learn anything useful from hundreds of lines of code. Yes, you too can create hundreds of lines of code, but
for now, start out simple. So with that in mind, I've simplified the lesson. In
the "Creating MisterHouse Tables" section, I show you how to add X10 Items
via the Web interface. Now you'll put one X10 item into use. Again, you've
already added this code to the user's code directory in Step 5 in the "Creating
MisterHouse Tables" section, and I'm displaying only a couple small chunks
of the code so you can get an idea of what it can do. There's more in the file,
so if you're curious, have a look inside `~mh/code/local/x10_macro.pl`.

```
my $MacroA9On  = new Serial_Item('XA9AJ');
my $MacroA9Off = new Serial_Item('XA9AK');

if(state_now $MacroA9On) {
  print " *** Macro A9 On\n";
  set $Front_Porch 'on';
  set $Desk_Lamp 'on';
}
if(state_now $MacroA9Off) {
  print " *** Macro A9 Off\n";
  set $Front_Porch 'off';
  set $Desk_Lamp 'off';
}
```

This code is a little more complicated than the simple set I use in this section, but not a whole lot more. Keep reading for an explanation of the code
snippet.

In the `x10_macro.pl` file, I've defined the Items `$MacroA9On` and `$MacroA9Off`. They're a little bit more than variables, but you can treat them as variables in this chapter.

I used the `Serial_Item` because the string I used will be received from the serial device. When an X10 device (like the console) sends the command `A9 Off`, MH sees the command and stores it as `XA9AK`. MH prepends the `X` to the command to make it clear that this is an X10 command. The `A9` is the X10 address (house code A, unit code 9). The `AK` is MH's way of storing `A Off` (`AOn` is stored as `AJ`, `ADim` as `AM`, and `ABright` as `AL`).

When your code checks the `$MacroA9On` object with `state_now`, it will return `true` only if MH has seen the X10 `A9 AJ` (`AOn`) received via the X10 interface.

When `state_now` is returned as `true`, the next lines of the code tell MH to print the message; turn on the `Front_Porch` light (it sends out the appropriate X10 command for the X10 address you defined for it earlier); and finally turn on the `Desk_Lamp`.

If MH sees `XA9AK` (`A9AOff`), it executes the second `if` statement and the commands between its curly brackets (`{}`).

## x10_test.pl

The next block of code is to be used for the telnet interface into MH. It isn't fancy, but it demonstrates the point quite well. You won't have to enter the code because you've already installed it earlier when you installed MisterHouse in Chapter 15. This time, this is the entire code:

```
$my_test = new Voice_Cmd 'Run test [A,B]';

if ($state = said $my_test) {
    if ($state eq 'A') {
        print_log "You ran test A, turning on the Desk
            Lamp";
        set $Desk_Lamp 'on';
    }
    elsif ($state eq 'B') {
        print_log "You ran test B, turning off the Desk
            Lamp";
        set $Desk_Lamp 'off';
    }
}
```

This code defines two commands: `Run test A` and `Run test B` (they're really voice Items). Yes, MH does support a voice interface, but unfortunately, Linux doesn't have a working speech-to-text voice interface. You can use Festival to make MH speak (text to speech). Currently, there is hope that the Sphinx project (`http://cmusphinx.sf.net/`) will solve this problem soon. Normally, the voice software would convert speech into text, and MH would execute the text command, if defined, such as `Run test A`. Instead, you can use other things to generate the text.

To use this code, open a terminal window and type the following:

```
telnet 127.0.0.1 1234
```

You will then be greeted by a prompt (`mh#`) where you can type your text commands (such as `Run test A`). When executed, the first command prints a message to the log file (`/var/log/mh.log`) and turns on the `Desk_Lamp` (which was previously defined in the `x10.mht file` as X10 address C2). The second command does the same, but this time turns off the `Desk_Lamp`. If you have an X10 device configured as C2, typing these commands will turn the device on and off. If no devices are configured, the commands are sent, but nothing is listening. No harm, no foul.

## Disabling user code

This information is going to seem a little backward, but it's important. In the "x10.pl" section, I show you how to create your own Perl code to control X10 based on events (yeah!). The first code example is a good (but annoying) example of how to turn the desk lamp on and off. After about four or five times, I found it to be really annoying. It's great that it worked, but what good is code that drives you crazy? So I show you how to turn off code that you've added to MH. After you've reloaded the code by clicking the Reload Code button, the new code will be active. To disable it, follow these steps:

1. **Bring up you browser with the MH URL and follow these buttons:**

```
Main screen
-> [Mr. House]
  -> [Setup Mr. House]
    -> [User code Activation]
```

You'll notice a screen with various items on it (see Figure 16-3).

2. **Click the Category Index link for X10 (or whatever category you put your new code into), and then find your file.**

Anything that is selected will be loaded; anything left deselected won't load.

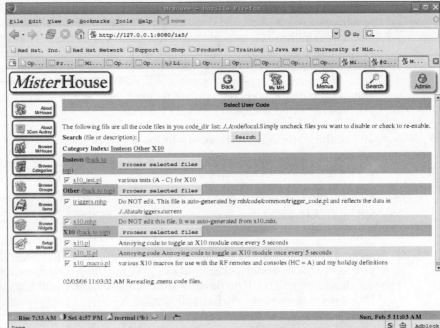

**Figure 16-3:**
The Select
User Code
menu.

3. **Select what you do or do not want and click any of the [Process selected files] buttons.**

4. **To disable the toggling lamp, deselect X10.pl.**

   Don't deselect the code until after you've let it run once or twice so that you can see how it's performing.

# *x10.pl*

But wait, there's more! Now it's time to create your own code. With your favorite editor, you will create a new file called ~mh/code/local/x10.pl that will turn the desk lamp on and off every five seconds. In this file, enter the following lines:

```
# Category=X10
#@ Annoying code to toggle an X10 module once every 5
          seconds

if(new_second 5) {
  set $Desk_Lamp 'toggle';
}
```

Enter the six lines as shown here. There are two spaces in front of the set command, but you can use as many spaces or tabs as you feel comfortable with. I do recommend using some kind of indentation in your code to make the code easier to understand by placing similar functions or commands in the indented section. You can also use blank lines to separate `if` statements and commands for ease of reading the code. Most of all, be consistent with your coding style. Okay, enough about coding style; now for the explanation:

The first line is a comment. All lines that start with a # are comments. Perl ignores comments in your code. The `Category=X10` string is used by MH to make it easy to find and group code together on the Select User Code Web page (see Figure 16-4).

The second line is also special to MH. It's still a comment, and Perl treats it as such, but MH interprets it as a description of the code file. It provides a description of what the code does. I recommend keeping the description as short as possible but still giving enough detail to know what the purpose of the code is. You can have multiple lines starting with #@, and they will be merged into the description.

The next command is an `if` statement. Inside the `if` statement is the `new_second 5` function. What this says is that every 5 seconds, the script must do the commands between these curly brackets. The command in this case is to toggle the X10 state of the X10 Item `Desk_Lamp`. So every 5 seconds, the desk lamp will turn on, and 5 seconds later, it will turn off as long as the script is running.

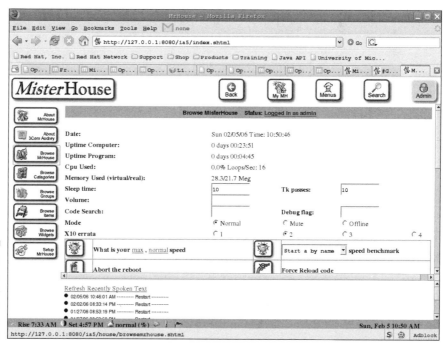

**Figure 16-4:**
MisterHouse,
Browse
MisterHouse
menu.

After you create the ~mh/code/local/x10.pl file, follow these steps to load it into the running MH and use it:

1. **Go to your browser and follow the buttons:**

```
Main screen
-> [Mr. House]
  -> [Browse M. House]
    -> [Force Reload code]
```

2. **If the lamp doesn't toggle on and off every 5 seconds (as it should at this point), find out what went wrong with MH by checking the /var/log/mh.log file with your favorite editor.**

At the end or close to the end, you can see a description of what's wrong and what you need to do to correct the problem.

3. **Open the x10.pl file and find the problem in the code. Fix the problem and use the Web interface to force a reload of the code, as described in Step 1.**

## x10_11.pl

Another important MH function is time_now, and it basically does what it sounds like it might do. If the time now is "12:00", the script tells MH it must do something. The time_now function takes a string with the time and/or date in it. The "12:00" or "12:00 PM" string means noon, and "00:00" or "12:00 AM" means midnight. The time_now argument format is actually pretty flexible. You can even use the string "6/6/06 4:00:01", which translates into June 6, 2006 at 4 a.m. and 1 second. In addition, MH has time-related variables, such as $Time_Sunrise and $Time_Sunset. These two variables relate to sunrise and sunset, respectively. Here's an example of their use:

```
if(time_now("$Time_Sunset-0:10")) {
   print_log "Sunset";
   set $Hutch 'on';
}
```

The 0:10 means 10 minutes, so when the time is 10 minutes before sunset, MH will print a log entry and then turn on the Hutch. The next chunk of code is a bit more complicated, but actually not any worse than other code in this chapter:

```
# Category=Lights

#@ routine related to the holiday X10 lamp control
```

```
my $DOY;
my $tmp;
$mhHoliday = new Generic_Item;

# Figure out which holiday it is
# But do it after midnight or when we reload or first
         start

if ($Reload || $Startup || time_now "12:01 AM") {
  # Remember that DOY starts at 0
  ($tmp,$tmp,$tmp,$tmp,$tmp,$tmp,$tmp,$DOY,$tmp) =
          localtime(time);

  # Holiday lights for a week before Oct 31 (297 - 304)
  if($DOY > 296 | $DOY < 304) {
    set $mhHoliday "holiday";
  } else {
    set $mhHoliday "normal";
  }
}

# Sunset, lots to do and so little time ...
if(time_now("$Time_Sunset-0:10")) {
  print_log "Sunset";
  set $Hutch      'on';
  set $xBench     'on';
  set $xTree      'on';
  set $Desk_Lamp 'on';

  if (state_now $mhHoliday eq "holiday") {
    # Holiday lights
    set $x01 'on';
    set $x02 'on';
    set $x03 'on';
    set $x04 'on';
    set $x05 'on';
  } else {
    set $Front_Porch  'on';
  }
}
```

So, starting at the top, here's an explanation:

> First I added a comment and assigned the code to a category. I make up
> the Lights category because this program controls my lights around the
> house. For example, my tea machine is in the Tea category, though I'd
> liked to have put it in the Breakfast category if I could just keep the
> toaster from burning the toast.

Next I've added my descriptive comment (#@) for the User Code Select Web page.

Then I define two variables, $DOY (day of the year) and $tmp. The variables themselves aren't remarkable, but the my that precedes them is. The my indicates that these variables have local significance. If you try to use the values of these variables in another user file, MH will complain that they aren't defined and sometimes won't run. Or to put it another way, you can reuse these variable names in another file, and the changes to the variables here won't change the variable there (and vice versa).

The next thing defined is an Item. (Remember that an Item is like a variable but with extra properties.) This Item is a generic Item or the *base Item* (the Item from which all other Items are derived, such as Serial_Item). Note that there is no my preceding $mhHoliday, which means that it's a global variable. I can use $mhHoliday in other files and the value will be the same across all the files. It also means that other files can change the value.

Okay, now you're back to familiar code, the sunset code (which I first introduce in Chapter 13). This time I added a little twist: In addition to the code that executes 10 minutes before sunset, I've added code that checks to see whether the day is a holiday. If it is ($mhHoliday equals holiday), then MH turns on additional lights. If not, MH just turns on the front porch light. Now, I could keep going, extending the code to do more, but my page space is limited, so you need to use your imagination and come up with your own code.

# Chapter 17

# Using the Web Interface for Remote Control

*I*n Chapter 18, I discuss methods and procedures for securing your access to your Linux box and MisterHouse (MH). In this chapter, I show you how to use your Linux box and a Web browser to access the controls of MH. One of the nice things about MH is that, in addition to other methods, it's Web based, and that makes it easy and somewhat intuitive to use. Another nice thing is that if you don't like something, you can change it, even the main page (see Figures 17-1 and 17-2). I don't describe how to change the front page, but I do describe how to create your own Web page. I also describe the various pages off the main Web page. I'm afraid that until you set up various settings and programs not all the pages will display anything useful. But don't worry — viewing the blank pages doesn't take anything away from MH.

## Exploring the MisterHouse Main Web Page

On the MisterHouse main Web page (see Figure 17-1), there are 18 buttons and an information bar. Basically, the page is split into three sections. The top section contains the following buttons:

✔ **MisterHouse:** The home button. The MisterHouse button gets you back to the main Web page from anywhere in the Web pages.

✔ **Back:** The Back button takes you back one page. If you attempt to use the browser's built-in Back button, you'll find yourself at the main Web page (which is slightly annoying).

✔ **My MH:** The My MH button takes you to the page where you can get to your custom Web pages. I explain that further later in this chapter.

✔ **Menus:** This button gives you access to various menus. These menus are useful for access from a WAP-enabled cell phone, a telephone (voice menu), or LCD keypads.

✔ **Search:** Search the Web interface for instances of text.

✔ **Admin:** Click this button when you want to log in as Admin. If you haven't set up your default admin password, the Web interface gives you admin access.

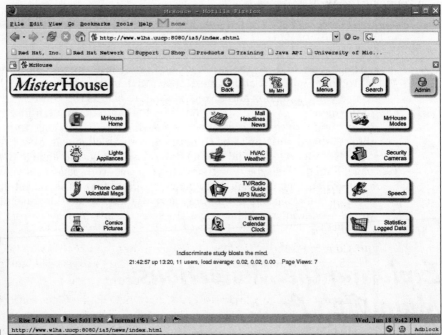

**Figure 17-1:**
The main Web page interface of MisterHouse.

The next group of buttons make up the main menu. This is generally the part of the Web pages that changes when you make your selection. So when you click a menu button, the top buttons and bottom status bar remain, but the center of the page displays the contents of the new page. This section of the main page consists of the following 12 buttons that pretty much get you to where you need to go to with little trouble:

- ✔ **MrHouse Home:** The MrHouse Home button takes you to the configurations submenus. After you get MH properly set up, you will spend very little time there.

- ✔ **Mail Headlines News:** Clicking the Mail Headline News button brings up your e-mail, links to News (CNN), to Newsgroups (Google), and to Postal Mailbox. I don't have the Post Mailbox set up, so I haven't used it yet.

- ✔ **MrHouse Modes:** The MrHouse Modes button takes you to a Web page to select MH's current mode, such as sleeping, occupied, or normal. You would use this in your code to help make certain decisions. You could add a party mode so that MH would know not to turn off the lights until MH was out of party mode.

- ✔ **Lights Appliances:** Next you have the Lights Appliances button. If you've already read Chapter 16, you might recall something about assigning X10 modules to groups. Well, this is the menu where you can click one of those group and get direct control of an X10, an Insteon, a UPB, an EIB, or other items. Here you can find out the state of the devices. (I use this button a lot.)

- ✔ **HVAC Weather:** This button is for weather/earth related data, such as weather reports, HVAC, sun, moon, and earthquake data. Don't laugh — there was a quake in New Jersey just the other day.

- ✔ **Security Cameras:** This button is for views from your security cameras. (I don't have my cameras properly set up, but I have two Chow-Chows, so I'm not overly worried about security.)

- ✔ **Phone Calls VoiceMail Msgs:** The next button is the Phone Calls VoiceMail Msgs button. If you have caller ID set up, you can record all the information from incoming calls along with announcing calls with text to speech.

- ✔ **TV/Radio Guide MP3 Music:** This button takes you to the TV guide, radio, Internet radio, and movie information.

- ✔ **Speech:** This button lets you view the speech logs (boring!).

- ✔ **Comics Pictures:** Next is a button I show you how to set up in Chapter 15. Every morning, I wake up, get my tea, let the dogs out, and read the comics. If only the rest of life were so easy!

- ✔ **Events Calendar Clock:** Next is the Events Calendar Clock button, which is basically your personal organizer (helpful!). This button gives you access to PDA Sync, a calendar, an address book, a to-do list, and a shopping list.

- ✔ **Statistics Logged Data:** The Statistics Logged Data button gives you access to the various logs and statistics MH has gathered.

Under the 12 buttons is a cute and cuddly saying that changes with each visit or refresh. Underneath that is the uptime string, which consists of the current time; the uptime in days, hours, and minutes; the number of current users; the load average (1 minute average, 5 minute average, and 15 minute average); and the number of page views.

At the bottom of the Web page is the MH status bar, which contains the sunrise time, sunset time, the current MH mode, number of email awaiting (if any), the current indoor temperature, the current outdoor temperature, the previous outdoor temperature, the inside and outside humidity, wind speed, wind direction, and the current time and date.

If you want to create your own main Web page, you can, but I don't go into that in this book because it's an advanced subject. (You have to make a lot of changes in the `mh.private.ini` file.) However, you can have a look at a page I found that looks good, `http://127.0.0.1:8080/mh4`. I've included an image of it in Figure 17-2 as an example of an alternative MH main Web page.

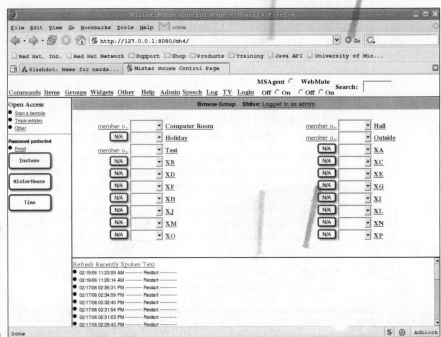

**Figure 17-2:**
An alternative main Web page interface.

# Accessing and Controlling X10

To access and control your X10 modules, you click a button on the main Web page to go to specific Web pages where you can see the X10 modules, find out which are turned on (or off), and make adjustments. To demonstrate, I take you on a quick tour of the Lights and Appliances Web page (accessed by clicking the Lights Appliances button on the main page), which is a page you'll likely visit often. When you visit the page, you can see various groups. These groups contain the current state MH thinks the X10 modules are set to, such as on or off. (Actually, this page isn't just for X10. It's also for any other device someone can build into MH, such as Insteon, UPB, or EIB.)

If you've set up the X10 modules in a logical order, such as assigning the groups to rooms, then you've made them much easier to use. I took the liberty of adding all the possible X10 addresses to the x10.mht file you install in Chapter 16. (If you haven't been through that chapter yet, don't worry. This chapter isn't dependent on Chapter 16, but you won't be able to look at the Web pages I reference except through the pretty pictures.) If you've been through Chapter 16, you will see quite a list (xA through xP), as shown in Figure 17-3. The names aren't the easiest to remember, but they're meant for playing with, and you can delete them if you see fit. No code is currently using any of the names assigned to the xA–xP groups.

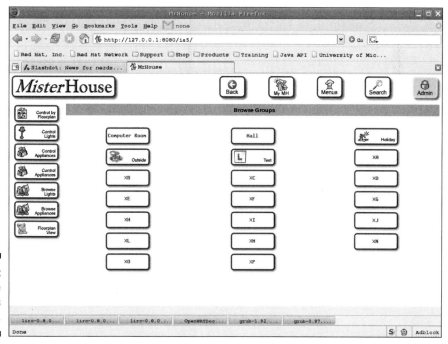

**Figure 17-3:**
The Browse
Groups
page.

If you click one of the groups, you'll see all the members of that group. I selected the Computer Room group (see Figure 17-4), and as you can see, it has only one member: Desk Lamp, which is the X10 module that the user code, test_x10.pl, toggles on and off every 30 seconds. If you disabled the test toggle code (see Chapter 16), the lamp will probably be off. I left the code enabled (very annoying) and captured the screen while it was on. MH tries to match the current state of the X10 module. Unfortunately, X10 can sometimes become deaf, or a user can manually change the state of the module, or the module might not be plugged in. X10 has no direct knowledge of the modules, so it does its best to guess. (I sent the command, so it must be on.) When the newer technology, such as Insteon or UPB, has caught on, this guessing will be a thing of the past. MH should be able to go out and ask the device how it's set, and the Web page will properly reflect its current state. Despite this shortcoming, X10 works pretty well, and the information on the Web page is usually accurate.

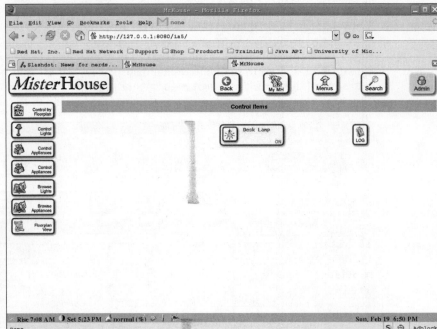

**Figure 17-4:**
The Control
Items
page of
MisterHouse.

If you want to change the state of the device, click the button and it will change state. If it was off, it turns on; if on, it turns off. A lamp module device will have an arrow on it to allow you to brighten the device. If the lamp is off, you must turn it on before you can dim or brighten it.

The menu buttons on the left side give you different ways to access lamp and appliance modules. A few buttons on the menu are redundant (sorry; it's the default), but the last button, the floor plan view, is the most interesting. You can create a custom floor plan of your house to view and control devices by using a graphic representation of your house's layout. You can see the current state of a device and click a device in its location on the floor plan to turn it on or off. Unfortunately, I haven't had time to learn how to use it, but I'm looking forward to figuring that out.

# Using the HTML Template

Some of the HTML (HyperText Markup Language) code used in MH is a bit lax on following the standards, and for now that's okay because the browsers

(Firefox, Mozilla, Opera, and IE) do not strictly enforce compliance with the HTML standard. But with the new standards becoming stricter with the rules about how pages are put together, browsers will be less likely to accept code that doesn't conform to the HTML standard. So in general, "do it once, do it right" is a good guideline to follow.

With that in mind, I've created a template to use for creating your Web pages (`template.html`). Whether the page is a static page or one created with Perl code on the fly, to really take advantage of HTML, you will have to know some HTML. You can also add JavaScript and Java, but that's way over the top for just starting out — sort of like hiring a NASA engineer to build a back-yard birdhouse.

## A brief history of the Web and HTML

The Web traces its history back to ideas from as long ago as 1945. The modern Web traces back to about 1989, when Sir Tim Berners-Lee proposed HyperText to CERN (the European Organization for Nuclear Research). By 1993, one of the earliest graphical browsers, Mosaic, was first released. Later, Mosaic would become Netscape. In 1994, the W3C (World Wide Web Consortium) was created to set the standards. Today users take HTML for granted because most users don't see it, but every page is made up of it in some form. The Internet wouldn't be the Internet without HTML. If you want to learn the nitty-gritty details of the protocols, visit the W3C Web site at www.w3.org. The W3C has all the details. I don't recommend visiting that site if you're just learning HTML, but after you've gotten a bit comfortable with HTML, it might more sense.

The first version of HTML that I can remember working with was 3.2. It was simple enough, and I really didn't know what I was doing. I basically looked at other Web pages. When I saw a feature that I liked, I tried to recreate that feature. Well, apparently so did a lot of other people. Browsers began supporting various HTML code that didn't follow the HTML standards so that the browser rendered most pages correctly. Sometimes there were competing proposed HTML standards where one browser did it this way and all the others did it another way. Or the worst offense would occur: creating new HTML tags that were not yet standard.

As of the writing of this book, XHTML (Extensible HyperText Markup Language) version 1.1 is the newest standard. Most modern browsers no longer render nonstandard HTML well but still support HTML 4.01, so it's still okay to use. Browsers don't drop the old standards the instant a new one appears. Instead, they support a group of standards: HTML 4.01 through XHTML 1.0 or even up to 1.1.

If you want to learn the latest and greatest, learn XHTML 1.1. If you just need to use it casually, HTML 4.01 will do for a while.

Don't spend too much time learning about frames, but do learn the proper use of `<div></div>` instead of tables. Frames are *deprecated* (which is a fancy way of saying "don't use that any more"), and tables are frowned upon for page layout but not for actual tabulated data. The proper method to use in place of both is to use the `<div></div>` tags . Unfortunately for you, MH still uses frames and will probably use them for some time. (Yeah, I know, do as I say not as I do. Sorry about that.) The good news is that for MH's use of frames, you can copy the default pages that use frames. This way you can remain consistent with the way MH does things now.

## Creating Web pages with an HTML template

When building new Web pages for MH, I recommend using this Web page as a template (included on the CD as `template.html`):

```
<!DOCTYPE HTML PUBLIC "-//W3C//DTD HTML 4.01
        Transitional//EN"
  "http://www.w3.org/TR/html4/loose.dtd">
<html>
    <head>
        <title>MY_TITLE</title>
    </head>
    <body>
        <p>Hello world!</p>
    </body>
</html>
```

The first two lines of this template inform your browser that this page loosely conforms to HTML version 4.01. The loose part allows for some breakage from previous releases of the HTML standard and gives you a bit of breathing room if you're new to HTML. The 4.01 standard is reasonably modern so that if you learn some new HTML code you can try it out. Don't worry; this template will work fine with MH.

The template is the shell you need to begin to create a Web page to display. In brief, these steps show you how to use this template:

1. **Open your favorite text editor and then open the template.**

2. **Replace MY_TITLE with your Web page's title.**

3. **Put the rest of your text between the HTML <body> (the opening tag) and </body> (the closing tag).**

   Between these two tags, you can use any standard HTML tags, but if you aren't yet familiar with HTML, just start by using the paragraph (`<p></p>`) tags and the `<pre></pre>` tags. The paragraph tags are for creating paragraphs like you would when writing a letter or other document. Just put your paragraphs between the paragraph tags. Any text you put between the <pre></pre> tags will be displayed on the page as it is currently formatted. For example, if you cut text from another document and paste it into the <pre></pre> tags, it retains its *pre*-existing formatting. I use that in the next section ("Introducing the My MH Web Page") to demonstrate how to use an external program and Perl to create page content for MH.

The template is valid and can be viewed in your browser. You would use a URL like this in your browser: `file://opt/mh/web/my_mh/template.html`. You need to use your path to the file, and the file will appear in you browser.

In the next section, I use the <pre></pre> tags. Normally HTML eats any extra spaces tags or new lines, but anything put between these tags is treated as pre-formatted text. Your spacing will be preserved as well as your line endings.

# *Introducing the My MH Web Page*

The main Web page (refer to Figure 17-1) has three frames. Can you see them? Don't worry if you can't; they're meant to be invisible to the user. The three frames are the top buttons, the main menu (middle), and the status bar (bottom). The top and the status line are generally kept constant throughout MH (but not always; so much for standards). When you click the My MH button, a new page appears (see Figure 17-5).

**Figure 17-5:**
The My MH
Web page
interface.

Can you tell how many frames there are now? There are now five: the original three plus two more inside the menu frame:

- ✔ **The top frame** (original), featuring the buttons across the top of the page.

- ✔ **The menu frame** (original) on the left — with a new set of buttons showing.

- ✔ **The status bar frame** (original) along the bottom.

- ✔ **The output frame** (new), middle-right. The output frame is where you want your newly created Web pages to appear.

- ✔ **The speech frame** (new), which is at the bottom but above the status line. The speech frame is where the speech log is displayed.

So that's five frames total in your Web browser. You don't need to know a lot about frames — just that they are there and anything you put in the frames doesn't need to use the template. Just drop your normal text and HTML tags in and you're off and ready to go.

When you first visit the My MH Web page, it's pretty boring. That's because it's your job to set it up. One way to accomplish this is to add the appropriate buttons on the left that call externals Web pages or programs and displays the output from them in the space on the right. And that's just what I show you how to do throughout the rest of this chapter. In this case, you're tweaking MH so that you can read a weather report for your area. First you need to install a few things, which I show you in the next section, and then you add a button that enables you to access the report (in the "Adding a Weather Report button" section).

## Installing a weather report page

Adding a weather report from the National Weather Service is very easy. First copy the program from the CD to your computer:

1. **Type** cp /media/cdrom/remote_control/nws.pl ~mh/web/my_mh/nws.pl **and press Enter.**

2. **Type** chmod a+x ~mh/web/ my_mh/nws.pl **and press Enter.**

3. **Type** cp /media/cdrom/remote_control/weather ~mh/bin/weather **and press Enter.**

4. **Type** chmod a+x ~mh/bin/weather **and press Enter.**

You also need to make sure you have the `Expect` package installed. So from the command line, do one of the following:

✔ `yum install expect` (for Fedora or SUSE)

✔ `apt-get install expect` (for Debian)

Next you need to get the city code for the location you're interested in getting the weather report for. To do this follow these directions:

1. **At a command prompt, type** telnet rainmaker.wunderground.com 3000.

2. **After the Welcome banner appears, press Enter.**

3. **When another prompt greets you, simply press Enter again.**

4. **At the main menu, press 1 (U.S. forecasts and climate data) and then Enter.**

5. **At the city menu, press 3 (Display 3-letter city code for selected state) and then Enter.**

6. **Enter the 2-letter state code (I chose NY) and then Enter.**

7. **Select a city code (such as jfk).**

8. **Now press X and then Enter.**

Now that you've selected your city code, you can try the command manually from the command line:

```
$ ~mh/bin/weather jfk

Weather Conditions at 05:51 PM EST on 19 Feb 2006 for New York JFK, NY.
Temp(F)     Humidity(%)     Wind(mph)     Pressure(in)     Weather
==============================================================================
   27            31%          WEST at 20       30.26        Partly Cloudy

Forecast for New York, NY
331 PM EST sun Feb 19 2006

.Tonight...Mostly clear this evening...then becoming partly cloudy.
Lows around 17. West winds 10 to 15 mph.
.Presidents day...Partly cloudy. Highs in the upper 30s. West winds
10 to 15 mph.
```

I've included only a small portion of the output, but you get the idea. I think that it returns some pretty good information. Turning the information into something that can be displayed on a Web page is very easy. With the programs at hand and a few simple changes, like adding a line to a Web page and a little Perl code, you can display this information from MH.

## Adding the Weather Report button

In this section, I show you how to add a new button to the weather report Web page, which will in turn call the weather program with the city information. (I show you how to install the program in the preceding section.) The Perl script will alter the returned information a little to tidy it up a bit; otherwise, it would look like it's double spaced. This is what the menu.html HTML information looks like before the changes:

```
<base target='output'>
<table height='100%' border='0'>
<tbody>
<td valign='top' align='left' width='100%'>
<a href='howto.shtml'><img src='/bin/button.pl?HowTo'
        border='0'></a></br>
<a href='my_menu1.shtml'><img src='/bin/button.pl?My
        Menu1' border='0'></a></br>
<a href='my_menu2.shtml'><img src='/bin/button.pl?My
        Menu2' border='0'></a></br>
</td>
</tbody>
</table>
```

Yes, that's the whole thing, but it's just the HTML for the left frame. Remember that you don't use the template for HTML that goes inside a frame.

To add the Weather Report button, follow these steps:

1. **Open that Web page in your favorite editor.**

   The file is located here: ~mh/web/my_mh/menu.html.

2. **Insert the following line before the </td> tag:**

```
<a href='nws.pl?jfk'
    title="National Weather Service for JFK">
<img src='/bin/button.pl?Weather' border='0'></a></br>
```

   You can make that all one line if you'd like. It was just too long to display on this page, so I broke it up to make it a little more readable.

3. **Change the city code (currently jfk, right after the first question mark) to whatever city code you selected and save the file.**

   The city code, jfk, is an argument being passed to the nws.pl program. If you needed to pass more than one argument, you would separate them with an ampersand (jfk&something). This will also require additional Perl code, so don't do that now.

   You can add more than one of these lines to the menu.html file. You would then change the city code on each line, and to make it more understandable, change the title string and the Weather argument being passed to /bin/button.pl. The button.pl script creates the image of the button on the fly. The word *Weather* will appear on the button in the first example.

4. **Change the button name to something else if you like by editing the button.pl script and replacing the word *Weather*.**

   Be careful not to put too much on the button because MH will shrink the font size to make everything fit.

   By adding the HTML code in Step 2 to menu.html, you're adding another option on the left menu. MH will create a new button called Weather. If you hover your mouse over the button, the title "National Weather Service for *[your location]*" will appear.

5. **Click the Weather menu button to execute the nws.pl Perl script (passing jfk as an argument).**

   The nws.pl script in turn calls the weather script, which goes out to the weather service (which might take longer than 60 seconds, depending on Internet traffic). The weather script returns the data it captured to nws.pl. At this point, nws.pl massages the data (more on that after I introduce the code) and builds a Web page, which is returned to MH to be displayed.

And with that, I can reduce the script to this much code:

```
my ($arg1) = @_; # Get the arguments from the command line
my $data = "<pre>";

# Get the weather
if($arg1) {
   $data = `~mh/bin/weather $arg1`;
} else {
   $data = `~mh/bin/weather`;
}
# Returns a bunch of ^M, delete them (\r = ^M)
$data =~ s/\r//g;
# Eat the first Newline
$data =~ s/\n//;

$data .= "</pre>";

return $data;
```

As you can see, it isn't a very long script. Here's an explanation:

The first line gets the argument, if any, passed to this script.

The next line declares $data as a local variable (you can't use it outside this script) and sets it to the string <pre>. Remember that the <pre></pre> tags are used to get the browsers to leave the format of the text alone.

Next the script determines whether $arg1 has been set to something, and if true, the script executes the weather command with the $arg1. If $arg1 hasn't been set, you have a blank $arg1, and the weather program executes without $arg1. The weather program will return the weather for the Trenton NJ area. The back ticks (`) tell the script to run this Linux command and capture its output.

The weather command will go out and pull back the weather information for the city code you request. This data is returned to this script and stored in the variable $data.

The next line in the script, containing $data =~ s/\r//g;, is really odd looking. It's Perl's way of doing a search and replace. The search and replace functions involves regular expressions. See the "Regular expressions (regex)" sidebar for some details.

The first argument between the slashes (\r or an ASCII carriage return) is to be replaced by the second argument between the slashes (in this case, nothing). So the script searches $data, replaces the first argument with the second argument, and returns the new modified string to $data.

The letter g towards the end of the line signifies to do this task globally (the entire string). The reason to remove this is that the normal line ending for internet data is a carriage return and a linefeed (\n). The <pre></pre> tags will treat the carriage return and linefeed as two line endings. This effectively double spaces everything, which is great for term papers but looks lousy on Web pages. (The normal line ending for Linux is a linefeed.)

The next command, $data =~ s/\n//;, then removes the first linefeed. The reason, I didn't like that first blank line (okay, so I'm picky) is the lack of a g at the end of this search and replace function. Without it, the command just performs the search and replace on the first match it finds.

The next command is $data .= "</pre>";, another interesting aspect of Perl. The .= signifies that the following string is to be appended to the string $data is set to.

The last line returns the string stored in $data back to MH.

If you could see the string that is sent back to MH, you would see this:

```
<pre>
Weather Conditions at 07:51 PM EST on 16 Feb 2006 for New York JFK, NY.
Temp(F)    Humidity(%)    Wind(mph)    Pressure(in)    Weather
========================================================================
   45          81%       SOUTH at 15      30.17        Mostly Cloudy

Forecast for New York, NY
829 PM EST Thu Feb 16 2006
```

```
...Wind Advisory in effect from 9 am to 6 PM EST Friday...

.Overnight...Partly cloudy...becoming mostly cloudy. Lows in the lower
40s. South winds 10 to 15 mph.
</pre>
```

I took the liberty to trim the data (it's much longer) but the final output to the Web page looks like Figure 17-6.

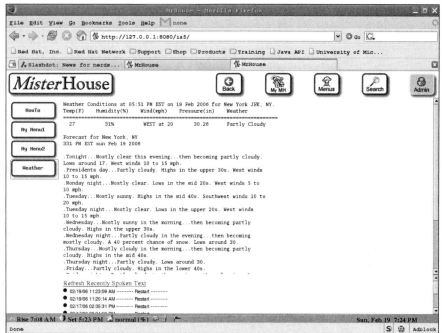

**Figure 17-6:** The National Weather Service script.

You might have noticed while running the weather command manually that there was a long pause between the time you pressed Enter and the time it took to display all the information. Well, MH would notice that, too, and you'll begin to see MH paused messages in the print logs. This is MH's way of letting you know that it was tied up waiting to do something. One solution is to move the page creation to outside MH but to put the finished page in the appropriate Web directory. You can do so by using a script with cron, instructing it to run the command at some odd hour, and parsing the output into a suitable format for MR. You would then have a button the points to the output Web page instead of a Perl script. This way, MH wouldn't pause when getting the information because it would have the Web page ready made. You could run the cron job once a day or a couple times a day.

## Regular expressions (regex)

I know of very little that is more UNIX-y than *regular expressions* (regex). Regular expressions are syntax rules for pattern matching. You're probably already familiar with some, especially if you've ever searched for a filename in a directory.

In Linux, you would simply type **\*foo\*** to search for all the files in the current directory that contain the snippet *foo* in their filename. If you use `*foo`, you'll search for everything that ends with foo; `foo*` gets you everything that starts with foo. The `*foo*` is a regex that follows the rules of the program you're using (most likely `bash` or `sh`).

Perl also has an extensive set of rules (*ai caramba,* do they got rules) for using regex with its scripts. These Perl regex rules cover grouping, quantifying, and an assortment of wildcards

rules. Plain and simple, they are extremely powerful and make searching and manipulating strings easy to do. Unfortunately they are also very complex. There are entire books (not just one) on the subject for just Perl. In the small MH Perl script I've created in this chapter, I used a very simple function to search and replace parts of a string I received back from a command under Linux. That command — `s/X/Z/` — says "search for X and replace it with Z but only do it for the first Z you find."

If I wanted to make the replacement for all instances of X, I'd change the command like this: `s/X/Z/g`. The g at the end of the command means *globally.* If you wanted to insert Z after X, you'd use this command: `s/X/\1Z/g`. The `\1` refers to the match string X. From here, more options can be added.

You can extend the script further to change other aspects of the data being returned. *Note:* Even though the browser will leave the text alone inside the `<pre></pre>` tags it will also properly interpret any HTML tags that are found there also.

You can create a whole page that contains information from other scripts running under MH. You could also add a new link to `menu.html` to take statistics from your firewall router (maybe using SNMP or by other means). You can keep a running total of your daily, weekly, monthly, and yearly transfer rates and byte counts. Or you could combine your home weather station information with the information from the National Weather Service to create a more useful weather page (current weather and forecasts). You can add graphs and pictures to further enhance the page. Before you think me to crazy and all this far-off fantasy stuff, remember that today's IP cameras are pretty cheap (pretty pictures from outside you window). You can get weather data from your personal weather station. Add in the weather report from this section and you've got yourself a better weather report than you can see on the TV.

# Chapter 18

# Remotely Accessing Your MisterHouse Controls

*W*elcome to the wild wild West, where bandits lurk around every boulder and con men try to hustle you out of your earnings. That sounds like the start of a bad western, but it could be a description of today's Internet. Actually, the Internet isn't that bad; the headlines do seem to focus on the negative (scams) while ignoring the positive (new services, entertainment, news, and research). But still, on today's Internet, you've got to be careful. The bad guys are creative and go to great lengths to try to access your system. And don't think for a minute that just because you aren't running Windows that you're invulnerable. As I write this, there are reports of the Mac OS X having a severe exploit, and several Linux apps (applications) can give the bad guys access to your machine. So what are you to do to keep the bad guys out? You use common sense, you don't panic, and you protect yourself from the outside in by setting up proper network protection, proper server protection and administration, and proper user tools.

Accessing MisterHouse (MH) from outside your home (no matter what you might think after reading the sidebar, "The bad guys break in") is possible. It doesn't take much to do it, either, and if you set it up properly, it's easy to use. Basically, I assume that you're somewhere else, like at work. You're using a Windows or Linux machine, and you want to impress your friends and co-workers. (This has very high geek value!) Basically, you start a secure shell application, ssh, to connect to your home server. Then you start up your browser and connect to MH. Yes, it's that easy to use, but the devil's in the details. In this case, the devil's in the following details:

1. **Setting up your firewall:** At home, you need to open up a port on your firewall and send that port to your MH server (port forwarding).

2. **Setting up your MH server:** You need to set up your Linux box with the proper iptables information to permit only certain IP addresses to access your MH server. I show you how in the "Locking Up with iptables" section.

3. **Setting up the ssh application you'll use to connect to your home:** You need to properly administer ssh and your ssh keys on the MH server. The "Connecting with PuTTY" section takes you through this step.

When you complete these steps, you'll be able to connect from almost anywhere in the world (depending on how tight your settings are).

## The bad guys break in

Let me tell you a little story of my first real encounter with the bad guys. First, understand that I've been using UNIX systems since 1985. When Linux first came out, I installed it on my home machine. I was running the sendmail MTA (Mail Transfer Agent) on a dialup line. I thought I had a pretty good understanding of the administration of sendmail, at least until I received a rather heated message from an unknown user that I was spewing out spam. What he reported to me was that someone had found my machine and was bouncing mail through it. It turned out to be a bug in sendmail (it was really buggy back then), but that didn't matter because my machine was helping a spammer. All this occurred in less than 15 minutes from when I started to dial up the Internet to when I received the e-mail that I had a problem.

**Lesson 1:** If you connect to the Internet, they'll find you. The faster the link is, the faster they'll find you. **Lesson 2:** Always keep up with your system's patches.

Now let me tell you a second story. A few years later, I needed to do a fresh reload on my Linux server/firewall box (a major upgrade from Linux 1.2 to 2.1). So I loaded the new version of Linux but neglected to disconnect from the broadband connection. (I was a beta tester for the @Home service.) Within seconds of finishing the installation, I noticed a whole lot of traffic on my cable modem. I was puzzled, so I checked the logs and found that my Linux box was under attack from several programs. One was an automated password guesser and the other a *port knocking program* (a program to check what network services are available). Although no one got in, I did have to quickly lock down my Linux box and install the most recent patches to secure it. After that, I purchased a hardware broadband router (a firewall/NAT box).

**Lesson 3:** Get a hardware firewall/NAT router to help protect your home network.

# Securing Your Home Network

Securing your network is an important step to take to keep people out while still allowing yourself in. You need to be able to access your network to be able to control and administer MisterHouse remotely. This section briefly explains a typical home network and gives some general security steps.

Networking your home is becoming more popular because there is usually more than one computer in the home. With wireless network products, networking is easier than ever. No messy cables are strung about the house (visible cables = very low Spouse Approval Factor!), and you can set it up in a few minutes. In a home with Linux, it isn't unusual for both Windows and Linux to exist on the same network. This works out pretty well for all involved because Linux can be a server, a desktop computer, or both quite easily. Linux can share printers, files, hard drive space, Internet access, and other things quite easily.

I used to share Internet access through my Linux server, but I found that if I took down the server for maintenance or for other reasons, my family lost Internet connectivity. A simple and effective solution to this problem is to get a broadband router. Today's broadband routers (also known as firewalls) provide excellent features, such as Internet access sharing, firewall protection, and routing capabilities. In Chapter 4, I explain how to put together and secure your network with a firewall that has Wireless networking (a WAP; wireless access point). Figure 18-1 is a good example of a typical home network setup. If you aren't using my exact setup, you need to open a port on your firewall to allow ssh to be port-forwarded to your Linux server's IP address. Normally the port for ssh is 22, but I recommend using a different port. I discuss this further in the section "Setting up encryption keys," later in this chapter.

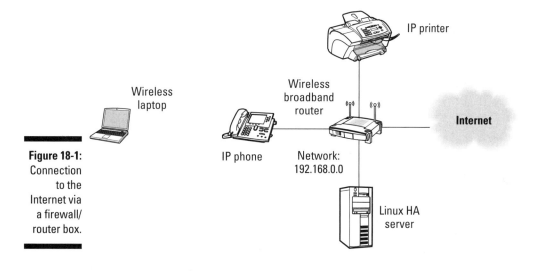

**Figure 18-1:** Connection to the Internet via a firewall/router box.

IP printer

Wireless laptop

Wireless broadband router

**Internet**

IP phone

Network: 192.168.0.0

Linux HA server

# Administering Linux

A large part of network security is performing proper configuration and maintenance of your server. These tasks fall under the heading of system administration, and performing the tasks in this section is critical to ensuring good network security. System administration probably ranks up there with cleaning out the garage on your to-do list, but it's actually pretty important, and it really isn't that hard. Remember that you aren't providing support for a huge corporation — just a small home network. Most of the system administration work is either initial setup or backups (and if you have Windows machine, deleting viruses and spyware). So administering your home machine is not so traumatic. Start out with these tips for good system administration practices:

✔ Use the root account only for system administration and not day-to-day user activities.

✔ Make sure all accounts have passwords.

✔ Use passwords that are not easy to guess.

✔ Lock unused accounts and groups so you can't log in to them.

✔ Disable any network services you are not using.

✔ Uninstall unused software.

✔ Use the software firewall, iptables, to further secure your server .

✔ Keep up-to-date with security advisories and software updates.

Although this isn't an extensive list, it's a good start. Take advantage of the tools for system administration, such as the System Monitor; the System Logs applications; and the Services, System Security Level, and Firewall tools. I don't cover how to administer your Linux box, but I do cover iptables in a moment. There are plenty of good books on how to properly administer your Linux box, such as *Red Hat Linux Networking and System Administration,* 3rd Edition, by Terry Collings and Kurt Wall (Wiley Publishing, Inc.). Also, let me mention SELinux, or Security Enhanced Linux, which just came out as I started this book. Basically, it's access lists for applications. Unfortunately, I haven't had a chance to become very familiar with it, but it promises to secure what the applications are able to access (more securely than Linux's file permissions do).

# Replacing telnet and FTP with ssh and sftp

telnet and FTP are tools that have been around since the early 1980s and are used to connect to another computer, execute commands, or connect to services and transfer files back and forth. One of the problems with telnet and FTP is that all the information is sent in plain text. By using a tool called a *sniffer,* such as tcpdump or Ethereal, someone could capture the session, save it, and analyze it to get the username and password. A *sniffer* is a network diagnostics tool that translates the information inside an IP packet into something you can decipher and make sense of. Its main purpose is for analyzing network problems. Of course, such a tool in the hands of the wrong people is not a good thing.

Today, a lot of network equipment still uses telnet to access, configure, and maintain the configurations. This is done on securely designed networks so that illegal sniffing shouldn't be possible. The use of telnet and FTP (other than anonymous FTP) is not a good idea for use on the wild west known as the Internet. There are too many unknown networks that the packets have to pass through before they get to their destinations.

To solve the problem of plain text transmission, ssh was born. As I describe further in the next section, ssh uses public and private keys to encrypt the contents of an IP packet. The encryption makes it much more difficult for nefarious-deed doers to nab the information inside an IP packet. The ssh is actually a suite of tools that includes

✔ **sshd:** Replaces telnetd, the server daemon.

✔ **ssh:** Replaces telnet, the remote user application.

✔ **scp:** Replaces FTP for copying files securely.

✔ **sftp:** Replaces FTP.

Although ssh and sftp are one-to-one replacements for telnet and FTP, they also have more features. With proper configuration, you can set up the ssh suite to permit you to connect to a remote system without requesting a password. (You can't do that with telnet or FTP.) This can be very useful in scripts where you would normally have to embed the password into the script to allow it to log in to a remote system.

One down side of this remote connection method is that if someone breaks into your account or steals your private key, he or she could get access to the remote system you share your ssh keys with.

In the next sections, I further explain the encryption keys that ssh uses, and then I show you how to access a system that is running ssh and how to set up your own keys.

## Understanding public and private keys

ssh uses encryption to hide the information inside the packets that are transmitted between the server and remote client. So by default, ssh is more secure than telnet because all information in a telnet session is transmitted in plain text. In addition, ssh allows you to use public/private key encryption for authentication to the ssh server. Public/private key encryption is not enabled by default and must be enabled if you want to use it. Basically, it works like this: At the start of an ssh session, when a user attempts to log in to the ssh server, the server requests the public key from the remote system, and the public key is then compared with the private key that is contained on the server. If the keys match, the user is allowed access. Setting up encryption keys is explained in the "Setting up encryption keys" section, later in this chapter.

## Accessing an ssh system

To access a system that has ssh running, you need to type this:

```
ssh user_id@somesystem.com
```

This connects your computer to the system *somesystem*.com as user user_id. Of course, if you don't have an account on that system, you won't get very far. But don't worry if you haven't set up your ~/.ssh/authorized_keys file before you log in. sshd will ask you for a password if you don't have a key or if your key mismatches.

One of the additional features that ssh provides is *tunneling,* which allows other applications to use the secure tunnel to connect to other services available on the server you are connecting to. To create a tunnel to get to the *destination*.com Web server by using ssh, you need to type something like this:

```
ssh user_id@somesystem.com -L 7000:destination.com:80
```

The line breaks down like this:

> user_id is your user ID.
>
> *somesystem*.com is the name of the computer you want to log in to.
>
> Your local IP port is 7000 (which is a safe port number to start with). *destination*.com is the name of the system the new service is connected to. (You could use an IP address instead of a name.) The port number of the service you want to connect to is 80. Port 80 is typically the Web server port.

I explain tunneling in more detail in the "Building tunnels" section, later in this chapter.

In addition to tunneling and connectivity, the ssh suite provides you with a way to transfer files with `sftp` and `scp`. To use `sftp` to transfer files, you type something like this:

```
sftp user_id@somesystem.com
```

This logs you in (you'll be prompted for a password if you don't have your keys properly set up), and then you can begin an interactive session as you would with your normal FTP. Another method of copying files is with `scp` (secure copy). To use `scp`, you type in something like this:

```
scp local_file user_id@somesystem.com:/path
```

This copies the file `local_file` on your local system to the directory `/path` on `somesystem.com`. If you want to copy a file from the remote system to your local system, you reverse the commands. `scp` works just like the local `cp` command and supports the use of all the wildcard characters. And don't forget the colon (`:`). If you do, you'll create a file on your local machine, or you might get an error.

# Setting up encryption keys

Now that you know how to use ssh, it's a good time to set up your keys. To create a key under Linux, you need to do the following:

1. **Open a terminal on the Linux server and type** ssh-keygen -t rsa -b 2048.

2. **When asked where to save the key, accept the default.**

   This is your private key file. Do not share this with other users, and do not store this on the Internet. You might want to make a backup copy of it and keep it safe and secure.

3. **When prompted for your passphrase, you can either enter one or leave it empty.**

   I always use a passphrase for security, but if no one else will ever use your system, you can skip the passphrase. (A *passphrase* is very much like a password except that a password tends to be a single word made up of letters, numbers, and special characters that should be relatively easy to remember but difficult to guess. A passphrase takes this one step further and instead of being just a word it's more like a sentence. Such as Cand13d App7e_Dre4m$, which looks like Candied Apple Dreams.)

4. **When asked to enter your passphrase a second time, leave it empty if you left it empty the first time (in Step 3); otherwise, type in your passphrase again.**

    Case and punctuation must match exactly.

5. **Copy the file `~/.ssh/id_rsa.pub` to your remote system's `~/.ssh/authorized_keys` file.**

    When you copy the contents of the file `~/.ssh/id_rsa.pub` to your `~/.ssh/authorized_keys` file on the remote system, make sure you enter it on a new line at the end of the current file and that this new entry is one continuous line. It might wrap on-screen (that's okay), but don't let your editor add new lines to break up the single line. If you do, ssh won't work, and you will still be asked for the prompt.

    Lastly, ssh is very picky about permissions. The `~/.ssh/authorized_key` file must not have write permissions for anyone else but the user (who is the file owner). Just be sure to generate the keys and copy the files while you're logged in as the same user and you won't need to worry about permissions.

Now that you can connect to other systems, you must make sure your system is set up properly to accept ssh connections. Most systems have ssh turned on by default so it's already running, but I recommend making a few changes to the `/etc/ssh/sshd_config` file:

✔ **Do not use port 22.** Port 22 is a well-known port for ssh. Unfortunately, a bunch of script kiddies have been banging away at every IP address on the Internet checking to see whether ssh is running and then trying every name in some kind of dictionary to get into the system. So leaving the ssh port 22 open to the Internet is asking for trouble. The solution is to not open your firewall on port 22 but on a different port and configure sshd to listen on that additional port. (sshd can listen on more than one port.) I recommend something greater than port 4000. In the following example, I arbitrarily chose port 13218. I've taken the liberty to trim the sshd_config file (a lot) and to present you only with the changes that need to be added. You can add these at the bottom of the file:

```
ListenAddress 0.0.0.0:13218

DenyUsers root bin daemon adm lp sync shutdown halt
         mail news uucp operator
```

The `ListenAddress` line tells `sshd` to listen on all your Linux server's IP addresses (usually `127.0.0.1` and whatever your Ethernet port's IP address is). The second line is all the users that are not permitted to log in via ssh. Be liberal with the users added to that list; this is just a sample.

✔ **Do not permit the user root to log in directly via ssh.** This is the most common method of attack on ssh. Instead, if you need to be root, use the `sudo` command or `su -` command. This makes it more difficult for

> outside users to get in as root directly. One of the advantages of using two ports is that your local users can still access ssh directly on port 22 or your alternative port.

After you've made the changes to the file, you need to restart sshd with this command:

```
service sshd restart
```

To use ssh with the new port assignment, add the option -p *port number*; for scp, add -P *port number*, like this:

```
ssh -p 13218 user_id@somesystem.com -L 7000:destination.com:80
```

This example uses the tunnel options, but you can ignore them if you want.

# Locking Up with iptables

If you want to directly connect your Linux server to the Internet (dialup or broadband), you should know iptables! *iptables* is the network packet filtering system for Linux. After your firewall, iptables rules are the next line of defense in your security arsenal. It looks at the incoming packet (a TCP/IP packet) and determines, from a set of rules you establish, what to do with the packet. It can ignore and drop the packet, return an error to the sender, let the packet pass, or mangle the packet (change certain values inside the packet), like when your Linux firewall does NAT, or Network Address Translation. It can do all these things to packets entering and leaving your computer.

My interest in iptables is just for ssh, but the principles apply to other ports, also. If you're interested in tools that will simplify using iptables, take a look at Firewall Builder at www.fwbuilder.org. Firewall Builder can take you a long way toward building complex iptables on your server. For now, I stick to just using iptables with ssh and sshd.

## Understanding the iptables.sh script

To permit and deny access to the sshd service, you use this iptables.sh script:

```
:
# =[ Variables ]============================================================
# Port I want processed.
PORT=13218

Permit_str=" ssh permit: "
```

```
Deny_str="ssh deny: "
# =[ Permit ]=============================================================
# Allow these site access to my machine
permit() {
    # I want to log just the start of the conversation
    /sbin/iptables -A INPUT -s ${1} -p tcp --dport ${PORT} -j LOG --syn \
       --log-level info --log-prefix "${Permit_str}" \
       --log-ip -options
    /sbin/iptables -A INPUT -s ${1} -p tcp --dport ${PORT} -j ACCEPT
}

# =[ Deny ]===============================================================
# Deny these sites access to my machine
deny() {
    /sbin/iptables -A INPUT -s ${1} -p tcp --dport ${PORT} -j LOG \
       --log-level alert --log-prefix "${Deny_str}" \
       --log-ip-options
    /sbin/iptables -A INPUT -s ${1} -p tcp --dport ${PORT} -j DROP
}
# =[ Permit list ]========================================================
#permit 127.0.0.0/8              # This gets denied, I used it to test
permit 10.2.3.4                  # A specific host out on the internet
permit 172.16.1.0/255.255.255.0 # local stuff
permit 192.168.102.20            # My laptop on my wireless network
permit 192.168.101.0/255.255.255.0 # Local stuff, entire 192.168.101.0 network
#

# =[ Deny list ]==========================================================
deny 0.0.0.0/0                   # Deny everyone else
exit 0
```

This is a shell script called `iptables.sh`, and it permits and denies IP
addresses access to port 13218 (my alternate ssh port). The way I have it
configured in the script is to add IP networks or hosts to the permit list by
adding the line

```
permit <IP address>
```

which is the command for a specific host, or

```
permit <IP network>/mask
```

which is for a specific network. Order is very important, which is why I've
placed the permitted IP addresses before the denied IP addresses; think of it
as "I'll permit this and deny everything else." You shouldn't need to add anything to the deny list because the deny statement will match any network not
permitted. You need to know the IP address or network number and mask of
the machine that you're trying to communicate from.

*If the IP address is a static address (doesn't use DHCP) and isn't behind a fire-
wall doing NAT,* you can just use its IP address. Don't worry; you won't need
the mask.

*If the IP address is behind a firewall doing NAT,* you need to figure out the IP address. You can try the URL www.whatismyipaddress.com from the computer of interest to get the IP address.

*If you know that the IP address is learned via DHCP,* you need to be a bit more inventive. Because the address might change at any time, you might need to include the entire network by using the network and mask. First, find out the IP address and mask that the machine currently uses. On Windows machines, use ipconfig; on your Linux box, it's /sbin/ifconfig; and on your firewall, you might need to find it in one of its menus. You can then use that as the argument to permit, like so:

```
permit 10.255.4.13/255.255.252.0
```

or

```
permit 172.31.94.62
```

The first permit is the IP address and mask of a host with an ISP that uses DHCP. The second is just a static host address. Please note that in all my example permit statements, I use private IP addressing. This is the IP address space that isn't allowed to be routed outside on the Internet (though most ISPs use this address space internal to their networks, legally). Do a search for **RFC1918** for the specifics. The private IP addresses consist of

- ✔ 10.0.0.0 - 10.255.255.255
- ✔ 172.16.0.0 - 172.31.255.255
- ✔ 192.168.0.0 - 192.168.255.255

The last address space is often used by home network equipment for its default address space. I'm sorry I couldn't put in real addresses, but if I did, they would be inundated with traffic, and that wouldn't be very nice.

## *Installing the iptables.sh script*

To install the script (which is included on this book's CD) you need to add it to your rc.local script. This script is run after all the other services are started up. To add it, do the following:

1. **Open a terminal.**

2. **Type** su - **and enter the password for user root**

3. **Type** cp /media/cdrom/chapter18/iptables.sh /etc/ **and press Enter.**

4. **Type** chmod u+rx /etc/iptables.sh **and press Enter.**

5. **Type** echo -e "\nif [ -x /etc/iptables.sh ]; then\n /etc/iptables.sh\nfi\n" >>/etc/rc.d/rc.local **and press Enter.**

Most of this is pretty standard except the last line. It's all one line, but it was too long to fit on the page. What you're doing here is copying the `iptables. sh` shell script to the directory `/etc/`. Then you change its permissions to be executable. Finally, you add a few lines of shell script to `rc.local` to execute `iptables.sh` on startup.

# Connecting with PuTTY

PuTTY is a telnet/ssh application that runs on UNIX (and Linux, of course) and Windows platforms. The reason I chose PuTTY was that it does a nice job of creating tunnels from the running platform to the remote system, and it pretty much operates the same on Linux as it does on Windows. In addition to providing telnet and ssh, it supports tunnels.

## Installing PuTTY

PuTTY is included on the CD, so you don't have to go looking for it on the Web. Pop the CD into your CD drive and then install PuTTY, following the appropriate directions:

- **Installing PuTTY under Windows:** Double-click the `putty-installer. exe` file in the `D:` drive (or whatever drive your CD is on) under the Windows directory. Walk through the directions in the windows, but make sure you create a desktop icon and a quick launch icon for PuTTY.

- **Installing PuTTY under Linux:**

    1. *Open a terminal session.*

    2. *Type **tar zxf /media/cdrom/chapter18/putty.tar.gz** and press Enter.*

    3. *Type **cd putty/unix** and press Enter.*

    4. *Type **sudo make -f Makefile.gtk install** and press Enter.*

When the installation is done, you're ready to start PuTTY:

- Under Windows, start PuTTY by double-clicking the PuTTY icon.

- Under Linux, simply type **putty &** in the terminal session.

For both Linux and Windows, you'll see a dialog box that looks like Figure 18-2. When PuTTY opens for the first time, there are no sessions defined. You need to create a session.

**Figure 18-2:**
The PuTTY
Configuration
dialog box.

To add a session, follow these steps:

1. **Type the hostname or IP address in the Host Name (or IP Address) text box.**

2. **Select the protocol you need to use.**

   • The protocol Raw will echo back everything you type.

   • The protocol Telnet is, well, for telnet (even if it isn't on port 23).

   • The protocol Rlogin is for rlogin, logically enough. (Don't worry if you don't know what that is.)

   • The protocol SSH is for secure shell access. It's the protocol you need if you want to use PuTTY with tunnels.

3. **Change the port number (if necessary).**

   If you need to change it, now is the time to do so. (Don't do it before you select the protocol; otherwise, your port number will change to the default for that protocol.)

   The port number must be the same as the port number that your firewall is configured for.

4. **Enter a name for the session (you make this up) in the Saved Session text box and then click Save.**

5. **Open the session by selecting it in the list, clicking Load, and then clicking Open.**

   Alternatively, you can just double-click the saved session in the list to open it directly.

6. **If everything is working properly, you will be asked for your login ID and then your password.**

If you're in your office, your employer might block ssh (as mine does). So you might need to check with your network administration folks to find out.

If you've already tried to open a session, close that PuTTY session and restart PuTTY. When it has restarted, select the hostname you just added and click Load. (Don't double-click the hostname or a new session will be loaded.) You need to make a lot of additional changes to properly support ssh and tunnels. I explain these changes in the next three sections.

## Generating ssh keys with PuTTYgen

Typically, when you use telnet, you must enter your login ID and your password. With ssh and PuTTY, you can create a key that can be used to log you in without asking for your password. In PuTTY, you use a program called PuTTYgen, which creates the public and private keys you need. To create these keys, follow these steps:

1. **Start PuTTYgen.**

   Under Windows, choose Start⇨Programs⇨PuTTY⇨PuTTYgen.

   Under Linux, open a terminal session and type **puttygen &**.

   In both cases, you start PuTTYgen and see the dialog box shown in Figure 18-3. Note the defaults.

**Figure 18-3:** The PuTTY Key Generator dialog box.

2. **Make some changes in the Parameters area.**

Here are my recommendations:

- *Type of Key to Generate:* Keep the SSH-2 RSA setting. The SSH-2 RSA setting is the strongest (most difficult to break) of the three, so it's a good idea to use it. If you must support SSH-1 (old equipment that supports only SSH-1), click that. I don't recommend SSH-1; it was found to have flaws and is considered weak.

- *Number of Bits in a Generated Key:* Change the number of bits to 2048. The security community keeps an eye on the raw power needed to attack the keys, and I think it will be possible to break 1024-bit keys within a year or so of this book's publication. The 2048-bit key will be good for a while longer. You could jump up to a 4096-bit key, but the amount of time it takes to process the key (generating it and using it) really slows things down. The 2048-bit key is a good compromise for now.

**3. After you're done making changes, if any, click the Generate button.**

The dialog box changes, and you will be asked to move the mouse around inside the application dialog box.

**4. Move the mouse all over the place.**

Don't worry — it's okay to do so. I recommend some slow movements and some fast ones, but mostly you should move it around randomly. This randomness helps to generate the key. The whole process takes a few minutes, so keep going until after the progress bar fills and clears. Then the key will be generated, and the dialog box will be redrawn with a lot of new information.

When the new information appears, you will be given the options to save your public key and your private key (see Figure 18-4).

**Figure 18-4:**
A PuTTYgen-generated key.

5. **(Optional) Enter a passphrase in the Key Passphrase text box (and again in the Confirm Passphrase text box).**

   It's usually a wise idea to create a passphrase to protect your key (you'll be asked for that passphrase whenever you use the key), but if you need to use one of the ssh tools to connect to a remote system via a script, not using a passphrase is probably a good idea. Adding the passphrase to a script just exposes the passphrase, which is needed, in the script.

6. **Click Save Public Key to save the public key.**

   A dialog box opens and prompts you for a name for the key. When saving the public key, you can name it whatever you like, but I recommend using the .pub ending.

7. **Click Save after you have entered the name of the file.**

   The public key file contains the public key to be added to your `~/.ssh/authorized_keys` file on remote systems.

8. **Click Save Private Key to save the private key.**

   If you haven't entered a passphrase, you will be prompted for one. You can choose to continue without entering a passphrase or enter one if you want. Click OK to continue. A dialog box opens and prompts you to name the key. When saving your private key, PuTTY uses the .ppk ending. Never share your private key with anyone. If someone has your private key, he or she can masquerade as you.

9. **Click Save to save the private key file.**

## Building tunnels

Before I show you how to configure tunnels, I start by explaining how tunnels work. The networking involved gets a little crazy because you use one network to get to another, and there is Network Address Translation (NAT) involved.

Figure 18-5 shows a typical user's home network to the left of the Internet cloud. There, the ISP has given the user one IP address, and the firewall is doing NAT to share that single IP address with all the computers in the user's home. NAT translates the network address of the user's PC to the network address the ISP has provided. This is the only address the ISP knows how to deal with for the user. When the user's traffic comes back, the router converts the ISP-provided address to the user's address. If someone on the Internet tries to communicate with the ISP-provided address, the conversation is ignored unless the router is configured to do something with it or the user has already started a session with that site and this is the return data. This helps with security by keeping attacks away from the user's PCs. (I describe this further in Chapter 4.)

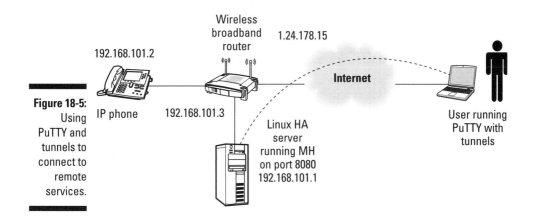

Figure 18-5:
Using
PuTTY and
tunnels to
connect to
remote
services.

To allow ssh traffic from the outside to go to the Linux home automation server, you have to configure the firewall to forward traffic on the port you are using for ssh from the router to the port on the server for ssh traffic. Also, the server is set up with iptables to further limit who is allowed to connect to the server.

When everything is set up, the user can start up PuTTY on his or her remote laptop and connect to the IP address of the router by entering the IP address or by utilizing one of the dynamic DNS services. A dynamic DNS service translates a hostname to the correct IP address. The firewall then connects the ssh session to the Linux HA server, and the user can log in and access Linux. At this point, any tunnels that PuTTY has configured will be available.

Now, here's where the tunnels come into play. If you want to use PuTTY to get to MH on your Linux server (the point of this chapter), you can use a tunnel to connect from your laptop's port 7000 (7000 is usually an unused port, so it's a safe port to start with) to the destination of `192.168.101.1:8080` (MH's IP address and default Web port). If you need to create a second tunnel to access the camera, you can use a source port of 7001 (just happens to be the next one available) and a destination address of `192.168.101.2:80`. PuTTY requires you to fill in the IP address (`192.168.101.2`) and the port number (`80`) in this fashion: `192.168.101.2:80`. (Port 80 tends to be the default port for most Web servers.)

MH uses a different address than a Web server, so you can have a Web server and MH running at the same time (just on different ports). Notice that the IP addresses are the actual IP addresses used on the home network. That's because the tunnels terminate on the server where the ssh session is connected to, and these are the IP addresses that the ssh server knows how to get to. Next, to access MH from your remote PC, start up your browser and type the URL `http://127.0.0.1:7000/`; this connects you to MH. To access your camera, type the URL `http://127.0.0.1:7001/`. Notice that `127.0.0.1` is being used in the URL. This is because the other end of the tunnel (on the laptop) knows only about `127.0.0.1`. So to build your tunnels with PuTTY, you need to know the following details first:

✔ The IP address or hostname of the system you want to connect to on your home network

✔ The port number of the service on the system you are going to connect to on your home network

✔ An unused port on your system

To build a tunnel, follow these steps:

1. **Start PuTTY.**

2. **Single-click a saved session and click Load.**

   If you added a session to PuTTY after installing it, you should see your session listed in the Saved Sessions area (refer to Figure 18-2).

3. **Click the Data category under Connection on the left.**

4. **In the Login Details text box, enter your Auto-login username (your login name on your Linux server).**

5. **Select the Auth category under SSH (on the left).**

6. **Select the private key you create earlier, in the section "Generating ssh keys with PuTTYgen" (the filename ends in .ppk).**

   If you have not set up your `~/.ssh/.authorized_keys` file under Linux, ssh prompts you for your normal login. Don't worry; it's still secure; ssh just doesn't recognize your key. You can properly set up your files after you log in.

7. **Fill in the Source Port text box and type the destination address and port number in the Destination text box.**

   For the Source Port, I recommend starting at 7001.

8. **Get back to the Session category by clicking Session at the top left and then click the Save button.**

   If you're satisfied with your settings, you can click the Open button and try out the ssh session and your tunnel via your browser.

# Part VII
# The Part of Tens

The 5th Wave          By Rich Tennant

"You're not going to believe this, but I'm standing in front of a 14.4k chimney. I'll be here all night downloading this stuff."

# In this part . . .

The *For Dummies* Part of Tens is like icing on a cake: You don't have to have icing to eat the cake, but it sure is nice. In Chapter 19, I give you ten suggestions for tasks you can automate. And in Chapter 20, I tell you about ten home automation gadgets that'll get your hands itching to tinker.

# Chapter 19

# (Nearly) Ten Cool Chores You Can Automate

### In This Chapter

▶ Automating your coffee pot, window shades, sprinklers, and greenhouse

▶ Playing gags by using the hackers' favorite fish

▶ Giving your kids or pets loving care even when you aren't at home

▶ Losing extra weight with a smart refrigerator

*W*ouldn't it be nice to wake up every day to the smell of coffee automatically made? Wouldn't you love to see the sunlight suddenly streaming into your bedroom window because your drapes automatically opened? And wouldn't it be nice if your dog could let himself in and out of the house whenever he needed, without your help? And how about keeping an eye on him or your babysitter and children while you're miles away at work? And wouldn't you enjoy having some help from home automation to lose weight? Does this sound like the Jetsons' house of the future? This chapter covers all of these chores and more — including helping to create a talking fish.

## Controlling a Greenhouse

Greenhouses come in all shapes and sizes. But whether your greenhouse consists of a few dozen pots or an acre or so of ground, automating the watering can be a real time-saver — and is probably better for your plants.

If your greenhouse has a drip irrigation system or sprinklers, you can get an X10 controller for it for about $100, more or less. It hooks up to one or more hoses and operates via your X10 system. The tricky part of watering your plants is knowing when to water and how much. Too much water can kill plants, as can too little. Plants need both water and air around their roots to grow properly. And you should never water your plants unless the soil is dry — unless you're growing cattails.

Testing the soil with a soil-moisture sensor to make sure it is properly dry is probably the best way to get good results and healthy plants. Soil-moisture sensors, sometimes called *tensiometers,* come in different shapes, price ranges, and sizes. A tensiometer can be buried in a pot or buried in the ground and connected to a controller, which can automatically water your plants when the tensiometer records that the soil is dry and stop watering when it records that the soil is saturated. You set the parameters of wetness and dryness. Chapters 13 and 14 have more information about X10.

For information on tensiometers, check out `www.aidlltd.com/tensiometers.html`. Also check out `www.aidlltd.com/plantdrip.html` for information about how to automate the watering of your potted plants.

# Watering Your Lawn with Your Computer

Why is it a great idea to water your lawn automatically? Because you not only save effort turning the spigots on and off regularly, but you can also use less water and get a better-looking lawn. Landscapers say that ideally, you want to water your lawn so that the water seeps down to at least 6 inches while also avoiding puddles. To do this, you might need to cycle your sprinklers. *Cycling* means turning the sprinklers on and off at short intervals so that the ground can have time to absorb the water. You can do this by hooking up an X10 sprinkler control system and then creating a macro in your X10 software (such as MisterHouse) to time the cycling. You might need to experiment a few times to find out the optimal cycling time for your lawn. (Just time how long it takes for puddles to form.)

The Rain 8 X10 sprinkler control system is available at `www.wgldesigns.com/rain8.html`. It is an eight-zone sprinkler controller, which means you can attach eight hoses, and you can download Linux configuration software created by Sean Maloney. It also has a rain sensor that can be added for about $25, or you can use MisterHouse to automatically download online weather information for your area and parse it to automatically determine whether it is raining or too windy or too cold to water.

# Checking for Snail Mail

If your home is like mine, you have to walk about half a mile to get to your mail every day — okay that's an exaggeration, but it's probably far enough to be annoying when you get there and the mailbox is empty. You can avoid this annoyance by installing a mail-detecting system. One way to do this is to place an X10 motion sensor, such as the Eagle Eye motion sensor available from www.x10.com, inside in the back of your mailbox and set it to the same house code and unit code as an appliance module (for instance, an appliance module with a light plugged into it). Be sure to plug in a transceiver to pick up the motion sensor's signal. Then your light will turn on when the motion sensor is activated. If you see that the light is on, you know you have mail. You can set your motion detector to turn the light off automatically after about four hours, if you are away for the day — or you can set it for less time. If you want to save electricity, you can turn off your light with a remote when you get your mail.

Also, if you want to keep an eye on your mailbox for security reasons, an X10 video camera aimed at the mailbox and connected to an X10 VCR could capture video of anyone using the mailbox. You might want to use a Nightwatch camera (also available from www.x10.com) because any mischief would likely take place in the dark.

# Hacking Your Bass (You Know, Billy the Bigmouth Bass)

Billy Bass is a realistic-looking plastic fish mounted on a plaque and can be controlled with a button or motion sensor to sing songs — moving its lips to the words and flapping its tail to the beat. Its repertoire includes such songs as Al Green's "Take Me to the River" and Bobby McFerrin's "Don't Worry, Be Happy." This bass caught the attention of a group of Linux hackers who are now working on modifying it to lip-synch to any user-recorded speech. After Billy can lip-synch, the next bass hack is going to be connecting him to a network for teleconferencing. Just think: Someday you might be able to talk into a microphone and control a talking fish! Or you could hook it to a speaker phone and all the words of a caller could be lip-synched by the fish. If there is an ultimate gag, this might be it. Anyone who wants to be a part of this giant leap for mankind can check out http://bigmouth.here-n-there.com.

# Opening and Closing the Window Shades

You can buy motorized drape controllers for anywhere from $99 to hundreds of dollars. One of the cheapest commercial drape controllers is probably the PLC 3142, which is available from Smarthome (www.smarthome.com/3142.html) and looks like a little white box on the wall with the cord for the drapes going through it. It works with drapes or vertical blinds, and you can attach a timer to it or plug it into an X10 appliance module for use with your X10 system. If you're a cost-conscious consumer who's addicted to tinkering, you could probably make your own by using a cordless screwdriver and wall-mounted charger or a rotisserie motor kit for barbecue grills. If you can find the parts you need inexpensively and have lots of drapes or shades to control, you can probably save plenty of money doing it yourself — although a PLC 3142 might look better on your living room wall than a rotisserie grill motor. Whatever works for you.

## Letting Fido Out When You Aren't Home

Depending on your home and how your dog has access to the outside, there might be lots of solutions for automatically letting him in and out. Here's a quick one that uses your automatic garage door:

1. **Update the wall switch of your garage door to an X10 WS13A wall switch (the wall switch for fluorescent lights or appliances, not the one for incandescent lights).**

2. **Place two X10 motion sensors, one on each side of the garage door (inside and outside).**

3. **With your X10 software, create a macro to open the garage door just high enough for your dog to scramble underneath each time either motion detector senses motion.**

   A dog can slip under an opening much smaller than any human can scrape through — unless you're raising Irish Wolfhounds.

4. **Program your macro to close the garage door after a while as long as no new motion is detected.**

   This allows your dog to come and go as he likes, without the unsightly look of a garage door partially open all day long and won't let in any would-be thieves, either.

For more about X10, take a look at Chapters 13 and 14.

## Watching Your Kids from the Internet

When you're away from home, do you want to know what your kids are up to? They might be young enough to require a babysitter or old enough to be on their own — but you might still want to keep an eye on them. Looking in at home, occasionally, can set a parent's mind at ease — or be the cause of an immediate phone call!

You can easily set up a webcam and place it in a likely location to view your kids — for example, on top of the Nintendo? (Maybe knowing that Mom and Dad are watching will dissuade them from that spot? Sure, if pigs could fly.) Instructions for setting up a single webcam and continuously uploading snapshots to a Web page are described in Chapter 8.

But a single webcam probably doesn't cover all the area you want to view. You might want several webcams — one for outside, one for the living room, and don't forget to put one on top of the refrigerator.

To get multiple cameras to interact with your computer, you can buy wireless cameras that send wireless video signals. These are available from www.x10.com. Wireless cameras require a video receiver to receive the image. This can be hooked up to a TV, but to view it over the Internet, you need a TV tuner card (or a graphics card with a built-in TV tuner) to which you can attach your S-video cables or coaxial cable, so that your computer can process the signal. Linux-compatible TV tuner cards are available from a variety of sources — for example, at this writing, you can purchase a Hauppauge WinTV401 PCI Interface TV/FM Tuner Card (also sometimes called a Hauppauge WinTV-dbx card) from www.newegg.com for under $70. Or you can buy a graphics card with a built-in TV tuner card. At http://linuxtv.org/v4lwiki/index.php/ATI and at http://linuxtv.org/v4lwiki/index.php/NVIDIA, you can find lists of ATI and nVidia cards with TV tuners supported by Linux.

Because your computer can process video signals only from one camera at a time by using this method, you can change which camera you want to view by plugging each camera into an X10 Appliance Module and using MisterHouse to send X10 signals to turn off all but the one camera you want to see.

 Cameras and computers can suddenly stop working for a variety of reasons, so don't rely on them for any reason relating to the safety and comfort of your children.

# Losing Weight with Home Automation

Yes, home automation is so much fun that you'll forget to eat. Okay, maybe not. But there's another way to lose weight by using your gadgets.

Nighttime snacking can rack up the pounds quickly. One method that has been found to be effective in combating this urge is to rig your refrigerator and cabinets with some kind of alarm that you can set to sound only during those crucial, evening snack hours. Or, if an alarm seems like overkill, how about a camera hooked up to a VCR? This makes everyone accountable to the entire family. In fact, you might want to hook up a camera and VCR to check on the eating habits of your family during the day while you aren't at home. (That could be an eye-opener.)

To hook up a refrigerator alarm, an X10 motion sensor in the refrigerator set to the same house code and unit code as an appliance module with a radio plugged in can do the trick. You can set it at a low-enough volume that it will startle the munchie marauder but not wake up the rest of the house. And you can set the motion detector to send an off command to turn the radio off after a minute. (That's usually the default anyway.) Or instead of using a radio, you can have your motion sensor activate a red and blue, rotating police light. That won't wake anyone up but still startle the snacker. If you use an X10 camera and X10 VCR, they could begin recording when any of the motion sensor activates, and set the motion sensor to send an off command after a few minutes.

# Heating Your Car Seat on Cold Mornings

Getting into an ice-cold car on a winter morning is no fun. Here's an idea from the friendly X10 community. How about heating your car seat with a small, electric heating pad plugged into an X10 appliance receptacle outside your home or in your garage? You can run an extension cord to the car and attach it to the heating pad. Then close the car door right on the cord to the heating pad. (This is probably fine because car doors have soft neoprene weather stripping around them.) Then schedule your heating pad to begin heating about an hour before you expect to need it. You can enjoy a nice warm drive without having to freeze your bottom until the heat kicks in.

Don't forget to unplug the heating pad before you go anywhere!

# Chapter 20

# Ten Gadgets Worth Checking Out

● ● ● ● ● ● ● ● ● ● ● ● ● ● ● ● ● ● ● ● ● ● ● ● ● ● ● ● ● ● ● ● ● ● ● ● ● ● ● ● ● ● ● ● ● ●

*In This Chapter*

▶ Streaming music clients

▶ Streaming media clients and servers

▶ Standalone print servers

▶ Ninja camera mounts

▶ Remote control your devices

▶ Socket rockets

▶ Universal remote controls

▶ Motion detectors

▶ Nokia 770

▶ Insteon controllers

● ● ● ● ● ● ● ● ● ● ● ● ● ● ● ● ● ● ● ● ● ● ● ● ● ● ● ● ● ● ● ● ● ● ● ● ● ● ● ● ● ● ● ● ● ●

*T*his book tells you about some cool devices and programs you can use to control things around your house or make your life easier or more interesting. This chapter shows you ten more gadgets or devices that you can put to use doing various tasks.

## *Streaming Music Clients*

I was originally planning to talk about the Apple AirPort Express here. The AirPort Express is a device that lets you stream music to powered speakers or a home stereo system. It's what I call a streaming music client, and many of these devices are available in addition to the Airport Express. Some music-only clients include these:

✔ Linksys WMLS11B

```
www.linksys.com/servlet/Satellite?childpagename=US%2FL
    ayout&packedargs=c%3DL_Product_C2%26cid%3D1115
    416831192&pagename=Linksys%2FCommon%2FVisitorW
    rapper
```

✔ Netgear MP101

```
www.netgear.com/products/details/MP101.php
```

✔ Terratec Noxon

```
http://entertainen.terratec.net/modules.php?op=modload
    &name=News&file=article&sid=228
```

✔ Roku Soundbridge

```
www.rokulabs.com/products/soundbridge/index.php
```

These devices all function similarly in that they all connect to your wireless home network. The music client devices then communicate with some type of server program that feeds selected streams of audio across the network to the music clients.

# Streaming Media Clients and Servers

Chapter 7 tells you about a wireless media client made by D-Link called the DSM-320. This device connects to a PC that runs media server software and can stream music and video as well as display slide shows of digital photos.

Besides the streaming media client device, you need to be running media server software on the PC or a device that holds the media you want to stream. Look for a media server program that is uPnP (Universal Plug and Play) compliant and a streaming media client that is also uPnP compliant. As long as you meet this requirement, the program will work on your Linux system. A media server called TwonkyMedia is available for download from `www.twonkyvision.de`. You can download a trial version and give it a try for 30 minutes (yes, 30 *minutes!*). If you like the program, you can buy it online fairly inexpensively. I highly recommend this program.

If you want to stream video and digital photos in addition to music, some of the streaming media client devices to look at are the D-Link DSM-320, the Netgear MP115, and the Philips Streamium SL300i. Many other manufacturers make music-only and media streaming devices. They're listed at the TwonkyVision Web site, and you can find them by clicking the Clients link on the left side of the home page.

# Standalone Print Servers

One problem that I had at my house was being unable to print to the laser printer on the third floor from my wife's PC on the second floor. This kind of problem is becoming a more frequent occurrence for many PC users because more households have multiple PCs. A fairly easy and inexpensive solution to this problem is available if you already have a home network set up: You can install a print server device that connects to your home network either wirelessly or with a cable. You then connect a printer to the device, and anyone connected to the network can use the connected printer.

Many printers sold for business purposes already have a built-in Ethernet connection, and if you have one of these printers, you're ahead of the game. Usually, though, a printer intended for home use doesn't have a built-in network port. If your printer doesn't have a network port, you can still connect it to your network by using a standalone print server.

Print servers are available with parallel port connections, USB connections, or both. They're available with RJ-45 ports that need to be connected to a wired network as well as wireless devices that don't need a physical network connection. You need to pick the device most appropriate for your printer connection type and network. Too many print server brands are available to list them all here. For a good review of many of the available print servers, go to `www.pcmag.com/category2/0,1738,28985,00.asp`. Find one that will suit your needs, set it up, and you'll be printing from anywhere.

# Ninja Camera Mounts

In Parts V and VI, you find out about X10 devices used for controlling and monitoring your home. Some of the X10 devices are video cameras that you place in different locations in your home so you can monitor what is happening. In most cases, the cameras are on fixed mounts, and you can see only what the camera is pointing at. But wouldn't it be cool to be able to move the cameras left and right and up and down?

You can if you use the Ninja camera mounts that are available for the XCam2 video cameras. With the Ninja installed, you can pan, tilt, and sweep the cameras to get the full view as well as set four presets to instantly move the camera to the preset location. The Ninja mounts are controllable locally by using a remote control or local PC, and you can control them across the Internet through a Web browser interface. Take a look at the camera mounts found here:

```
www.x10.com/products/x10_vk74a.htm
```

# Remote Control Your Devices

Picture this scenario if you will. Night has fallen, and you're at home in your pajamas. You just finished locking up and have gone upstairs to bed. Then you realize that you forgot to turn off the lights in the living room. So back down the stairs you go to turn off the lights. But wait, isn't this a book on home automation, and shouldn't you be able to turn off the lights remotely? Yes, you should be able to, and you can — but only if you've installed the equipment that enables you to do so.

One of the nice features of automating your home is the ability to control any device from anywhere. You can install switches and outlets that you can control remotely, either through a hard-wired connection or through radio frequency (RF) transmitters. It isn't that expensive to do, and if you're automating your house, why not include remote control for your lights and appliances? You'll be glad you did, and your friends will be really impressed when they visit you and you show off your system. Go to `http://linuxha.` `sourceforge.net` to read more about home automation with Linux, including remotely controlling devices in your home.

## Socket Rockets

What a strange name . . . or perhaps not. A *socket rocket* is a specific type of device that screws into a standard light bulb socket. You then screw the light bulb into the socket rocket. After this simple installation, the light is now controllable by any X10 remote controller. The socket rocket is a type of remote control device designed to allow for retrofitting of remote control into existing lights and lamps. You can easily make all the lights in your house remote controllable just by screwing one of these rockets into the light bulb socket of each lamp. Socket rockets cost about $20 each, and you can find out more about them here:

```
www.x10.com/automation/x10_lm15a.htm
```

## Universal Remote Controls

This section tells you about two remote control devices you can use to control any infrared (IR), and sometimes radio frequency (RF), controllable device. These remotes are typically known as *universal remote controls* because you can use them to control nearly any device by teaching them the necessary control functions. In most instances, you just need to put the universal remote control into learning mode, point the original remote for the device at the universal remote and press the button for the function you want. Here are two great universal remotes to know about:

 ✔ **The Sony RM-AV3000:** This universal remote is sort of a cross between a tabletop and hand-held remote. This remote has 22 physical buttons for selecting specific component types, such as DVD or VCR, that are pre-configured. In addition to the hard buttons, it offers an LCD touch screen panel with buttons for controlling the devices you selected by using the hard buttons. You can change the configuration for any of the hard buttons so it can control any device, not just what it was initially programmed to control. You can also change the control assignments of the LCD buttons to add or remove functions. This remote is capable of learning commands from other remote devices, as I explain earlier. The remote costs about $200 retail. You can find a detailed review of this remote here:

```
www.remotecentral.com/av3000
```

✔ **The Philips ProntoPro NG TSU7000:** This device costs about $1000 for the IR version, and for another $150, you can get one that can also control RF devices. The Philips remote has a much larger LCD touch screen than the Sony unit and fewer physical buttons. The unit comes preprogrammed to control many types of devices, such as VCRs, DVDs, and other A/V equipment. Of course, you can change the programming to control different devices. And you can teach the Philips remote new control codes by using your original device remote and pressing the buttons while pointing at the Philips. Go to this URL for a detailed review of this remote:

```
www.remotecentral.com/tsu7000
```

# Motion Detectors

Have you ever gone into a room with your hands full and couldn't turn on the lights? Wouldn't it be great if the lights turned on automatically when you entered the room and turned off when you left the room. Well, stop wishing; it is easily possible.

You can install a motion detector in any or all of the rooms in your house. Then, when you enter a room, the motion detector will send a signal to the controller that monitors the detector. The controller then sends a signal to the lights in that room, telling them to turn on.

As long as you're in the room and moving, the lights will stay on. When you leave the room, the lights don't immediately turn off. The controller monitors the motion detector, and when the detector no longer senses movement in the room, it stops sending a signal to the controller. Depending on the controller's program, it could immediately send the signal to the lights to turn off, or it could wait for some programmed delay. No matter how it does the work, it's still pretty cool. This URL provides information on all types of motion sensors:

```
www.x10.com/automation/motion_sensors.html
```

# Nokia 770 Internet Tablet

One device that people are using more frequently to control home automation systems is the Nokia 770 Internet Tablet. With this device, you can browse your favorite sites and read your e-mail from wherever you are. Whether you're relaxing at home or enjoying your kid's soccer game, if you have broadband access over WI-FI, the Nokia 770 Internet Tablet gives you instant wireless access to the Web and the ability to control your home from anywhere.

The Nokia 770 Internet Tablet is easy to use and easy on your eyes, too, with a truly portable design, fashionably discrete brushed metal cover, and an ultra-sharp widescreen display that's optimized for viewing online content. This device is a little pricey (around $400), but it does give you a lot for the money.

One of the best features of the Nokia 770 Internet Tablet is that it runs on the Linux-based Internet Tablet 2005 software edition. Later this year, a launch is planned for an operating system upgrade — the Internet Tablet 2006 software edition — that will support additional services, including Internet telephony (VoIP) and instant messaging. Get more information about this device in a PC Magazine review at

```
www.pcmag.com/article2/0,1895,1820232,00.asp
```

# INSTEON System

INSTEON is the latest development in the home control and automation arena. It combines two networking technologies — wireless radio frequency (RF) and the home's already installed power lines — to create a redundant control network. This redundant network is less susceptible to interference typically found in a home environment. In addition, each INSTEON device acts as a repeater by retransmitting signals it receives, making communications more reliable.

INSTEON is designed to be an inexpensive, yet more robust, replacement for X10 home automation devices. Users with existing X10 networks can easily migrate to an INSTEON-based network while still using their existing X10 devices. All INSTEON devices will accept communications from X10 devices on the network. INSTEON devices contain a unique identifier that identifies them to other devices on the network. As new devices come onto the network, each device identifies itself and a peer-to-peer network is created, with each device aware of the other devices. Because each device is capable of identifying itself and other devices on the network, no complicated network controllers are necessary, so network setup is easy.

# Appendix

# About the CD

● ● ● ● ● ● ● ● ● ● ● ● ● ● ● ● ● ● ● ● ● ● ● ● ● ● ● ● ● ● ● ● ● ● ● ● ● ● ● ● ● ● ● ● ● ● ● ● ● ● ● ● ●

*T*he CD that comes with this book is packed with the software that I discuss throughout the book, plus scripting and configuration files. In this appendix, I give you the requirements necessary for using the CD, and I describe the software it contains. Enjoy!

*Note:* The software contained on the CD is designed specifically to run on Linux.

## System Requirements

Make sure your computer meets the following minimum system requirements. If your computer doesn't match up to most of these requirements, you might have problems using the contents of the CD.

- A PC with a Pentium or faster processor.
- A Linux distribution with a 2.4 or 2.6 Linux kernel such as Fedora FC 5 or Debian 3.1.
- At least 32MB of total RAM installed on your computer. For best performance, I recommend at least 128MB of RAM installed.
- One or more free serial ports.
- At least 500MB of free hard drive space.
- A CD-ROM drive.

If you need more information on the basics, check out these books published by Wiley Publishing: *PCs For Dummies,* 10th Edition, by Dan Gookin, or *Linux For Dummies,* 7th Edition, by Dee-Ann LeBlanc.

## Using the CD with Linux

To install the items from the CD to your hard drive, follow these steps:

1. Log in as root.

2. Insert the CD into your computer's CD-ROM drive.

3. If your computer has Auto-Mount enabled, wait for the CD to mount. Otherwise, follow these steps:

   a. *Command line instructions:*

   At the command prompt, type

   ```
   mount /dev/cdrom /mnt/cdrom
   ```

   This step mounts the cdrom device to the mnt/cdrom directory. If your device has a different name, change cdrom to that device name — for instance, cdrom1.

   b. *Graphical:* Right-click the CD-ROM icon on the desktop and choose Mount CD-ROM. This step mounts your CD-ROM.

4. Browse the CD and follow the individual installation instructions for the products I list in this appendix.

5. To remove the CD from your CD-ROM drive, follow these steps:

   a. *Command line instructions:*

   At the command prompt, type

   ```
   umount /mnt/cdrom
   ```

   b. *Graphical:* Right-click the CD-ROM icon on the desktop and choose UMount CD-ROM. This step un-mounts your CD-ROM.

After you have installed the programs that you want, you can eject the CD. Carefully place it back in the plastic jacket of the book for safekeeping.

# What You'll Find

In this section, I list the products included on the CD and describe each. You can find all these items on the CD in a directory structure.

*Shareware programs* are fully functional, free, trial versions of copyrighted programs. If you like particular programs, register with their authors for a nominal fee and receive licenses, enhanced versions, and technical support. *Freeware programs* are free, copyrighted games, applications, and utilities. You can copy them to as many PCs as you like — free — but they have no technical support. GNU software is governed by its own license, which is included inside the folder of the GNU software. There are no restrictions on distribution of this software. See the GNU license for more details. Trial, demo, or evaluation versions are usually limited either by time or functionality (such as being unable to save projects).

### MisterHouse: www.misterhouse.com

MisterHouse is an open source (GPL-licensed) home automation program that runs on a number of operating systems (even that other one, MAC OS X). It was originally written by Bruce Winter in Perl, but it has been enhanced by the community. Bruce still maintains the code, and it gets updated on a regular basis. It's the Swiss Army knife of home automation programs (and it's twice as sharp). Most people start out by using it to control their X10 modules, but it can do a lot more: monitor the weather, get the daily news, monitor the security of your home, pick up your e-mail, monitor your wireless access point, control your stereo — I think you begin to get the point. After you've overcome the initial shock of what it can do and start focusing on what you want it to do, you'll be surprised at what it supports and the support it gets.

### Asterisk: www.asterisk.org

Asterisk is an open source telephony and IP PBX application. It was originally written by Mark Spencer of Digium, Inc. Mark now maintains and contributes to the code along with the Asterisk community. It can be used for small to large businesses or for home use. It's flexible enough to act as an answering machine with extra capabilities, such as torturing telemarketers with forwarding calls to voice menus or mail boxes. Or you can use Asterisk to handle a lot of users.

### NdisWrapper: http://ndiswrapper.sf.net

NdisWrapper is an open source network driver wrapper package that allows you to use Windows drivers in the Linux kernel for wireless network cards. Many wireless network cards don't have support for Linux. This is especially likely to occur with laptops, which allow little choice concerning what hardware you can add. To get around this limitation, a few members of the Linux community figured out a way to use the Windows NDIS (Network Driver Interface Specification) to interface the Windows driver to the Linux kernel. When you can't find a native Linux driver, at least you have this to fall back to.

### Heyu: www.heyu.org

Heyu is a text-based program to control X10 modules by issuing commands via the CM11A X10 serial controller. It can schedule and issue X10 commands based on time or events. It also keeps track of the state of X10 commands that have been issued. It's licensed free of charge for non-commercial distribution, personal, and internal business use. Originally it was written by Daniel B. Suthers, and it is now maintained by Charles W. Sullivan. T

### MythTV: www.mythtv.org

MythTV is a GPL-licensed PVR (personal video recorder, like a TiVo) software suite that runs under Linux. In addition to its playback and record capabilities, it allows you to schedule recordings in advance. MythTV also supports plug-ins, which allow it to be extended by other programs. It was originally written by Isaac Richards, and he now maintains and contributes to the software. Visit the Web site for the latest updates:

### Quagga: www.quagga.net

Quagga is a GPL-licensed routing suite that includes daemons for `rip` (IPv4), `ripng` (IPv6), `ospfd` (IPv4), `ospf6d` (IPv6), and `bgpd` (BGPv4+, support for multicast and IPv6). Quagga is a fork of the GNU Zebra routing suite. The current maintainers are Paul Jakma, Vincent Jardin, Andrew Schorr, Hasso Tepper, Greg Troxel, and David Young.

### OpenWrt: www.openwrt.org

OpenWrt is a GPL-licensed Linux distribution for wireless routers. Currently, the most popular routers are the Linksys WRT family of routers, but there is also support for wireless routers from Netgear, Buffalo, and Motorola. OpenWrt is meant to be light on resource but flexible enough to suit the needs of most users. It accomplishes this by creating external packages that can be loaded to suit the user's needs. Linksys released its Linux source (in accord with the provisions in GPL). Then the OpenWrt community used that source as the base for its Linux distribution.

### PuTTY: www.putty.nl

PuTTY is an open source (MIT-licensed) implementation of ssh for Win32 computers. PuTTY includes many standard ssh utilities to securely access machines (such as your Linux server) across the Internet. It was originally written by Simon Tatham and is now also maintained by Owen Dunn, Ben Harris, and Jacob Nevins.

### BlueLava: www.drophat.com/bluelava

BlueLava is a GPL-licensed CGI script that interfaces to the command line utility BottleRocket (an interface to the X10 CM17A transmitter). It was created by Bruce A. Locke and is maintained by Ian Wilkinson. BlueLava allows you to control X10 modules from a Web browser.

### WPA-Supplicant: http://hostap.epitest.fi/wpa_supplicant

WPA-Supplicant is an open source (GPL-licensed) program which is the middleman between your wireless card and your WAP (wireless access point). It provides support for WPA (WiFi Protected Access) and WPA2, which provide better protection from hacking than WEP does.

### BottleRocket: www.linuxha.com/bottlerocket

BottleRocket is an open source (GPL-licensed) command line interface for UNIX systems to use the X10 Firecracker (CM17A) to transmit X10 signals to X10 wireless devices. Its authors are Ashley Clark, David Anderson, Jason

White, Warner Losh, and Tymm Twillman. I currently maintain it. Visit the Web site for the most recent updates:

## LIRC: www.lirc.org

LIRC (Linux Infrared Remote Control) is an open source (GPL-licensed) suite for recording and playing back recorded IR signals from remotes such as those used for TVs or entertainment systems. This enables your Linux box to send and receive almost any IR signal. The current maintainer is Christoph Bartelmis. The developers are Manuel Estrada Sainz, Heinrich Langos, Karsten Scheibler, Jim Paris, and Milan Pikula.

## TwonkyMedia: www.twonkyvision.de

Twonky is a commercial media server program that allows you to share your music, pictures, and video with standard UPnP-enabled client devices. (UPnP stands for Universal Plug and Pray, er, *Play.*)

## One-wire weather: http://oww.sourceforge.net

Oww (One-wire weather) is software to receive and interpret live sensor data from the One-wire weather station (now being sold by AAG Electronica). It supports a barometer, a solar radiation sensor, a humidity sensor, an anemometer, a wind vane, a rain gauge, and temperature sensors. It is written and maintained by Simon J. Melhuish.

## ForecastFox: http://forecastfox.mozdev.com

ForecastFox is an extension that provides quick weather reporting on one of the bars of your Firefox browser. It provides support for international weather reports (not just North America). A simple click of an icon opens a new tab, which displays a more detailed report. This extension uses AccuWeather.com for its weather information. The project owner is Jon Stritar, and its active developers are Richard Klein and Alexander Slovesnik.

## Scripting and configuration files

I've provided you with a number of configuration files and scripts that I've used in various chapters. I've always hated typing in long scripts or programs because I often made mistakes (was that an O or a 0?), so I decided to spare you the pain. The instructions to access the scripts are found in the chapters, and each script and configuration file comes complete with comments (and some advanced examples that are commented out). The CD has a few other bonus files, such as Firewall Builder. There were a few topics that didn't fit into the book. All files are open source, so improvements are encouraged. You can browse these files directly from the CD or copy them to your hard drive and use them as the basis for your own projects. If you create anything interesting, drop by the Web site (`www.linuxha.com`) and share.

# If You Have Problems (Of the CD Kind)

I tried my best to compile programs that work on most computers with the minimum system requirements. Alas, your computer might differ, and some programs might not work properly for some reason. Sometimes, the problem is just that a few files are in a different place. Other times, you might be missing some basic utility (didn't think you'd need the C compiler, huh?). If you run into problems, drop by the Web site (www.linuxha.com) and post the problem. It might be that others have run into the same problem (couldn't be a typo, could it?). Either way, I'll do my best to help you get the CD content up and running as quickly as possible.

If you're trying to use these programs under Windows, that will cause problems. These programs were designed for Linux specifically. You might consider the suggestion that I've seen on much of Windows software: Requires Windows 98 or better. Upgrade to Linux; you'll be glad you did.

If you have trouble with the CD-ROM, please call the Wiley Product Technical Support phone number at (800) 762-2974. Outside the United States, call (317) 572-3994. You can also contact Wiley Product Technical Support at http://support.wiley.com/. John Wiley & Sons will provide technical support only for installation and other general quality control items. For technical support on the applications themselves, consult the program's vendor or author.

To place additional orders or to request information about other Wiley products, please call (877) 762-2974.

# Index

Video Out card, 18
Video settings (MythTV), 124
Video Sources setting (MythTV), 119–120
videoconferencing. *See also* Ekiga
    CamStream, 34
    described, 34–35
    overview, 151–152
videos played on MythTV, 128
viewing information with MythWeather,
    209–210
VoIP (Voice Over IP), 153, 158
vtysh, 99

• *W* •

Wall, Kurt *(Red Hat Linux Networking and
    System Administration)*, 316
WAN information
    DHCP connection type, 76
    None connection type, 75
    overview, 75
    PPPoE connection type, 76
    Static connection type, 76
    wireless access point (WAP), 75–77
WAP. *See* wireless access point (WAP)
warm house, waking up to a, 219
watching recordings on MythTV, 126
watching TV on MythTV, 125
watchquagga, 99
WAV format, 137
weather, 34
weather applets, 19, 199–203
weather data
    Firefox Web browser, 19, 203–207
    Internet, getting weather reports from,
        19–20
    MythWeather used to obtain weather
        updates, 20
    overview, 18
    StormSiren used to obtain weather
        updates, 20
    weather applets on Linux desktop, 19
    weather station, getting reports from
        your own, 19
Weather Display, 188
weather monitoring with MisterHouse
    (MH), 264
Weather Report button, adding, 308–312
weather report page, installing, 306–307

Weather settings (MythTV), 124
weather station. *See also* Oww (One-wire
    weather)
    building, 188–189
    cable for, 193
    configuration, 191–197
    getting reports from your own, 19
    hardware for, 187–188
    installing software for, 189–197
    Internet, putting your weather data on
        the, 198
    mounting, 197–198
    overview, 187
    software for, 187–188
Web pages created with HTML template,
    304–305
Web parameter (MisterHouse), 274
webcams. *See also* CamStream
    described, 34–35
    Ekiga, 34
    finding webcam driver, 142
    installing software by using Synaptic,
        144–145
    OrbitView program, 156
    overview, 141
    pan feature, 155–156
    setting up Synaptic software repositories,
        143
    Synaptic used to install driver for, 142
    tilt feature, 155–156
    used for home security, 156
Weeder Technologies boards, 280
whole house blockers, 245
window shades, automating opening and
    closing, 335–336
Winter, Bruce (MisterHouse), 261
wired networks compared, 41
wireless access point (WAP)
    configuration, 81–84
    described, 39–40
    LAN information, 73–74
    Linksys WRT54GL, 67–69
    OpenWrt, 69–70, 78–81
    overview, 67
    requirements for, 71–73
    WAN information, 75–77
    wireless information, 77–78
wireless channel number, 47
wireless network interface card (NIC), 40

# Wiley Publishing, Inc.
# End-User License Agreement

5. **Limited Warranty.**

   **(a)** WPI warrants that the Software and Software Media are free from defects in materials and workmanship under normal use for a period of sixty (60) days from the date of purchase of this Book. If WPI receives notification within the warranty period of defects in materials or workmanship, WPI will replace the defective Software Media.

   **(b)** WPI AND THE AUTHOR(S) OF THE BOOK DISCLAIM ALL OTHER WARRANTIES, EXPRESS OR IMPLIED, INCLUDING WITHOUT LIMITATION IMPLIED WARRANTIES OF MERCHANTABILITY AND FITNESS FOR A PARTICULAR PURPOSE, WITH RESPECT TO THE SOFTWARE, THE PROGRAMS, THE SOURCE CODE CONTAINED THEREIN, AND/OR THE TECHNIQUES DESCRIBED IN THIS BOOK. WPI DOES NOT WARRANT THAT THE FUNCTIONS CONTAINED IN THE SOFTWARE WILL MEET YOUR REQUIREMENTS OR THAT THE OPERATION OF THE SOFTWARE WILL BE ERROR FREE.

   **(c)** This limited warranty gives you specific legal rights, and you may have other rights that vary from jurisdiction to jurisdiction.

6. **Remedies.**

   **(a)** WPI's entire liability and your exclusive remedy for defects in materials and workmanship shall be limited to replacement of the Software Media, which may be returned to WPI with a copy of your receipt at the following address: Software Media Fulfillment Department, Attn.: *Linux Smart Homes For Dummies*, Wiley Publishing, Inc., 10475 Crosspoint Blvd., Indianapolis, IN 46256, or call 1-800-762-2974. Please allow four to six weeks for delivery. This Limited Warranty is void if failure of the Software Media has resulted from accident, abuse, or misapplication. Any replacement Software Media will be warranted for the remainder of the original warranty period or thirty (30) days, whichever is longer.

   **(b)** In no event shall WPI or the author be liable for any damages whatsoever (including without limitation damages for loss of business profits, business interruption, loss of business information, or any other pecuniary loss) arising from the use of or inability to use the Book or the Software, even if WPI has been advised of the possibility of such damages.

   **(c)** Because some jurisdictions do not allow the exclusion or limitation of liability for consequential or incidental damages, the above limitation or exclusion may not apply to you.

7. **U.S. Government Restricted Rights.** Use, duplication, or disclosure of the Software for or on behalf of the United States of America, its agencies and/or instrumentalities "U.S. Government" is subject to restrictions as stated in paragraph (c)(1)(ii) of the Rights in Technical Data and Computer Software clause of DFARS 252.227-7013, or subparagraphs (c) (1) and (2) of the Commercial Computer Software - Restricted Rights clause at FAR 52.227-19, and in similar clauses in the NASA FAR supplement, as applicable.

8. **General.** This Agreement constitutes the entire understanding of the parties and revokes and supersedes all prior agreements, oral or written, between them and may not be modified or amended except in a writing signed by both parties hereto that specifically refers to this Agreement. This Agreement shall take precedence over any other documents that may be in conflict herewith. If any one or more provisions contained in this Agreement are held by any court or tribunal to be invalid, illegal, or otherwise unenforceable, each and every other provision shall remain in full force and effect.